# The Templars and the Assassins:
# The Militia of Heaven

by

James Wasserman

Including

*In Praise of the New Knighthood*

by Saint Bernard of Clairvaux

Translated by Lisa Coffin

Inner Traditions
Rochester, Vermont

First Edition Published 2001 by
Inner Traditions International
One Park Street
Rochester, VT 05767

ISBN: 0-89281-859-X

Library of Congress Cataloging-in-Publication Data
Wasserman, James
The Templars and the Assassins : the militia of Heaven /
by James Wasserman ;
including In praise of the new knighthood
by Saint Bernard of Clairvaux translated by Lisa Coffin.—1st ed.
p. cm.
Includes bibliographical references and index.
ISBN 0-89281-859-X (alk. paper)
1. Military religious orders—History. 2. Templars. 3. Assassins (Ismailites)
4. Occultism—Religious aspects. I Title.
CR4701 .W37 2001
271'.7913—dc21
2001017256

Book design and typography by STUDIO 31
www.studio31.com

Printed and bound in the United States

10   9   8   7

# The Templars
## and the Assassins:
# The Militia of Heaven

*This book is dedicated*

*to my children,*

*and to the*

*Immortal Spirit of Liberty.*


*It is offered in loving memory of my mother and father.*

# Acknowledgments

I wish to thank my wife, Nancy, who has cheerfully endured the countless hours and dollars spent in research and writing, and who has been of great help with the conception, editing, and production of this book. I am especially indebted to my dear friend Dr. Christopher S. Hyatt, who originally suggested I write it. Chris Bamford, Cathy Finne, and Robert Brazil engaged me in stimulating conversation. Bil Padgett, Khem Caigan, Robert Brazil, and Henry Suzuki helped in the acquisition of research material. Genevieve Mikolajczak provided essential help as usual. J. P. Lund made a series of important editorial suggestions. Sean Konecky offered erudite criticism that improved this work. I thank Paul Shoenfeld, a true practitioner of the writer's craft, who contributed to the creative process through our regular conversations. The quality of Laura Senie's language skills was exceeded only by the fortuitous timing of her arrival. Kristin Overson wielded her editorial scalpel with precision. The example of scholarly integrity embodied by David Vagi in his research on ancient Rome was an inspiration to me, as was his good-natured acceptance of the rigors of scholarly research. Dr. Gerald Epstein generously shared his insights into Western monotheism. Dr. Michael Aquino's expressions of confidence in me were greatly appreciated, as was his critical acumen in reviewing the manuscript. My friend Martin Starr offered quiet encouragement throughout. Thanks to Richard Gernon and William Breeze for their help with the original outline of this work which appeared in *The Equinox* 3, no. 10, in 1986. Stella Grey, Bill Koegl, James Strain, Michael McCarthy, Tony Carlsen, and Amir Modak all offered assistance. I am grateful to Peter Lamborn Wilson for reviewing my understanding of the complexities of Islamic doctrine. Herb Golub helped me sprint past the last hurdles. The importance of the contribution made by Emma Gonzalez cannot be overstated and is most visible in the maps. Lisa Coffin generously allowed the use of her translation of Saint Bernard's letter, without which the passions that led to the growth of the Templars would have remained less visible. The enthusiasm expressed by Jon Graham of Inner Traditions International touched me deeply. Rowan Jacobsen's editorial skills and sensitivity helped accomplish that mysterious alchemical transmutation by which a manuscript becomes a book. Finally, my thanks to Ehud Sperling, founder and publisher of Inner Traditions, for his friendship and support these many years.

# Contents

A thousand years ago the eerie stillness of what is now the Israeli desert was shattered by the thunderous cacophony of armored horses' hooves racing to battle. The clash of swords and lances striking armor and shield resounded through the field. Battle cries mixed with the screams of the wounded, the blasts of trumpets, the shouted commands in many foreign tongues. Muslim battled Christian for possession of a strip of land upon which both their religions were founded. Some thousands of miles away in a mountain fastness south of the Caspian Sea in modern Iran, a Persian adept sat wrapped in a rigid posture of meditation while his mind's eye gazed upon another deadly scene. One of his most trusted disciples, disguised as a Sufi mystic, had just approached the litter of the powerful Seljuk vizier. His dagger plunged into the vizier's heart seconds before he too was struck down by the guards. Hasan-i-Sabah, the legendary Old Man of the Mountain, must have experienced a moment of relief, since the death of his sworn enemy would lessen the Turkish threat to his headquarters at Alamut. Fate would again smile kindly on the besieged Assassin community as the Seljuk sultan himself passed away within weeks of his slain vizier.

The richness of the historical truths about the Order of Assassins and the Knights Templar intertwines inexorably with the myths that have stimulated the imagination of so many minds through the centuries. Both the Assassins and Templars were destroyed as heretics some seven hundred years ago. While the Assassins (more properly known as Nizari Ismailis) survive to this day under the leadership of the Aga Khan, the primary period of their history under discussion here was obliterated by their Mongolian and Mameluke conquerors in 1256 and 1273, respectively. They were slandered by Sunni heresiologists who considered them religious criminals and by medieval Christian historians who considered them pagan idolaters. The Templars similarly have no surviving documentary corpus, despite the probability that as a medieval religious order they kept scrupulous records of their doings. The Templars were also written in dark ink by historians of the power structure that had tortured and murdered them and destroyed their Order. Since history is characteristically written by the victors, we make haste at the outset to state that our study is of the vanquished.

This book begins with an introduction to secret societies in which the mystical secret society is examined and distinguished from both the political conspiracy and the religious hierarchy. The balance of the book is divided into four parts.

Part 1 attempts a broad overview of the historical conditions in Europe and the Near East from the birth of Christ through the Crusades. Focusing primarily on the West, this overview will help identify the major religious, political, economic, and cultural developments that led to the European invasion of the Holy Land. While some readers may find it overly detailed and seemingly out of place, it will set the stage for some of the complex interactions in the events that follow. Those with a firm grasp of European history may prefer to proceed directly to part 2.

Part 2 is an investigation of the Order of Assassins. After presenting some of the legendary tales that survive to this day, I undertake a detailed look at Islam from the birth of the Prophet through the birth of the Nizari Ismaili sect. The particular 166-year period of political success in Persia known as the Alamut Imamate is discussed in detail, as is the Syrian Assassin community with whom the Crusaders interacted. Brief highlights of the subsequent history of Nizari survivors through modern times follow.

Part 3 is a history of the Knights Templar that begins with a close look at the origins of the Order and the Rule initially drafted by Saint Bernard of Clairvaux. The subsequent history of the Order is divided into chapters that correspond to the Crusades in which the Templars fought during the two hundred years since their founding. The destruction of the Order is closely investigated, as is the eternal question of the Order's guilt or innocence.

Part 4 is an afterword that briefly surveys the development of the Western esoteric tradition from its roots in prehistory through the eclipse of the pagan Mysteries under the Christian religious hegemony during the six centuries known as the Dark Ages. We then observe the reintroduction of occultism to Europe immediately following the Crusades, a development that continues to the present day. Particular attention is paid to the critical points of convergence between East and West, especially those that may be traceable to the interaction between the Assassins and Templars.

Appendix 1 presents a modern analysis of the purported Nine Degrees of Wisdom of the Ismaili initiation as the system has been variously posited since at least the tenth century. Appendix 2 offers a new translation of Saint Bernard's critical letter, *In Praise of the New Knighthood*, in which he first proclaimed the ideal of the warrior-monk that so inflamed the European psyche in 1136 and forever inspired the mythos of the Knights Templar in Western culture.

In view of much of the literature that has grown around these two orders, and much occult writing in general, it may be wise to state at the outset that I have taken great pains to avoid speculation and fantasy in this book. Legends are identified as such, and the reader is invited to form his or her own opinion about many of the truly unanswerable questions that are presented here. I believe the legitimate scholarly facts of the histories you are about to read will be sufficient to provide a suitable launching pad for the flights of fancy inherent in the nature of the Assassins and Knights Templar. I hope the reader will accept the difficult challenge of surveying the compressed mass of data and the many unfamiliar names and terms that follow. I especially hope that this effort will be rewarded with a deeper insight into these holy warriors — ostensible opponents, mirror images.

CHAPTER ONE

# AN INTRODUCTION TO SECRET SOCIETIES

The existence of Higher Consciousness is the prime postulate of both religion and the occult. Human beings are separated from their divine nature by the seemingly impassable barrier of the rational mind and ego. Yet we share an implicit awareness that a higher state exists and that we are capable of communion with a source of power far greater than any we can access by physical means. The search for union may well be considered the root motivation of human existence. Merely intellectual attempts to discredit or deny it pale before its universality. In the words of Iamblichus, the fourth-century Neoplatonist, "[A]n innate knowledge of the Gods is coexistent with our very existence; and this knowledge is superior to all judgment and deliberate choice, and subsists prior to reason and demonstration."[1]

## INITIATION

Legends of a Fall attempt to explain *why* a chasm exists between the human mind and divine consciousness. This great mystery is a fundamental concern for both religion and philosophy. The existence of such a chasm is, however, simply accepted as a basic premise in esoteric doctrine. *The purpose of initiation is not to explain the Fall but to overcome its effects.*

The goal of initiation, the primary "secret" of the wisdom tradition, is gnosis — direct, tangible, personal experience of God within the human body in the here and now. A "gnostic" is one who "knows," who cultivates the discipline of contact with divine consciousness. Unlike those who follow religions that either seek, guarantee, or threaten their adherents with the presence or absence of an after-death state of grace, the gnostic fully intends to experience grace within his or her lifetime.

The Mysteries defuse the exclusivity of the Word so often claimed by religion.[†] The individual becomes the knower. "[U]nless you make

[†] The use of the word *Mysteries* in this book applies to that broad-based network of autonomous religious-philosophical schools that flourished throughout the ancient world. Discussing this ideal, Manly P. Hall writes, "The Mysteries claimed to be the

yourself equal to God, you cannot understand God: for the like is not intelligible save to the like. Make yourself grow to a greatness beyond measure, by a bound free yourself from the body; raise yourself above all time, become Eternity; then you will understand God."[2]

## MYSTICAL SECRET SOCIETIES

Mystical secret societies dedicated to initiation and spiritual liberation have existed in all ages and cultures. From the mythic invocation of the aboriginal tribesman to the ecstatic whirling of the dervish, the aim of these societies is the same — the programmed alteration of individual consciousness within a group setting.

The closest modern analog to the term "secret society" might be the "special interest group." People of varied vocations and avocations, from agriculture to zoology, develop forums devoted to their specialties. They communicate via newsletters, the Internet, social clubs, and so on. Members assume at least minimal prior knowledge of the subject matter at hand. Their individual commitment and willingness to explore their chosen field serves as the common denominator by which they interact. The goal of their association is increased personal development within the chosen specialty area, assisted by contact with similarly motivated individuals.

Members of mystical secret societies share a desire for the attainment of states of higher consciousness through participation in group ritual and the communication of magical and mystical knowledge with others of similar interests — knowledge that, by definition, conveys a sense of awe. The interpenetration of divine and human, the realization of truths that stem from a higher point of origin, the power implicit in

---

guardians of a transcendental knowledge so profound as to be incomprehensible save to the most exalted intellect and so potent as to be revealed with safety only to those in whom personal ambition was dead and who had consecrated their lives to the unselfish service of humanity. Both the dignity of these sacred institutions and the validity of their claim to possession of Universal Wisdom are attested by the most illustrious philosophers of antiquity, who were themselves initiated into the profundities of the secret doctrine and who bore witness to its efficacy" (Manly P. Hall, *The Secret Teachings of All Ages* [1925; reprint, Los Angeles: Philosophical Research Society, 1975], p. 20.). The Mysteries provided for the spiritual needs of the masses with ceremonies of external worship and simplistic creeds, while more advanced souls were guided through the progressive levels of the secret doctrine.

that knowledge — all suggest a sense of reverence, even fear, to the generally bewildered consciousness of the "normal" rational mind.

## DOCTRINES OF MYSTICAL SECRET SOCIETIES

The most common type of mystical secret society operating within the Western esoteric tradition is the hierarchically structured order. All of the groups to be discussed in this book are (or were) graded organizations. While these groups may vary widely in their particular spheres of activity — pursuing such diverse interests as alchemy, metaphysics, or fraternal work — they all share the following distinguishing characteristics:

1. An inner doctrine is at the heart of the secret society. All of the group's teachings point to the inner doctrine, which is progressively revealed through the initiatory degrees of the society.

2. A hierarchical structure presides over the incremental unveiling of the inner doctrine. As one progresses toward the top of the hierarchy, one presumably knows more than those below. Also, it is assumed of those further up in the hierarchy that loyalty to the society and commitment to its principles have been tested through the years of membership.

3. A set of moral values particularly stresses loyalty to the membership, service to the society, respect for the hierarchy, and aspiration toward the inner doctrine. The patience required for the gradual illumination peculiar to the secret society itself is considered part of its moral teaching.

4. The development of a stable foundation upon which the candidate may continue to build is encouraged by the society's method of progressively revealing secrets — that is, gradually unfolding the inner doctrine over time and through the degrees of advancement within the hierarchy. The practical value of this style of teaching to the society is that it separates the committed from the merely curious.

5. Oaths required for the receiving of these secrets are standard. Historians of the occult, and some occultists themselves, have scoffed at

the majestic and terrible oaths with which the most commonplace knowledge was revealed to initiates. The technique serves to weed out the unfit, however, and to develop the virtue of silence within the fit. During the historical periods discussed in this book, secrecy meant the difference between life and death.

6.  A curriculum provides the intellectual and psychospiritual methods by which the candidate is better prepared to understand the inner doctrine. These will include the study of recommended literature and the practice of meditation and ritual.

## Teachings of Mystical Secret Societies

Numerous time-proven techniques have been developed to transcend the normal, ego-bound state of three-dimensional, emotion-driven consciousness and to achieve experiential knowledge, or gnosis. All the secret societies and spiritual movements surveyed in the following pages have in common a curriculum of instruction. While the details and emphases vary, they all share the following assumptions:

1.  The existence of Higher Consciousness and the assertion that certain practices and disciplines allow the individual access to higher levels of awareness.

2.  The employment of mental and psychic practices, loosely grouped under the term "meditation," to induce this access. Meditation is the process by which the mind is trained to function free of the distractions of the senses. Meditation may include such things as exercises to achieve stillness of mind, prayer, magical invocation, programmed visualizations, practices of remembrance, astral projection, and so on. There are many variations in the techniques of meditation. At one end of the spectrum, the practitioner will be motionless, locked in silence, with eyes closed. At the other extreme of meditation are the techniques of magick, where the practitioner may be whirling in a dance while intoning sonorous invocations in a room filled with sensory cues to reinforce the one idea of the ceremony.

3. The concept of a physical link to the psyche. Forms of exercise such as *haṭhayoga,* as well as rhythmic breathing and dietary regimens, possibly including the ingestion of alchemical composites, are all employed to strengthen and purify the body. Drugs may be used by some systems or prohibited by others. The object of these practices is to limit distractions.

4. The teaching of certain moral or ethical behaviors. These teachings are designed to free the seeker from the mental conflicts and psychic obsessions that inhibit one-pointed effort. Moral values may vary widely. For example, among the sects we will encounter in this book, the Cathars were strictly forbidden the shedding of blood, which, for the Assassin or Templar, was an act worthy of esteem. Any number of the groups discussed herein would look unfavorably upon stealing, yet, to the devotee of the Thug sect in India, stealing was an act of worship to the goddess Kali.

5. Recognition of the value of the intellect. Intellectual studies are part of the Western training for achieving expanded spiritual awareness. The natural facility of the rational mind can be harnessed to align with the spiritual quest. The mind is a key component of the self to be placed in service to the ultimate goal.

6. A sexual doctrine. Sexual codes are included in all spiritual secret societies. Sex is a widely misunderstood means by which consciousness may be raised beyond its normal limitations. The occultist perceives the basic life force as a bioelectrical sexual energy, known to Wilhelm Reich as *orgone* or to the yogi as *kuṇḍalinī*. Management of this force is the root of yoga and meditation, its raising and directing the purpose of magick, its purification the goal of alchemy. Sex is the mirror of divine unity manifested as polarity — "divided for love's sake, for the chance of union."[3] Mystics throughout the centuries have taught a great many shades of sexual behavior, ranging from strict ascetic restriction to enthusiastic sensual indulgence. While these techniques may at first glance appear contradictory, they rest upon the common assumption of the sanctity and power of sexual energy.

## HIGHER INTELLIGENCES

Innumerable myths and legends concern teachers of Wisdom who have appeared throughout history to bring the gifts of civilization and spirituality to a benighted and ignorant humanity. These extraordinary guides and helpers have been variously identified as gods, angels, spirits, extraterrestrials, saints, mahatmas, buddhas, Inner Plane Adepts, ancestors, or just naturally talented geniuses. Advanced antediluvian civilizations such as Atlantis and Lemuria have also been posited.

Members of mystical secret societies may believe they are in contact with Higher Intelligences who are guiding the societies through invisible channels. These Intelligences are often perceived as having enlisted themselves in support of the secret society in order to share their wisdom with aspirants psychically attuned to the emanation of their energies. The society may then be conceived of by its membership as a three-dimensional manifestation for the evolutionary workings of Higher Consciousness.

## POLITICAL SECRET SOCIETIES

A different type of secret society is the political one whose primary goal is worldly power and whose members seek anonymity for these ambitions. At the simplest level of the political conspiracy are such criminal organizations as the Mafia, whose activities, if revealed, would result in prosecution. Revolutionary secret societies, such as the Bolsheviks or the Irish Republican Army, have also been a common phenomenon in political history.

Far more dangerous, in the opinion of the author, are the internationalist societies of the last hundred years (such as the Bilderbergers, the Council on Foreign Relations, and the Royal Institute of International Affairs) that are patiently and inexorably striving to build a world government. The membership of such groups is composed of politicians, business people, media leaders, and foundation executives who are able not only to shape public opinion, but to define the very terms of public debate. "The great political issue of our times is not liberalism versus conservatism, or capitalism versus socialism, but Statism — the belief that government is inherently superior to the citizenry, that progress consists of extending the realm of compulsion, that vesting arbitrary power in government officials will make the people happy — eventually."[4]

The goal of the modern statist is a level of control that surpasses the dreams of empire of the ancient Egyptians, Macedonians, and Romans. The primary building block for this political ideology is the individual willing to enforce his beliefs on others. Motives may range from genuine idealism to an arrogant contempt for the rights of others. The "good of the many" — as interpreted by the self-appointed experts and social planners — will inevitably result in the destruction of the liberty of the individual.[†] The incessant modern clamor for "democracy" neglects the fact that the ultimate symbol of uncontrolled majority rule is the lynch mob.

## HIERARCHICAL RELIGIONS

Another type of association that merits consideration is the established religion, such as Catholicism, that contains a hierarchical system of power and is founded upon divine revelation. A progressive illumination of the individual, however, is not the rationale for the structure of the Church hierarchy; rather, function, organization, and efficiency are its motivating principles. One accepts more operational responsibility, succeeds at the task, and becomes imbued with greater authority. A cardinal or a pope does not necessarily understand more of the inner doctrine of Christ as he rises within the structure of the Church, nor does an informing gnosis electrify his ascent. Members of the Church

---

† The reader is invited to compare the founding principles of the American Republic as expressed in the Declaration of Independence, Constitution, and Bill of Rights with the U.N. principles enshrined in such agreements as the United Nations Declaration of Human Rights, the International Covenant on Civil and Political Rights, and the International Covenant on Economic, Social and Cultural Rights in support of this unequivocal statement. Briefly stated, in the American system, the inalienable rights of the individual are derived from God and protected *from* the government as indicated by phrases such as "Congress shall make no law . . . " The "rights" enumerated in the U.N. movement are each *conditional* upon the will of the state, as this quote fom the International Covenant on Civil and Political Rights should make abundantly clear: "The above-mentioned rights shall not be subject to any restrictions except those which are provided by law, are necessary to protect national security, public order (ordre public), public health or morals or the rights and freedoms of others, and are consistent with the other rights recognized in the present Covenant."

hierarchy are no more likely to achieve sainthood than a congregant. For every pope or bishop who has been canonized (ideally, for true spirituality), there exists a lay person — such as Saint Francis of Assisi, Saint Joan of Arc, even our modern Mother Theresa — whose life stands as witness to their embrace of Christ.

The lines of demarcation between a mystical secret society, a political conspiracy, and a hierarchical religion often appear faint because they have various structural elements in common. For example, political conspiracies and mystical secret societies share secrecy as an operative mechanism. Hierarchical religions and mystical secret societies share graded structures of leadership and the root motivation of spiritual aspiration. The distinction between mystical secret societies and political conspiracies becomes substantially blurred in the case of the Assassins and Templars, as we shall see.

## CULTS

Much ink and many broadcast hours were expended on cults during the final decades of the twentieth century. The word *cult*, according to the *Oxford English Dictionary* (1933), originally comes from the Latin root *cultus*, meaning "worship," and *colere*, "to attend to, to cultivate, to respect, etc." It means: "1. Worship; reverential homage, rendered to a divine being or beings. 2. A particular form or system of religious worship *esp.* in reference to external rites and ceremonies. 3. Devotion or homage to a particular person or thing, now *esp.* as paid by a body of professed adherents or admirers." As one example of the latter, the *OED* gives "The cult of beauty as the most vivid image of Truth." Since the Jonestown fiasco of the late 1970s, however, the word *cult* has become a virtually meaningless media term intended to connote religious fanaticism.

All modern organized religions were originally cults. The chief danger facing a cult and its members today, as always, is that of becoming a target for entrenched interests. The dominant reigning party in any society tends to exterminate cults in a self-serving and self-righteous manner, because cults become both embarrassments to and competitors of the prevailing dogma and social order. This was certainly true of pagan Rome, which persecuted the new Christian cult. When the Christians finally rose to political power in 323, they returned the favor with centuries of violence, culminating in the Inquisition.

The modern corporate-socialist state, into which the United States is fast plunging, well demonstrated its power by its treatment of the Branch Davidians in 1993. The televised holocaust at the Mount Carmel center outside Waco, Texas, recalled the brutality of the Middle Ages. Like the Assassins, the Branch Davidians were a small religious group outside the norm of society. Like the Knights Templar, their beliefs were shaped by the New Testament. The destruction of the Branch Davidians at the hands of federal police was accompanied by a campaign of vilification and disinformation that rivaled the propaganda of the French monarchy against the Templars and the medieval Sunni establishment against the Assassins.

The human race still has a long way to travel in its journey toward the Light. And a fair case may be made for questioning the ineluctable reality of humanity's evolution. The pervasive psychological weakness and endemic dependency of human beings in modern society is a case in point. The rude virtues of yesterday — courage, self-reliance, individual morality — could arguably be considered a more advanced cultural model than today's collectivist gestalt. A look even further back in time, to the mountain fastness of Alamut, may allow us to share for a moment in the clear-eyed visionary independence of an uncompromising people who refused to surrender their integrity to the demands of their environment.

PART ONE

# SETTING THE STAGE

✠

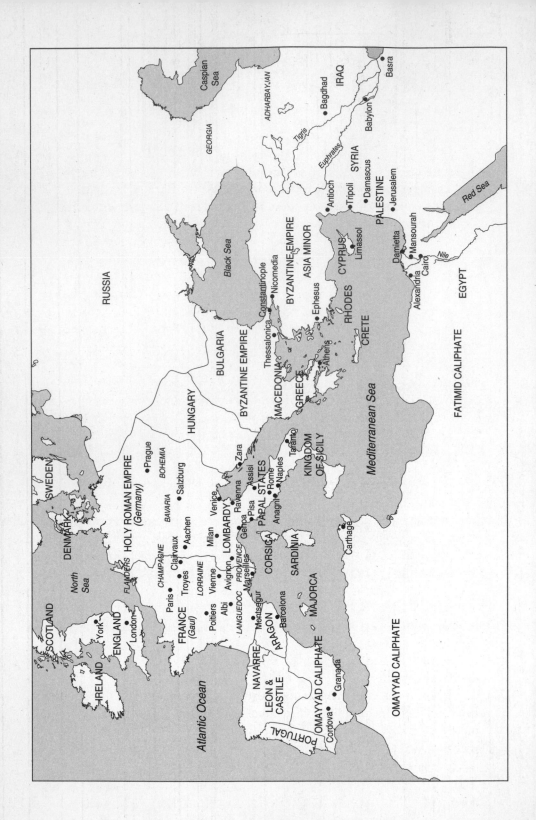

# CHAPTER TWO

# Historical Background of the Crusades

B efore beginning our inquiry into the Assassins, it will be helpful to examine some of the historical developments that led to the Crusades. The European invasion of the Holy Land in 1095 represented the height of political influence for Christianity, which had risen from being a minor cult within the Roman Empire to a position before which kings and peasants alike trembled. We shall also explore certain broad themes in medieval history and their roots in the Roman Empire, for Rome was the birthplace of feudalism, which provided the context for both knighthood and chivalry. Furthermore, the Roman Empire built the foundation upon which the European nation-states were erected only moments before the inauguration of the Crusades. A review of the schism between Eastern and Western Christianity (also rooted in the Roman Empire) will shed light on the animosity and treachery we shall encounter between Christians during the Crusades, and help explain the many alliances formed between Christian and Muslim. This survey focuses mainly on Europe; the evolution of Islam, crucial to the story of the Assassins, will be explored later.

## The Birth of Christianity

The Near East has functioned as the birthplace of numerous religions and spiritual movements, including the world's three great monotheistic faiths: Judaism, Christianity, and Islam. Prior to the inception of these, dating back to prehistory, the indigenes have worshipped such deities as Oannes, Osiris, Enki, Adonis, Dionysus, and Attys, among others. As a well-worn trade route, the Holy Land has traditionally been an area of unusual religious and cultural cross-fertilization. For millennia, it has also been the scene of nearly constant political upheaval.

In 143 B.C.E. Simon Maccabee began the Jewish conquest of Palestine, and there he established the kingdom of Judea. The Romans completed their conquest of the Greek empire by 63 B.C.E. and annexed Judea to Syria. After a Jewish revolt in 43 B.C.E., the Romans reestablished Judea under King Herod. Although Jewish himself, Herod was hated because he sought to Romanize the realm. He was, however, able to complete a magnificent restoration of the famed Second Temple. (The First Temple had been built by King Solomon in the mid-tenth century B.C.E. and housed the mysterious Ark of the Covenant. Solomon's Temple was destroyed in 587 B.C.E. when the Babylonians, under King Nebuchadrezzar, conquered Jerusalem. In 538 B.C.E., King Cyrus II of Persia defeated the Babylonians and allowed the Jews, led by Zerubbabel, to return to Jerusalem, where they completed the Second Temple in 515 B.C.E.). Upon Herod's death in 4 B.C.E., Jewish nationalists revolted. Extensive Roman reprisals caused immense suffering. Another rebellion in 70 C.E. resulted in the destruction of the restored Second Temple and the death of an estimated 600,000 to 1,200,000 Jews at the hands of the army of the Roman caesar Titus.

The decades of Roman occupation kindled Jewish messianic hopes. The Messiah would end the reign of evil, subdue the heathen, and bring forth the acceptance of Jewish Law and the Jewish God by all peoples on earth. Poverty, disease, and injustice would disappear. The Final Judgment would cast the evil into Hell, while the righteous would be rewarded with unending bliss.

Thus, the story of Christ fit seamlessly within the framework of the time: His messianic mission, healing powers, performance of miracles, and moral teaching through parable, and the example he provided by his religious faith, echoed the intense spirituality of Palestine. Whether Jesus was a solar myth, the apotheosis of Jewish eschatology and messianic hope, a historical master of the spiritual path, a Jewish revolutionary, or the Son of God, the Christian religion continues to exert a powerful influence two thousand years after his birth.

The Mediterranean world at the time of Christ was alive with astrologers, magicians, clairvoyants, healers, fortune-tellers, interpreters of dreams, saints, and wonder-workers. The Egyptian and Palestinian deserts were home to numerous ascetics living either in solitude or in monastic communities. The pagan Mystery religions had prepared the way for the acceptance of Christ. The dying god whose sacrifice redeemed the community, who was resurrected from the grave, and who, from his kingdom in the afterlife, could act as the intercessor between humanity and the cosmic, impersonal deity was a familiar figure. The Eucharistic Mass had been a feature of the Greek Mysteries of Eleusis. The Egyptians worshiped various trinities, taught the doctrines of a last judgment and personal immortality, and worshiped a divine mother and child. The cult of the Great Mother Cybele, as well as the cult of Isis, were spread throughout the Mediterranean. The great battle between God and Satan had long been a tenet of Zoroastrian dualism. Deified emperors such as Julius Caesar, and god-men such as the Pythagorean philosopher and miracle worker Apollonius of Tyana, gave credence to the idea of apotheosis. Among the most important new faiths of the Roman Empire in the first century C.E. was the worship of the Persian deity Mithras, son of Ahura Mazda (the god of light), who battled his antagonist Ahriman (god of darkness). Mithras came to mediate in favor of mankind. His birth was celebrated on December 25, and his worship included the consecration and consumption of wine and bread. Mithraic eschatology included the belief in a final judgment over which Mithras presided, eternal damnation of unclean souls in the realm of Ahriman, and the union of the pure with Ahura Mazda in his heavenly realm.

Saint Paul (died ca. 65) carried the teachings of Jesus to the pagan world. Paul's preachings of the physical resurrection of Jesus, his appearance to his disciples following his crucifixion, his ascension to Heaven, and his promise of eternal life to those who accepted him met with little resistance. The apostolic miracles and healings performed in Christ's name further spread the faith. After the aforementioned Jewish revolt in the year 70, the young Christian cult, indifferent to political concerns, severed its remaining ties with Judaism.

Despite periodic episodes of violent persecution during the next three centuries, Christianity spread rapidly through the dying Roman Empire. This may more accurately be interpreted as an effect of Rome's decay rather than a cause. The degeneration of the pagan faiths at this time caused Christianity to be seen as an inspiring model of moral behavior. Christian theology, like its Jewish parent, spoke of an ever watchful and judgmental deity who demanded moral behavior. Its teaching of equality and compassion, self-restraint and forgiveness, and the ennobling example of the love and self-sacrifice of its savior were widely embraced.

## EARLY CHRISTIANITY

The early years of Christianity were a period of chaotic, experimental, and anarchistic religious creativity. By 384, eighty separate Christian sects could be found in the Roman Empire. Certain heresies developed at this time that will figure largely in Templar history. Among these was the *agape*, or love feast. Greek and Roman Christians would gather for the Sabbath sacramental dinner in which wine and bread would be blessed as the blood and body of Christ. Then the "kiss of love" would be exchanged among the faithful. Contemporary historians complained that these gatherings frequently degenerated into orgies. By the third century the *agape* had disappeared from mainstream Christianity.

Early Christianity was also open to influence from other faiths. For example, Greek philosophy introduced numerous doctrinal variations to Christianity that would also bear fruit as future heresies. And Gnosticism easily adapted Christian language into its rich mix of Greek and Oriental thought. In the second century, Gnostic Christian philosophers such as Basilides (who conceived the Gnostic formula of the Supreme Deity known as Abraxas), Valentinus, and Bardesanes taught emanationist doctrines that placed the Christ figure within a recognizable pattern of cosmic spiritual hierarchies. The Gnostic preacher Marcion was excommunicated when he denounced the God of the Old Testament as an unforgiving tyrant opposed to Christ's gentle message. He taught that Jehovah's role was to imprison man in a material body, while Christ could provide spiritual liberation. Marcion also stated that Christ's crucified body was a mere phantasm.

One of the greatest challenges to the new faith arose in 242, when the Persian mystic Mani of Ctesiphon proclaimed himself messiah. He divided the world into good and evil, darkness and light. He identified the earth as the kingdom of darkness under the reign of Satan. The only hope for man lay in intense ascetic practices by which he could remove the shackles of the dark force from his soul and arise to the kingdom of light. After thirty years of preaching, Mani was crucified and his body stuffed with straw by the Persian authorities on the recommendation of Magian religious leaders. His martyrdom fueled the spread of Manichaeism.

As Christianity continued to mature, the Church grew from a community of believers who chose their own priests, deacons, and acolytes to a more complex and stratified organism. Ecclesiastical councils, or synods, developed during the second century to help regularize the religion. By the third century, only bishops were allowed to attend these councils, and their judgments determined all matters of faith and policy. Early spiritual enthusiasm had led to numerous scriptural variations and apocryphal revelations. The standardization of the Bible became an important second-century development. Incompatible elements of mysticism were neatly excised from the canon. The exclusive right of bishops to ordain priests followed next. The concept of sin became an ever more obsessive concern. By the late second century the practice of the Mass was widely instituted, recalling the eucharistic rites of pagan Mystery religions. The sacraments of baptism, communion, confirmation, penance; the rite of marriage; the cleansing of extreme unction at death; and the ordination of priests were all instituted at this time.

The early church fathers of the second and third centuries, like Ignatius of Antioch, Tertullian of Carthage, and Clement and Origen of Alexandria, built the doctrinal philosophy of Christianity into a sophisticated theology that resulted in increasing numbers of well-educated converts. The new religion was growing at an astonishing rate. Historian Norman Cantor estimates that there were as many as fifteen million Christians in the Roman Empire by the end of the third century, totaling some twenty-five percent of the population.[1]

Patriarchs reigned over aggregate sees from their seats in Constantinople, Jerusalem, Antioch, Alexandria, and Rome. The power of the Church gradually shifted from its base in Jerusalem and became more decentralized. Through the second and third centuries, Rome became the preeminent Christian center in the West. The Patriarch of Rome was known as the "pope," or "father." The doctrine was advanced that the Roman church had been founded by Peter, who had received Christ's appellation as the "rock" upon which His church would be built. According to this interpretation, the Roman patriarch should reign supreme as Christ's vicar on earth. This belief has been the unquestioned reality of Western Catholicism ever since. By the beginning of the fourth century, Rome counted one hundred thousand Christians and produced the first Latin translation of the New Testament. By the fifth century, the supremacy of the Roman bishop, or pope, was fully established in the West. The pope stepped into the leadership void left by the powerlessness of the late Western Roman emperors. While the Roman state continued its decline, the Roman Catholic Church grew.

An often bitter rivalry sprung up between the Eastern patriarch in Constantinople and the Western patriarch in Rome after the division of the Roman Empire by Diocletian at the end of the third century. By the year 300, Asia Minor was the leading center of Christianity and the majority of its citizens were adherents of the new faith. In 303,

Armenia became the first country to adopt Christianity as the state religion. In 451, the ecclesiastical Council of Chalcedon proclaimed that the authority of the bishops of Rome and Constantinople were equal. The struggle between Eastern and Western Christianity is examined in greater detail later.

## THE DECLINE AND DEATH OF ROME

When the Roman god Mars was overcome by the beauty of a sleeping vestal virgin, he fathered the twins Romulus and Remus, who grew to manhood and built their kingdom on the hills of Rome in 753 B.C.E. Thus is the legendary derivation of one of the greatest and longest-lasting empires the world has yet known. At its peak, Rome spanned the European continent and beyond. It included Spain in the west and the British Isles in the north, reached throughout North Africa in the south, and extended to most of Asia Minor in the east.

From Rome we inherit the concept of republican government, in which a barrier is provided to the autocratic rule of the king on the one hand and the democratic excesses of the majority on the other. Rome separated the legislative and executive powers and included a system of checks and balances that later found expression in the American Constitution. Rome imbued Western civilization with a body of law that stimulated economic, scientific, and cultural growth by its protection of property and individual achievement. Rome's commercial activities facilitated cross-cultural communication on a hitherto unknown scale. Roman civilization preserved the philosophic genius of Greece and Egypt, trained generations of students in its widespread educational system, and built roads, bridges, aqueducts, and other vast public structures. Having flourished as the home of innumerable pagan faiths, Rome became the birthplace of the Christian Church, whose civilizing influence is unequaled in history.

The Roman Republic began in 509 B.C.E. with the overthrow of the last king of the Tarquinian dynasty. A group of noble families formed a senate through which the state was governed. Two consuls were appointed by the senate and functioned as the executive branch. Their terms of office were limited to one year. After four centuries, the country was ravaged by the Social Wars of ca. 91–88 B.C.E., when a series of military leaders or warlords arose who denied the authority of the senate. They became dictators who ruled through strength of arms.

A triumvirate was formed in 60 B.C.E. of the three most powerful Roman generals, Pompeii, Crassus, and Julius Caesar. After the death of Crassus, Caesar and Pompeii warred for control. Julius Caesar emerged victorious and was proclaimed dictator for life by the senate in 44 B.C.E.[†] In 27 B.C.E., the senate declared Caesar's nephew Octavian as augustus. The Roman Empire had replaced the Roman Republic.

By the turn of the second century C.E., however, Rome was in her death throes; Rome's four-century decline lasted longer than the life of many nations. From the Age of Augustus forward, the autocratic power of the emperor increased as the rule of law and republican principles progressively gave way to tyranny. The emperor became estranged from the senate — the traditional root of Roman power — while he cultivated the favor of the lower classes through public handouts. The lost vitality and self-indulgence of this period proved no match for the aggressive barbarian spirit in the surrounding provincial territories. Late Rome's addiction to abortion and infanticide was, in part, responsible for her falling birthrate. This decline in births was especially ill timed because it accompanied the decimation wrought by the bubonic plague during the third and fourth centuries. It is estimated that the empire lost twenty percent of its citizens between 250 and 400.[2] The catastrophic effects of all this led to an abandonment of farmlands throughout Italy.

Neighboring barbarian tribes, generically identified as Germans, demanded Roman territory to house their expanding populations. The Germans were a primitive nomadic people, initially from Scandinavia, whose polytheistic religion included elements of animism, human sacrifice, divination, and the sacred kabbalistic alphabet known as runes. Warrior chieftains ruled, maintaining loyalty through successful conquest and the resulting opportunity for plunder. German kings were generally elected by tribal councils. The Germans also made use of a primitive jury system to judge accused criminals. In spite of these democratic institutions, the German tribes had no concept of a state or citizenship, no system of reciprocal responsibilities between leaders and the common people, such as that on which the Roman state had thrived. In time, German warriors took over the Roman army. German farmers became the Roman agricultural class. The provincial territories prospered as Rome grew more weary.

---

[†]A particularly short-lived designation, since he was assassinated some thirty days later.

The overall decline of Rome was mirrored by the decrease in patriotism. The glory of the Roman Republic had long been exemplified by its concept of the citizen-soldier-legislator. A large percentage of the citizens of the republic were small farmers, ready and willing to leave their plows and take up arms in defense of their country. Lucius Quinctius Cinncinatus embodied this ideal when he answered the call of duty and led the Romans to victory in 458 B.C.E., then returned to the simplicity of his farm immediately thereafter. Citizenship was a privilege in republican Rome, as was the honor of service in the Roman military, which was reserved exclusively for citizens.

As the dictatorship characteristic of the imperial period continued, however, this citizenship requirement was no longer the case. Rome evolved the concept of the professional soldier. Military service became a career path for ambitious citizens who saw it as a steppingstone to the position of governor and senator. In time, the same would apply to ambitious provincials. Roman citizenship also became progressively less exclusive, until 212 C.E., when the emperor Caracalla (r. 198–217) declared that all free men within the borders of the empire were automatically Roman citizens in order to increase his tax base.[3] Soon after, during the reign of Gallienus (253–68), the political breakdown of the Roman state had reached an unprecedented level of chaos. Uprisings, betrayals, and calls to civil war had so decimated the empire that Gallienus was forced to bar Roman senators from positions of command within the army.[4] The increasingly alienated Roman citizen had little interest in a supportive personal relationship with the state. Middle-class Romans avoided military service. Provincial recruits and slaves swelled the ranks of the Roman army. By the year 200, German soldiers may have comprised five to ten percent of the army. By 400, they numbered as high as fifty percent.[5]

## The Importance of Diocletian

Diocletian (r. 284–305) formally divided the empire in 285. He judged Rome a dangerously indefensible locale and moved his capital to Nicomedia in Asia Minor, several miles from Byzantium. While the senate still met in Rome, the seat of government had been removed from Italy. In 286, Diocletian appointed a comrade-in-arms, Maximian, coemperor of the West, although Diocletian retained veto power over him. The two emperors, known as augusti, each had a caesar beneath him who was his primary aid and designated successor. Thus the unitary rule of the Roman Empire was formally divided into a quaternary power, and the role of the senate was largely bypassed.

During the previous fifty years, the office of emperor had been declining in power and prestige. Diocletian attempted to reverse this trend by reinstituting emperor deification and embracing the oriental model of courtly behavior. He proclaimed himself the embodiment of Jupiter, divinely ordained to lead.

Diocletian created the conditions that were to result in the feudal system. He built the central management of the economy to a stranglehold of administrative expense and bureaucratic inefficiency. His policies of taxation so demoralized the wealthy that they abandoned their properties and left Rome for the countryside. Italy lost its manufacturing base to foreigners. The government mints had been debasing the coinage for over two decades, which resulted in gross inflation. Peasants were forced by imperial decree to remain on their farms. They were considered so intrinsically bound to the land that they were transferred along with property ownership. Diocletian enforced the same policy on industrial workers.

Under Diocletian, the conflict between Rome and Christianity was further exacerbated. Christian refusal to acknowledge the superiority of the emperor and the state had long strained the characteristic tolerance Rome showed to earlier faiths. The Romans viewed Christians as shrinking from the duties of good citizenship and patriotism and resented their aloofness. Christians believed their loyalty was to God and avoided interaction with what they perceived as the evils of Roman society. Their neglect of the Roman gods had long caused them to be blamed for many ills that befell the state. Their antimilitaristic stance, in the midst of the very real dangers to which Rome was increasingly exposed, further caused them to be viewed with hatred.

By 303, Roman hostility against Christianity came to a head, and Diocletian was persuaded to launch a full-scale persecution that lasted eight years. Churches were destroyed throughout the empire, property was confiscated, and an estimated fifteen hundred Christians were killed. Many more, including the bishop of Rome, recanted their faith. So severe were the Diocletian persecutions that the sympathies of the pagan population were aroused. In 311, the government relented and an edict of tolerance was put forth.

## CONSTANTINE AND CHRISTIANITY

On October 27, 312, the day before the great battle against his chief rival, Maxentius, for control of the West, young Constantine had a vision in which a flaming Christian cross was revealed as the sign under which he would conquer. On the morning of the battle, he dreamed that he should paint the sign of an X surmounted by a P on the shields of his soldiers. (This sign is known as the Christogram, the Greek monogram of Christ formed from the first two letters of the Greek word *christos*, chi and rho.) Constantine triumphed and entered Rome as the undisputed emperor of the West. By 324, he seized control of the Eastern Empire as well, establishing himself as sole emperor. The long-awaited political victory of Christianity had arrived.

Constantine was concerned with enforcing regularity of doctrine in order to prevent political divisiveness among his religious allies. He would accept no interference from theological disputes. One such that faced him almost immediately was the Donatist schism of 315. Donatus, the bishop of Carthage, criticized the behavior of many bishops during the Diocletian persecutions. He stated that if a bishop had compromised his oaths or recanted his beliefs because of the persecution, his further religious activities were rendered null and void. In other words, the spiritual condition of the individual who administered the sacraments was more important in the eyes of God than the sacerdotal office he held. Not surprisingly, many Church leaders vigorously disagreed. The supporters of Donatus countered by establishing a rival ecclesiastical hierarchy that was soon stamped out by Constantine, although the Donatist heresy would continue to resurface.

The greatest contemporary challenge to the unity of the Church, however, was the Arian heresy. Arius was an Egyptian priest who stated in 318 that Christ was neither the same as nor coeternal with God the Creator. Instead, Christ was the first created being and reigned as Logos. The Holy Spirit was created by the Logos and was thus even further from consubstantiality with God. The idea that God ruled the heavens and earth by creating successive emanations to handle various tasks was very much in line with the philosophic thought of the day — and is a key to many of the religious ideas that will be found in this book. Arius's supervising bishop, Alexander, vigorously protested against the emanationist doctrine and ordered Arius to cease his teaching. Arius refused. While Constantine considered the matter "quite trifling and unworthy of such fierce contests,"[6] he was forced to deal with

it. The intellectual battle raged so violently that pagan theater drama-
tized the controversy to mock Christianity.

In 325 Constantine convened the Council of Nicaea. Three hundred and eighteen bishops attended along with many lower clergy.
Athanasius, archdeacon under Alexander, successfully argued for the
doctrine of the Trinity. He forced Arius to admit that if Christ was a
created being, he was liable to sin. The matter was resolved when all
present, with the exception of Arius and two bishops, signed the statement known as the Nicene Creed — drafted with the aid of Constantine. Arius was anathematized by the council and exiled by the
emperor. His books were ordered burned and their possession became a
capital offense. Constantine financially rewarded the attending bishops
after their work was finished. The Council of Nicaea celebrated the
marriage of church and state, whose child would become the Dark
Ages.

In 324, Constantine officially founded the city of Constantinople
(modern Istanbul) on the site of the ancient city of Byzantium. He
spared no expense in building this lavish testimonial to his embrace of
Christianity and the end of paganism. He also built the Church of the
Holy Sepulcher in Jerusalem over the site said to be the Savior's tomb
and to contain a fragment of the True Cross on which Jesus had been
crucified. Yet the first Christian emperor was less than a saint. For
example, in 326 he ordered the execution of his first wife, his son, and
his nephew for reasons that remain unclear. On his deathbed in 337,
Constantine summoned the bishop Eusebius to administer the sacrament of baptism and so cleanse him of mortal sin.


## AFTER CONSTANTINE

Three and one-half centuries of despotism had destroyed the civic
virtue that was once the strength of Rome. The ethical degeneration of
late Roman society presaged our modern plunge toward secular human-
ism and moral relativism. Apathy and indolence replaced the patriotism and love of liberty that had motivated the hard men who built that
admirable republic. Those who now sought political office were attracted to collecting the graft that had become attendant on government
service. The lust for empire placed impossible demands on the army,
which remained logistically overstretched and a constant drain on the
economic resources of Roman society. Productive middle-class citizens

supported a legion of tax collectors who redistributed income into the hands of the extremely rich, the extremely poor, and the corrupt and inefficient bureaucracy. Population decline among the overburdened productive sector led to an inequality of population density in favor of immigrants. Increasing lawlessness and excessive taxation caused many free peasants to abandon their independence and willingly submit themselves to the protection of wealthy landowners. This trend continued to encourage the development of feudalism.

The last breath of paganism came during the short reign of Constantine's nephew Julian, "the Apostate," who held the throne from 361 to 363. Julian was imbued with the faith and asceticism of that rare soul who achieves spiritual greatness. He viewed Christianity as a hateful religion. He sought to restore the former glories of paganism with all of his power. Julian established a church with himself at the helm. Although generally tolerant of Christians, he denied them all state privileges and demanded the return of funds and property seized by Constantine. Julian was killed in battle at the age of thirty-two during an attempted conquest of Persia, thus ending any hope for reversing the tide of the victory of Christianity.

In 390, Christianity enjoyed a new political triumph. The Roman emperor of the East, Theodosious I, "the Great," had murdered seven thousand citizens of Thessalonica as punishment for killing his governor. Refused admission to the Church, he finally consented to be stripped of all royal insignia and to seek forgiveness for his sins in an act of public contrition imposed by Ambrose, the bishop of Milan, later canonized. In 392, Theodosious issued an edict banning paganism in the Roman Empire. In 394, he quelled a retaliatory pagan revolt and religious tolerance officially ceased to exist in the Roman Empire.

The persecution of Gnostics, pagans, and Jews ensured no philosophic rivalry to Christian ideological consolidation. In 391, an angry Christian mob destroyed the priceless Alexandrian library. This dealt a major blow to the intellectual spirit of paganism. Heresy became a catchall term for religious speculation. It would be several centuries before the power to turn this policy into mass murder was achieved, but rehearsals for the Inquisition were well under way.

In 410, weakened and frightened, Rome fell to the raw fury and vigor of Alaric and his army of Goths. The effete, luxury-loving Romans were no match for the rugged Germanic tribes. In 455, Rome was sacked again by the barbarian Vandals. In 472, the German armies achieved political control of the Western Roman Empire. Goths, Huns,

Picts, Celts, Angles, Visigoths, Saxons, Jutes, Teutons, Franks, and Ostrogoths overwhelmed the remains of Roman culture and civilization. Latin, the linguistic high-water mark of Rome, became a dead language. Its dilution by the tribal tongues of Rome's many conquerors resulted in the Romance languages of modern Europe.

In the Eastern Empire, the situation was quite different. The Byzantine emperor, ruling over the remains of the Roman Empire from his capital at Constantinople, was the wealthiest and most powerful Christian ruler in Europe during the Middle Ages, despite the vast cultural differences that seemed to place him so far from the West. The Eastern emperor Justinian (r. 527–65) codified the laws and statutes enacted since Constantine. The Code of Justinian was a milestone in the history of Western jurisprudence, regularizing and normalizing what had been a patchwork of tradition, fiat, and interpretation. It became the basis for the twelfth-century revival in both civil and ecclesiastical law in all of Europe except England. The centralized power of the monarchy recognized by the Justinian code proved an ideal model for the rise of medieval kingship.

Justinian declared Christianity the sole legal faith of the Roman Empire. He stipulated that the Church was subservient to the emperor. In 529, he closed the doors of the Neoplatonic academies in Athens.[†] Justinian rebuilt Constantinople, undertaking one of the most ambitious architectural enterprises in history and establishing the Byzantine style of art, a creative fusion of Roman, Greek, Oriental, and Christian antecedents. His cathedral of Santa Sophia still stands as the greatest achievement of Byzantine architecture.

On the other hand, Justinian's obsession with reuniting the Roman Empire severely weakened the Byzantine Empire. His armies invaded Italy, now under the domination of the Ostrogoths, ostensibly the emperor's loyal regents. Justinian's campaigns caused immense suffering in Italy as the Ostrogoths mounted a strong defense that lasted three decades. In order to win the alliance of the pope, Justinian launched a persecution against the Christian Monophysites of Egypt and Syria. Justinian's persecution so alienated this sect from Constantinople that

---

[†] This was the same year Saint Benedict founded the monastery of Monte Cassino. His Benedictine Rule would serve as the guide for most of the monastic communities of Christendom and was the foundation upon which the Rule of the Templars would be erected six centuries later.

when the Muslim conquerors arrived some decades after, they were welcomed as the lesser of two evils.

Monophysites believed Christ had only one nature, that he was altogether divine despite the fact that he took on incarnation and experienced the human cycle of birth, suffering, and death. This belief was in sharp contrast to the Nestorian heresy, which had been formally condemned at the Council of Ephesus in 431. The Nestorians believed Christ was actually two persons, one divine and one human. Roman Catholic doctrine, officially proclaimed at the Council of Chalcedon in 451, stated that Christ had two natures, one human and one divine. Thus the two extreme positions were regarded as heresy while the middle position was sanctioned as official doctrine. The denial of Christ's humanity would reappear in the medieval Cathar heresy.

Persian military expansion brought war to the Eastern Empire in the last half of the sixth century. The seventh century opened with invasions by northern tribes, such as the Avars and Slavs, tempted by the emperor's focus on Persia. In 614, the Persian king Khosrow II declared war on Byzantium and a holy war against Christianity. Persian armies sacked Jerusalem and massacred some ninety thousand Christians. The Church of the Holy Sepulcher was burned and the fragment of the True Cross carried to Persia. The conquests of Alexander the Great nearly a thousand years earlier were avenged as Persia briefly reclaimed its ancient power and glory. The Byzantine emperor Heraclius was finally able to regroup his forces and defeat Khosrow in 628. Khosrow's son made peace with Heraclius, yielding back Egypt, Palestine, Syria, Asia Minor, and western Mesopotamia and returning the fragment of the True Cross. Heraclius rebuilt the Church of the Holy Sepulcher. He was later able to defeat the Avars.

Exhausted by battle, neither the Persians nor the Eastern Romans were ready for the appearance of the Prophet Muhammad and the faith of Islam he founded in 622, a religion of the Book spread by the sword. The ferocity of the Muslim warrior in battle was exceeded only by his single-minded purpose — to achieve glory in the eyes of Allah. By 640, the Eastern Roman Empire had lost Syria, Egypt, and North Africa to Islam. The persecution of the Jews launched by Heraclius had alienated many citizens of Alexandria, Antioch, and other Mediterranean cities and caused them to welcome the more tolerant Muslim conquerors. The Muslims attempted to take Constantinople from 673–78, and again in 717, but were driven back both times. Constantinople

stood up against a third Islamic campaign launched in 960. (In anticipation of one of the most important psychoreligious themes of the Crusades, the Byzantine emperor Nicophorus unsuccessfully entreated the
patriarch Polyeuctus to promise martyrdom to Christian soldiers who
died in battle against the Muslims.)

## CHRISTIANITY AND THE DARK AGES

The sixth century marked the beginning of the Dark Ages in western
Europe. While the Byzantine Empire generally prospered, despite its
loss of territory, western Europe spent the six centuries after the death
of Justinian in chaos, war, cultural degeneration, superstition, ignorance, and poverty. The majority of western Europe, including Italy,
Gaul (modern France), and Spain, had fallen to the barbarian tribes
who had earlier overtaken Rome. Plague and famine decimated Europe.
By 550, Rome, which once had a population of one million people, was
reduced to forty thousand souls, half of whom were maintained by papal
alms.

Life was harsh and brutal. The peasantry, although free, were poor,
uneducated, and politically impotent. Skin disease was epidemic
because of the Church's prohibition against nudity and bathing. Lice
and similar vermin tormented all, regardless of social class.[7] By the
beginning of the seventh century, literacy was reserved for the clergy.
Science, medicine, and literature were replaced by magic, superstition,
and religious texts. Eighty percent of the population during the Dark
Ages never moved more than ten miles from their place of birth. As a
result of poor nutrition and medicine, the average life expectancy was
thirty years, while the average height for men was not more than five
feet three inches. Throughout the ninth and tenth centuries, Europe
endured a perpetual state of war, decimated by continuous aggression
from Scandinavian, eastern European, and Germanic tribes, as well as
Muslims. Savagery and faith, ignorance and piety, agriculture and
aggression — this mixture embodied the intellectual stagnation of the
Dark Ages.

The rude and unlettered barbarian tribes who had eclipsed the rule
of the Roman Empire were led by the Roman Church. The Church
provided the glue by which these scattered tribes became a united force
capable of protecting the Continent against the military expansion

of Islam and the Oriental hordes. Its priests, bishops, and monastic communities provided political as well as spiritual leadership among far-flung and isolated towns and villages. Ecclesiastical councils served as courts of justice. Christian monasteries preserved learning and literacy. Norman Cantor estimates that ninety percent of those who attained literacy between 600 and 1100 received their education in a monastic school.[8] The Church extended the hand of charity to the poor and suffering.

On the other hand, the Church was responsible for inculcating pernicious doctrines that infested Europe for centuries. Original sin was no mere philosophical or religious speculation. The concept of sin informed the entire social, political, and legal structure. Since the human condition was fallen to begin with, justice was, by definition, impossible. Social improvement was not a goal. This was a reversal of earlier Jewish beliefs in the goodness of God and the possibility of reformation of society through adherence to the Divine. To the medieval Christian, life was a test and trial in preparation for death. If one were good, the joys of Paradise followed the loss of the body. The soul-chilling horror of eternal torment in Hell awaited the wicked. Suffering cleansed and purified the soul in preparation for its after-death reward. Contrition, confession, and penance were introduced in the sixth century by Pope Gregory I, "the Great" (later canonized), as the sole means by which the sin-befouled human being could advance through the intermediate state of Purgatory.

Nature herself was evil. She was the source of the insistent, instinctual sexual drive to reproduce. Those conceived by the sin of sex were sinful at birth. Celibacy became a spiritual ideal rather than a spiritual technique. The attempt to promulgate and enforce rigid antisexual behavior on the masses led to a raging rebellion within the European psyche. Insanity and disease are the inevitable consequences of sexual repression, and they took a horrid toll during the Middle Ages. Because sickness of the body was seen as God's punishment for wickedness, the medical arts were confined to Arab and Jewish practitioners and to women, who studied herbs and the healing properties of nature. These were among the many who fell in that great battle against Satan and the flesh known as the Inquisition — the central command center for the centuries of murder, torture, and hysteria that followed its establishment.

While Christianity endured repeated episodes of corruption with-

in its leadership, and while some of its doctrines were clearly responsible for much of the suffering and weakness of Western civilization, it
also served a higher purpose. Through the exalted story of Jesus and his
holiness, sacrifice, and resurrection, Christianity provided the moral
teachings designed to lead many generations of human beings to a
higher stage of spiritual evolution.

## FEUDALISM

"In theory, feudalism was a magnificent system of moral reciprocity,
binding the men of an endangered society to one another in a complex
web of mutual obligation, protection, and fidelity."[9] The savagery of
the invasions by northern Europeans during the fifth through tenth
centuries encouraged the collectivization of the population under a
largely autonomous land-owning nobility. The invasions inclined aristocrats to leave the targeted cities and establish themselves at their
country estates. Feudalism grew in France, England, Italy, and Germany
during the sixth century as weak monarchs rewarded jealous aristocrats
and efficient generals with greater land holdings in return for their services and support in administration and war.

Independent peasant farmers, or *villeins*, attached themselves to
the larger centralized landowners. Ninety percent of the feudal economy was agricultural. The rich gradually purchased peasant lands and
instituted an elaborate system of tenant farming in return for military
protection and the physical safety offered by fortified castles. A series of
villages grew up around the great estates. These rural villages allowed
independent peasants and bound serfs to enjoy the protection and con-
venience of living close to their fields without the dangers of isolation.
The villages provided opportunities for social interaction, while their
marketplaces allowed for the exchange and barter of goods and services.

Feudal society was organized as a hierarchy that included at its lowest level the slave. This class included white warriors captured in
battle, such as the Slavic invaders, or the North African Muslims purchased by Mediterranean slave traders. The Church forbade the
enslavement of Christians but held large numbers of slaves who had
been donated along with grants of land.

European slavery diminished as serfdom increased. The serf was a
farmer who tilled a plot of land in exchange for a lifetime of guaranteed

employment and protection, as long as he produced the required amount of crops, money, labor, and military service. He was essentially the property of his lord. He could be evicted at will. The lord could sell his labor to another. In order to pass along his land and serf status to his children, the serf required the consent of the lord. In France a serf could abrogate the arrangement by giving up his land, but in England he was denied even that freedom. The lord had numerous legal rights over his serfs, among which was the demoralizing practice of *jus primae noctis*, or *droit du seigneur*, the lord's right to deflower the wife of a peasant on her wedding night unless an adequate fee could be paid instead. In practice, leniency most often gave rise to greater productivity, and a sensible lord was a fair one — while a wise serf was supportive of his lord's prosperity, recognizing it as his own. It has been estimated that in late medieval Germany, a serf had to pay up to two-thirds of his produce to his lord.[10] (Since this percentage is the modern equivalent of both rent and taxes, it gives pause for thought.)

Vassals or retainers were free men of limited means who attached themselves to lords by an act of homage and a vow of fealty, and who provided military service or personal attendance in exchange for protection, land (a fief), and sometimes serfs. (The word *vassal* comes from the Celtic word meaning "boy." During the sixth and seventh centuries, vassals were essentially teenage gangs attached to various warlords. They would be sent to do the nefarious bidding of their noble masters, receiving financial support in return. As the concept of the mounted cavalry evolved during the eighth century, the position of the hired warrior was elevated. The enormous expense associated with arming and equipping the mounted knight caused nobles to endow them with lands and peasants by which they could earn their own support.)

Vassalage extended throughout the feudal hierarchy. For example, a lesser lord could become the vassal of a greater lord. A person could take the oath of vassalage to more than one lord. The secondary oath was of simple homage, while the primary lord received the oath of "liege homage" or full allegiance. All lords were vassals of the king. As the feudal decentralization of the ninth and tenth centuries progressed, each layer of vassalage took more political and judicial power into its own hands. By the tenth century, the specifics of feudal contractual obligations were fairly standardized.

The feudal lord was, in theory, a wealthy and skilled administrator whose responsibilities included offering military protection to those in his care, organizing the agricultural and industrial activities of his estates, and providing military service to his liege lord — the king — in times of war. The feudal lord provided, at a small fee, the heavy and expensive equipment needed by the peasant community, such as wine presses, mills, and ovens. He maintained lands for hunting, woods for fuel, and the farms on which the serfs earned their own and his livelihood. The lord was responsible for the maintenance and construction of roads, bridges, and canals. His castle included a common area large enough for all members of the surrounding villages to gather for defense, food, and water during attack. He provided funds for the armored, mounted warriors who served as his elite military corps.

The Catholic Church, although initially resistant, played a large part in the feudal system. It began to imbue feudal óaths and the ceremonies of vassalage with religious content. The Church accumulated many estates, complete with serfs, as offerings from the faithful. Bishops were ritually invested with their sacramental symbols of office by kings, who received clerical oaths of fealty and reciprocated with gifts of tracts of land. In time, the Church became the greatest feudal landholder in Europe.

The king occupied the top of the feudal hierarchy. He was the lord of all vassals. His position was buttressed by several millennia of tradition inherited from the Mediterranean roots of Western civilization regarding the sacred kingship of the realm. Yet the position of feudal kings depended far more on the willing support of their vassals than in either earlier or later centuries. The autonomy of feudal lords functioned as a check on European monarchs for a thousand years. The state was protected by the military power of the organized, independent forces of the lords. The king was first among relative equals. In exchange for the continued loyalty of his nobles, he gave land and money. In theory he owned all the land in his realm, while in practice his own landholdings were often no larger than those of his lords.

The tug-of-war between king and nobles is the story of the establishment of the nation-state. As commerce began to develop in Europe during the waning years of the Dark Ages, a wealthy class arose outside the traditional boundaries of the feudal system. This new merchant class demanded centralized stability to rein in the chaos. For example, the road tolls levied by feudal lords competed with highwaymen to discourage travel and commerce. Kings were too impoverished to provide protection for life and property — the sole legitimate function of government. The wealthy merchants achieved their goals by financing the centralized power of the king against the nobles. Popes also found that dealing with individual kings could be less unpredictable than trying to work with groups of barons, so they too encouraged the growth of the monarchy. Finally, the fractious nobles were all too frequently unwilling to maintain order and discipline among themselves, as centuries of privilege had inbred arrogance. The tide of history was turning against them, and by the end of the thirteenth century, the French king had triumphed over both nobles and pope to reign supreme over his realm. By 1500, monarchy was the primary form of government in Europe.

## CHIVALRY

Chivalry, which developed from a combination of Germanic military codes, Muslim warrior ideals, and Christian devotion, marked the creative high point of feudalism. Its myths were spread and its praises hymned by wandering troubadour minstrel poets throughout the Languedoc region of southern France beginning in the late eleventh century. The elite mounted and armored cavalry in service to feudal nobles and devoted to the arts of war were imbued with an inspiring ideology.

While the concept of a military elite remains a contemporary archetype, it was a more formalized and widespread cultural phenomenon during the period of chivalry. For example, the medieval tournaments began as training exercises in the techniques of battle. In time, tournaments evolved into elaborate affairs that could last up to a week, serving as festive communal events of great pageantry and offering opportunities for social and commercial interaction as well as entertainment. Poetry, song, and dance added to the romance of these gala events. Heraldry was a by-product of the tournament. The armored and vizored knights developed graphic symbol sets, unique emblems painted on shields or embroidered on banners, to identify themselves.

The order of knighthood was open to the noble-born candidate, who was received only after completing a long apprenticeship. At the age of seven or eight, the youth began his training as a page. He went on to become a squire between the ages of twelve and fourteen. Vows of Christian fealty overlay the institution of knighthood. The ceremony of induction began with a day of fasting, a ritual bath of purification, a night spent in solitary prayer, confession, and communion. The knight-to-be's sword was blessed by a priest. His liege lord then administered the oath of knighthood and the accolade of reception.

Protection of the weak, courtesy, truthfulness, defense of the Church, chastity, honor, and courage were all elements of the code of chivalry. Romantic love — the idealization of the beloved — was another aspect. The knight pledged himself to a noble lady to whom his efforts were dedicated. While service to the chivalric lady shared many aspects with the devotion accorded to the Virgin Mary, there was a definite sexual element. Medieval marriage was based more on property than love. When troubadours hymned their love for a lady, she was often a married woman. A joyless marriage frequently left open the door to an adulterous tryst with her devoted knight or poet.

Chivalrous Grail literature popularized by twelfth-century troubadours introduced themes of the mystic quest interspersed with images of romantic love. Personalized romantic love was heretofore unknown in Western culture. The medieval celebration of emotional and sentimental love, accompanied by the chivalric idealization of the feminine, was a marked departure from the utilitarian impersonality with which women had previously been viewed. The elevation of the uniqueness of romantic love necessarily focuses attention on the needs and wants of the individual. This represented a complete rebellion against the collective and rigidly stratified feudal social structure.

There was, of course, a darker side to the culture of knighthood. In theory the purpose of the knight was to protect his homeland against foreign invasion. The reality, however, was of interminable infighting among rival feudal lords. Feudal battles were more common but less deadly than modern wars. Elaborate rules and customs defined the art of war, and ransom was a frequent consequence of the less-than-lethal medieval battlefield. This practice had the net effect of allowing for more fighting. In addition, the aggressive mounted troops were often guilty of the excesses common to an armed elite set over an unarmed citizenry. The Church attempted to protect the people from the bullying and battling of the knights and nobles by instituting the Peace of God movement as early as the eleventh century. Nobles were encouraged to arbitrate their differences and forswear fighting on certain days.

The introduction and widespread use of the longbow in the fourteenth century struck the first blow against the mounted knight, as a skilled archer was easily able to dispatch the horse of the heavily weighted armored knight and force him to fight on foot, where he was most ineffective. The introduction of gunpowder in the fifteenth century spelled the end of the medieval knight.

## The Holy Roman Empire and the Growth of Europe

The Merovingian dynasty ruled France from 486 through 751, progressively weakening in power. Charles Martel (the Hammer) was a brave and resourceful general under the Merovingians. His military prowess saved Europe from the Muslim invasion during the eighth century. In 751, his son Pepin III approached Pope Zacharias for his blessing in overturning the last Merovingian king. Pepin had wisely allied himself with the vastly influential Benedictine monk Saint Boniface, who had worked tirelessly to unify the Catholic faith and clergy under the pope.

The pope was in desperate need of political support. He was involved in one of the periodic flare-ups with the Byzantine emperor on doctrinal matters and gladly welcomed the armed power of the state to buttress his spiritual authority. Boniface traveled to Rome in support of Pepin's aspirations. The pope assented, and Pepin was elected king of the Franks (a generic name applied first to a specific European tribal group, next to the French and German citizens of the Holy Roman Empire, and finally, quite loosely, to all European Crusaders). At the ceremony of coronation, Boniface, serving as the pope's representative, anointed Pepin with holy oil and crowned him king, inaugurating a new conceptual stage in the politico-religious development of western Europe.

Upon the death of Pepin, the kingdom passed to his son Charles the Great, Carolus Magnus, or Charlemagne, universally considered the greatest of medieval kings, who ruled from 768 to 814. Charlemagne was an extraordinary man who stood some six feet four inches tall, was deeply religious, and possessed a keen intellect, a tremendous thirst for knowledge, and unbounded energy. He was married four times, kept several mistresses, and fathered eighteen children to whom he remained loyal and protective. In 773 he aided the pope against the Lombards, assumed the crown of Lombardy, and obligated himself as the temporal protector of the Church. His kingdom included the modern countries of Italy, France, and Germany. His capital was at Aachen. He was a brilliant strategist and fierce soldier who refined his military prowess through fifty-three campaigns.

Charlemagne was also an able administrator. He erected a system of education during an otherwise backward era, learned to read, and strove mightily to learn to write. He strengthened his army through superior organization and by providing the psychological support of patriotism and religious sanction. He encouraged agriculture, industry, and finance. His court included administrators, church officials, scholars, and judges. He sought inclusion and participation by others in decision making, convening large assemblies of property owners for semiannual policy-making sessions. He attempted to protect the peasantry from enforced serfdom, while enabling the aristocracy to exert a strong measure of self-government. The growing literacy he encouraged helped Europe to emerge from the barbarism of the Dark Ages.

In 799, Pope Leo III was physically attacked and imprisoned. He escaped and fled to Charlemagne for protection. Charlemagne arranged for the pope's safe return to Rome under armed escort. In 800, Charlemagne entered Rome and, on December 1, convened an assembly of Franks and Romans that dropped all charges against the pope. A great celebration was arranged for the Christmas holiday. As Charlemagne knelt to pray, Pope Leo placed a jeweled crown on his head and consecrated him Emperor and Augustus of the Romans, a title reserved since 476 for the Eastern emperor at Constantinople, the official head of the Roman Empire. This was a bold move for which there was no prior source of authority or tradition. It is not known who originated the idea of the coronation, or even whether Charlemagne was aware he would be crowned when he knelt.

The creation of the Holy Roman Empire was an act that strengthened both king and pope for one thousand years. Church and state were united. The divine right of kings was acknowledged by the Church, as was the king-making power of the Church by the king. The king was strengthened against the nobility, while the Church was strengthened against the king. Of course, the Roman Church's relationship with Constantinople was further damaged.

Charlemagne interpreted his new role as the revival of the true and all-powerful ruler of the ancient empire of Rome and acted accordingly until his death in 814 at the age of seventy-two. The Carolingian kings who followed him were, however, unable to maintain the high standard he had set for wisdom, power, and courage. The Scandinavian invasions of the ninth and tenth centuries especially highlighted their impotence. The Carolingian dynasty ruled until 987, when Hugh Capet was unanimously elected king of France as the first of the Capetian dynasty.

The establishment of England as a single country was initiated under King Egbert of Wessex in 829, half a century after the Danish invasions. Most of England north of the Thames was still under Danish control in 871, the year that Alfred the Great took the throne and continued the unification of the nation. By 899, he had defeated the Danish invaders. A century later the Scandinavian attacks resumed, motivating most free peasants to surrender their property and independence to the great landowners in exchange for military protection. In 1016, Prince Canute of Denmark became king of England. He was a wise leader who improved and civilized the country by accepting Christianity, building churches, acculturating himself to the mores and history of his Anglo-Saxon subjects, and appointing Englishmen to all high offices of the realm. He later became king of Denmark and Norway, ruling all three countries from his capital at Westchester. In September of 1066, the Norman forces of William the Conqueror arrived in an armada of fourteen hundred vessels. William was crowned king of England on Christmas Day, 1066. The tribal mixture of Angle, Saxon, Celt, Gaul, Jute, and Dane that heretofore composed the English nation was now enriched with Norman blood.

The Norman conquest led to the political unification of England as the first stable monarchy of Europe. William strengthened the nation with an intelligently structured and innovative administrative apparatus. This included his policies of taxation, military recruitment, control and support of the clergy, and record-keeping efforts. The English judicial system (from which the American system is primarily derived) was also unique. It rejected the centralized monarchical model of the Justinian Code and adapted the German tribal model of community-based law. The common law now rested in the hands of the legislative apparatus of both the king and the community, rather than being an expression of the will of the absolute monarch as under Justinian. The English-Germanic system worked to decentralize power through juries, while the Justinian system centralized power in the hands of the judge as a representative of the emperor.[†] Ideally, the king is as much a subject of the common law as is any other citizen. This principle was first formally embodied in 1215 in the Magna Carta, a history-making con-

---

[†] "Judicial activism," that is, the seizure of legislative power by the judiciary, derives from the Justinian system. Under common-law principles, the power to make laws resides exclusively with the people through their representatives in the state and national legislative bodies. The judiciary is limited to interpretation and administration of those laws, rather than being allowed to indulge in broad extemporizations that effectively create new law.

tractual agreement between the king and the aristocracy in which the king was forced to recognize certain rights of the nobility that were not to be infringed. In time, the restriction on monarchy instituted by the Magna Carta would result in the American Constitution, the greatest and longest-lived formal check on tyranny in history.

Denmark, Sweden, Norway, and Finland were inhabited at this time by Norse tribes whose population had outgrown the limitations of their icy territories. In 800, they began the two and one-half centuries of Viking conquests. Teutonic Norsemen launched campaigns against Scotland, Ireland, Iceland, Greenland, Russia, France, Sicily, and England. The mythology of these brave and fearsome warriors included a heavenly reception in the great hall of Valhalla for those who died honorably in battle, an idea that would reappear among the religious themes that energized the Crusades.

Germany began to emerge as a nation after the Treaty of Verdun in 843, which elevated one of Charlemagne's grandsons, Louis, or Ludwig, as the nation's first king. He ruled over the remains of the barbarian tribes of Goths, Vandals, Burgundians, Franks, and Lombards who had earlier spread throughout the Roman Empire and had since been joined by the Slavic Wends, Saxons, Thuringians, Bavarians, and Swabians. The Magyar attacks in 900 proved the weakness of the central German government, which was forced to rely on the armies of its provincial dukes for military survival. This contributed to the strengthening of the feudal system in Germany. Soon after, however, Otto I, "the Great" (r. 936–973), persuaded a number of provincial dukes to participate in his coronation. When these dukes later rebelled against him, he appointed his chosen friends to their own duchies, thus weakening the power of the nobility and advancing his royal ambitions. In 962 he was crowned Roman Emperor of the West by Pope John XII. From 955 to 1075 Germany was the most prosperous country in Europe.

Spain had been invaded by the Moors in 711, and southern Spain remained under Islamic dominion for 500 years thereafter. Muslim expansion into France was checked first by Charles Martel in 732 and again in 759 by Pepin the Short. In Spain, however, the Muslims were a welcome change from the primitive Visigoths. Islamic cultural achievements in art, architecture, and poetry accompanied a generally fair and effective political administration. Muslims introduced scientific agriculture and metallurgy. Cordova in the tenth century was considered the most sophisticated city in Europe, with paved sidewalks, lighted streets, great bridges, a large freshwater aqueduct, beautiful gardens, and a world-renowned university.

Northern Spain was home to the displaced Christians. Its population included the Goths, Suevi, Berbers, and Celts who had been driven from the south during the Muslim conquest and had succeeded in halting the northern Islamic advance in 718. Christian Spain was poor and weak in contrast to the south. Political disunion was fomented by the feudal structure of a weakened king and an independent and aggressive nobility. Agricultural ineptitude kept the people of the north poor and ill fed. The *reconquista* of Spain lasted well into the thirteenth century as Christians fought to expel the Muslims. After a two-century lull in this effort, the Christian conquest of Granada in 1492 finally ended the political power of Islam in Europe.

Italy had three separate areas of political influence. In the north lived the Lombards who had migrated from Scandinavia in the sixth century. In the eighth century, their southern advance toward Rome was halted by Pope Gregory III. In 774 Charlemagne conquered Lombardy and annexed it under Frankish rule. Central Italy was held by the Church, headquartered in Rome. Here, competition among the Roman nobility for control of the papacy was a continual strain. Pagan Rome never accepted the dour celibacy preached by its Catholic clergy, remaining ever true to its sensuous and artistic past. Southern Italy was gradually invaded by the Normans beginning in 1036. At first they hired themselves out to rival southern Italian nobles. Eventually they grew numerous enough to battle among themselves. In 1053, Robert Guiscard established himself as king of southern Italy, from which he launched successful campaigns against the Byzantines, Venetians, and Germans.

## EMERGENCE FROM THE DARK AGES

The medieval view of the approaching millennium was increasingly fraught with anxiety as the tenth century progressed. The Revelation of Saint John had declared the importance of the one-thousand-year period. Interpretations ranged from the eradication of the wicked to the establishment of the reign of Satan, from the second coming of Christ to the destruction of the earth — whatever cataclysmic alterations of normal events could be construed to be the meaning of Saint John's text. Included in the psychology of millennial mania was the yearning for the ultimate resting place in death that characterizes the psyche at war with itself. When the year 1000 came and went rather uneventfully, a sense of anticlimax, even cautious optimism, replaced fear. European Christianity began to awaken to the possibility of options.

Tentative social developments of the mid-tenth century flourished in the eleventh. Frontiers receded as the great forests were cleared and swamps were drained, providing lumber for renewed construction and lands for agriculture. The use of water-powered mills to grind grain and water-powered sawmills to prepare lumber increased the supply of food and shelter. The horse collar and stirrups improved transportation. The widening vistas of emergence from the Dark Ages encouraged increased mobility as nobles, merchants, ecclesiastics, scholars, and pilgrims were willing to brave the dangers posed by both the robber barons in their great castles and the bands of brigands who infested European roads.

Cities grew as centers of commerce and crafts. Merchants and artisans sought to protect themselves by forming guilds and corporations. Rights of self-government were purchased by groups of these wealthy bourgeois who were increasingly able to exert political control of the cities they built. Venice, Genoa, and Pisa became the international commercial centers of western Europe. Navigational improvements encouraged sea trade. Western Europeans began to penetrate the Mediterranean, long controlled by Byzantines and Muslims.

Churches and monasteries were built throughout the eleventh century as the Christian consolidation of Europe was bearing fruit in increased piety. The popularity of the pilgrimage to the Holy Land as an act of religious devotion became widespread. The devotee could walk in the very footsteps of Christ and the many other heroes and heroines of the Bible. The pilgrimage also served as a convenient alternative to prison as a means for the expiation of sin. The culprit could be both effectively distanced from the community for a period of years and allowed the opportunity for genuine repentance. European pilgrims, young and old, rich and poor, traveled in large numbers throughout Europe and the Near East in search of spiritual growth and religious experience.

## JERUSALEM

Jerusalem was the major destination of the medieval pilgrim. A tax paid to the Muslims enabled Christians to travel safely to the various holy shrines in Palestine. Yet, as the pilgrimage increased in importance in medieval Europe, a growing sense of frustration developed among the Christian faithful against the four and a half centuries of Muslim rule of the Holy Land.

Prior to the seventh-century Muslim conquests, Jerusalem had long been under the control of Europe. Alexander the Great had taken the city in 334 B.C.E. during his Persian campaign. When Alexander's empire was divided after his death, the Ptolemies took Egypt and Palestine. The region remained under Hellenic dominion until Rome began her conquest in 190 B.C.E. Jerusalem then became part of the Roman Empire until the short-lived Persian conquest of 614. It was reclaimed by Heraclius in 628. In 638, however, the Muslim army took the Holy City, and it had been in their hands ever since. By the eighth century, Arabs predominated in the population.

Muslim conquerors were fairly benign rulers of occupied territories. Jews and Christians were regarded as "people of the Book" and afforded religious freedom. In fact, taxes were lower than they had been under Greek and Roman rulership. The Christians who lived in the Holy Land had no allegiance to Roman Catholicism or the pope. They were either under the authority of the Patriarch of Jerusalem, affiliated with the Greek Orthodox Church and the Byzantine emperor, or members of the various local Gnostic groups.

Jerusalem is as sacred to Islam as it is to Judaism and Christianity. In 691, the Omayyad caliph Abd-al-Malik erected a group of structures known as the Venerable Sanctuary near the site of the Church of the Holy Sepulcher. He built the Dome of the Rock to house the rock viewed by the Jews as the center of the world. It was upon this rock that Abraham was said to have intended to sacrifice Isaac in response to God's command, where Moses received the Ark of the Covenant, and over which Solomon and Herod had built their temples. From this rock Muhammad had ascended to Heaven astride his winged steed; if one had enough faith, the Prophet's footprints were still visible. This rock was also where Muhammad's encounters with Abraham, Moses, and Jesus took place.

## Constantinople and the Byzantine Empire

Byzantium, the ancient capital of the Byzantine Empire, was founded in 657 B.C.E. Strategically poised as the gateway between East and West, Asia and Europe, it has remained a major urban center ever since. Renamed Constantinople and dedicated in 330 as the capital of the Roman Empire, it was also known as New Rome. The Eastern Roman or Byzantine Empire stood for over one thousand years as the vital defender of Europe against the ingress of Asian conquerors. It also served as the repository in which classical Greek culture was preserved for the modern world. The stability of its government and administrative apparatus and the richness of its arts far exceeded any similar accomplishments of the West. Constantinople finally fell to the Ottoman Turks in 1453.

From the fifth through the fifteenth century, Constantinople remained the greatest commercial market and shipping center in the world. It served as the hub for immense amounts of both trade and cultural interaction between Europe and the Holy Land prior to the Crusades. The state of war that existed after the First Crusade was undoubtedly a most unwelcome handicap to late-eleventh-century Byzantine and Near Eastern business interests.

Constantinople's population was both Greek and Roman. By the seventh century, Greek had become the language of government, literature, prayer, and common speech. Yet Byzantine civilization was more Asian than European. The classical Greek spirit had been substantially modified as a result of its extensive contact with the Near East. The mystical and philosophical creativity of the Greek mind was more easily complemented by similar characteristics of Eastern thought than by the unsophisticated rigidity and orthodoxy of primitive Western Christians. The proximity of Greece to Constantinople, which lay just across the Aegean Sea, may also help to account for the oriental cast of mind of Byzantine Greeks. An overland trip between Athens and Rome was more than twice the distance of the trip from Athens to Constantinople.

## Eastern and Western Christianity

The medieval popularity of the pilgrimage in western Europe engendered a fascination, to the point of obsession, with Constantinople and the Byzantine Empire. Here were housed the major relics of the Christian faith, all of which were outside the control of papal Catholicism. The Crown of Thorns itself was believed to be in the possession of the Greek Orthodox Church.

The division between the Eastern Orthodox and Western Roman Churches had continued to escalate since Diocletian's third-century division of the Roman Empire. As Christianity continued to grow in power, doctrinal variations between the Roman and Orthodox faiths inexorably widened. The language barrier between the Latin-speaking West and Greek-speaking East further exacerbated their differences.

In politics, the Roman Church perceived a conflict between the powers of the Church and the powers of the state and concluded that any questions of loyalty must be decided in favor of God. The popes were ever locked in a struggle for power with princes and kings. Latin Christianity demanded autonomy for the Church. Such was its power that, by the sixth century, Pope Gregory I could threaten European princes and demand their obedience to God's law. (It should be noted that this spurning of the state by the Roman Church was the policy of a more mature institution. The rise of Christianity had been greatly facilitated by its contact with the state, as the examples of Constantine and Charlemagne most notably demonstrate. The state had often proven its value to the Church in such distasteful activities as the persecution of heretics, whether the Arians of the fourth century or the Cathars of the thirteenth.)

In contrast, the Eastern Empire was a theocracy. The religious hierarchy of the Eastern Church was traditionally under the rule of the emperor, recognized as head of the Church. Eastern Orthodox Catholicism accepted the state as an ordained force under God. Allegiance to the political leader was a spiritual obligation, and political dissent was blasphemy. While the emperor was dependent for his position on the Church, the patriarchs were appointed and deposed by the emperor. The balance of power was truly delicate.

Greek theologians accepted the immanence of the Kingdom of God — through piety, the believer could experience salvation on earth. To the Roman Church, the kingdom of God was a transcendent event reserved for the future. Biblical support for these conflicting positions was claimed by both sides, each choosing to emphasize different passages of either the Gospels or the Acts of the Apostles. The argument for the hegemony of the Roman bishop based on Peter's scriptural authorization fell on deaf ears in the Eastern Church, as did the Roman doctrine of the infallibility of the pope. The Eastern Church accepted the emperor as a designated representative of the Kingdom of Heaven, Christ's vicar on earth. The Byzantine vision of society as the image of Heaven was never duplicated in the West, even in the doctrine of the divine right of kings. While western Europe may have accepted the king as God's ordained political regent on earth, the popes jealously guarded the spiritual leadership of the Church by physically conferring that ordination.

During the seventh-century Islamic conquests of Alexandria, Antioch, and Jerusalem, the patriarchs of these regions were displaced. Thus the Patriarch of Constantinople became the true head of the Eastern Church, as the Roman pope had assumed control of the West. As the Arab conquests extended into the eighth century, the military problems besetting the Roman emperor in Constantinople left him less able to defend his Western protectorates. Rome, although officially and traditionally under the political dominion of the Byzantine emperor, sought the protection of the growing power of the Frankish rulers. The ultimate repercussion of Rome's overture to the Franks was the establishment of the Holy Roman Empire in 800.

The division between the Eastern and Western churches continued to intensify. The central Christian symbol, the cross, differed in each: the Greek cross was equal-armed, while Rome used the familiar Calvary style. Vestments and ritual ornaments also differed and the Greek faithful stood as they prayed while the Romans knelt. Greek priests were encouraged to marry, while celibacy was enjoined upon the Roman clergy. Political conflicts further increased the animosity between the churches. The rejection of the Byzantine emperor in favor of the Frankish king infuriated the Eastern patriarch. The pope's coronation of Charlemagne as a rival Roman emperor in 800 brought the conflict to a boiling point. In 863, the pope excommunicated the patriarch. In 867, the patriarch excommunicated the pope. The death of both protagonists, however, temporarily prevented further conflict.

In 1054, the Great Schism finally occurred between Rome and Constantinople. The patriarch Michael Cerularius was an ambitious leader. He made military alliances and incited popular sentiment in his favor. He closed churches in Constantinople that celebrated the Latin rite, excommunicated the clergy who continued to practice it, and widely criticized the pope on doctrinal grounds. Pope Leo IX wrote him demanding his submission to Rome and sent papal legates to Constantinople. A bull of excommunication against the patriarch was issued on July 16, 1054. Christianity was irreparably divided.

In 1057, the Byzantine general Isaac Comnenus rose to become emperor. His nephew Alexius Comnenus took the throne in 1081. Alexius faced a very difficult military situation that had been worsened by the Turkish seizure of Jerusalem in 1076. Turkish forces were on the march to Constantinople. In 1095, during the Council of Piacenza, Alexius appealed to the Christian West to come to the aid of the Christian East. He offered to join the Eastern to the Western Church in return for Western aid against the Muslims — thus setting the stage for the Crusades.

## Papal Reform

In addition to his battles with the Eastern Church, Pope Leo IX was also actively concerned with introducing a series of reforms to the Roman Church. A long period of papal corruption, lasting for most of a century and a half, had brought the Church to a moral low. When Leo assumed the papacy in 1049, he exerted every effort to return the Church to its proper spiritual role and the papacy to a position of respect. He roundly condemned and sought to eradicate the practice of clerical marriage and concubinage that had spread throughout Europe in violation of Church policy. Wielding the ultimate papal sword, the threat of excommunication, he worked tirelessly.

Leo's death in 1054 was followed by two decades of papal weakness until the accession of Pope Gregory VII, who reigned from 1073 to 1085. For three decades before becoming pope, Gregory had been an active member of the reform movement. He had been largely responsible for the decision by the Lateran Council of 1057 to move the election of the pope to the college of cardinals and thus out of the hands of the German emperor and Roman nobility. As pope, he renewed Leo's battle against clerical marriage and simony (the dispensing of ecclesiastical positions and favors in return for financial contributions). By 1074, he began to proselytize for a crusade that he proposed to lead in person. His goals were to rescue the Holy Land, heal the Great Schism with Constantinople, and unite all Europe as a theocratic republic.

## The Rise of the Antipope

Gregory is best known for his battle to end royal or lay investiture, the practice by which secular kings chose bishops and invested them with the symbols of their episcopal authority. Gregory identified this as a source of worldly corruption. He was determined to bring every aspect of the Church under the authority of the pope. Secular rulers were justifiably opposed to his plan because of the extent of the lands and revenues with which they had endowed their appointed bishops, as well as their traditional authority in the matter dating back to the days of Constantine.

Gregory's greatest rival was the young German emperor Henry IV. Gregory railed against lay investiture at the papal synod of 1075. Henry angrily renounced his obedience to Gregory and publicly called on him to step down as pope. Gregory excommunicated him and declared him deposed as emperor. He further threatened any noblemen who supported Henry with excommunication. The political repercussions of this motivated Henry to present himself before the pope and plead for absolution. He journeyed to northern Italy, where Gregory was resting en route to an assembly whose purpose was to replace Henry as king. Henry waited outside the castle where Gregory was staying, literally standing in the snow for three days, appealing for a papal audience. Gregory finally absolved him.

By 1080, Gregory again excommunicated Henry and again declared him deposed, and began working with a group of rebellious German nobles to set up an antiking. In retaliation, Henry's German bishops declared Gregory removed as pope. They chose as his successor Guibert, the archbishop of Ravenna. Henry laid siege to Rome from 1081 to 1083. In 1084, his troops took the city. Guibert was crowned as Pope Clement III in Saint Peter's Church, and he reciprocally crowned Henry emperor. Gregory remained powerless to intervene.

Gregory envisioned an imperial papacy in which the spiritual and religious authority of the pope would reign supreme over all secular rulers and nations, much as God ruled the world. He was canonized in 1606. His efforts to establish the Church as a spirit-centered secular power would be continued by several of his more ambitious successors, two of whom, Urban II (r. 1088–99), who initiated the First Crusade, and Innocent III (r. 1198–1216), a major supporter of the Templars, figure largely in the history that follows.

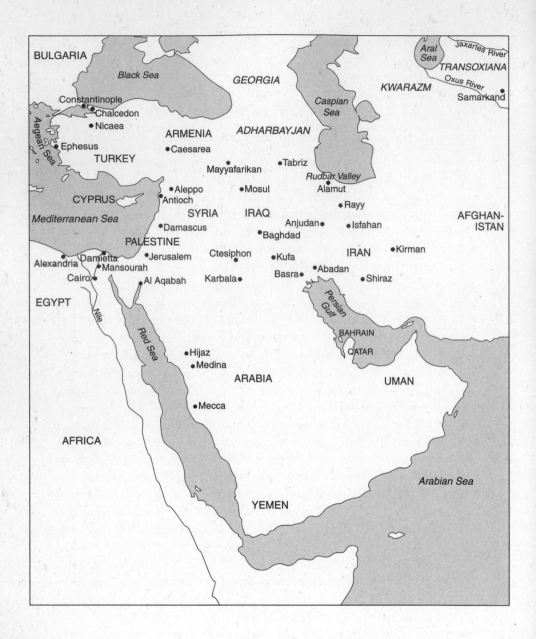

PART TWO

# THE ORDER OF ASSASSINS

✠

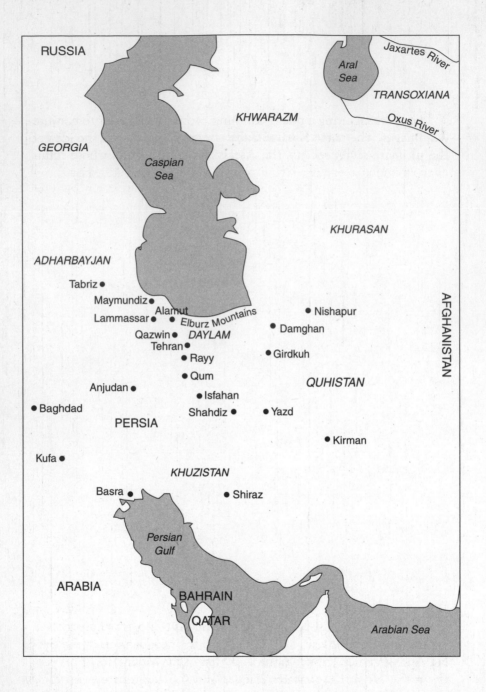

RUSSIA

Jaxartes River

Aral
Sea

TRANSOXIANA

KHWARAZM

Oxus River

GEORGIA

Caspian
Sea

KHURASAN

ADHARBAYJAN

Tabriz ●

Maymundiz ●
Lammassar ● Alamut ●
Elburz Mountains

● Nishapur
● Damghan

Qazwin ●
Tehran ●
DAYLAM

● Rayy

● Girdkuh

● Qum

Anjudan ●

QUHISTAN

● Isfahan

● Baghdad

Shahdiz ●    ● Yazd

PERSIA

● Kirman

Kufa ●

KHUZISTAN

Basra ●          ● Shiraz

Persian
Gulf

AFGHANISTAN

ARABIA

BAHRAIN

QATAR

Arabian Sea

# CHAPTER THREE

# THE ASSASSIN MYTH

L ike sparks igniting a pile of kindling, words have power to conjure images. The name Hasan-i-Sabah immediately evokes the idea of the ultimate secret society, the Assassins or Hashishim, whose influence extended over a significant portion of Persia and Palestine a thousand years ago. Hasan's legend has endured in the West through modern times. He has been embraced by hip culture — a common reference in the writings of William S. Burroughs, he even made an appearance in the movie *Performance*, where the character played by Mick Jagger offers a tantalizing look at the Old Man of the Mountain.

The popularization of the Assassin myth throughout the European world was the result of contact with Islamic culture during the Crusades. One of the earliest elements in European lore was contributed in 1175 by Burchard of Strassbourg, the envoy to Egypt and Syria of the Holy Roman emperor Frederick Barbarossa. He described the dwellers of the Syrian mountain region as *heyssessini* — men who lived without law, ate pig's flesh, shared their women, and practiced incest with their mothers and sisters. He described the feared Master of the sect, ruling his network of young killers, as the scourge of both Muslim and Christian leaders. The Master was said to have possessed beautiful and inaccessible mountain palaces in which young men were raised from earliest childhood and schooled in all the languages and customs of the time. They were taught absolute obedience and loyalty to the Master and told that the reward of their service would be the joys of Paradise, which he had the power to offer them. At his command, they gladly accepted the golden dagger personally handed them to slay the Master's designated enemy.

In 1192, the Syrian Assassins claimed their most important Christian victim, Conrad of Montferrat, the Latin king of Jerusalem. His successor, Count Henry of Champagne, the nephew of King Richard the Lionhearted, was approached by the Assassins to negotiate an accord. Henry described his visit, around 1194, to the headquarters of the Syrian Assassin chief, known as the Old Man of the Mountain, at his castle in the Nosairi Mountains. Henry and the Master were strolling through the grounds of the fortress when the Old Man said that he did not believe the Christians were as loyal to their leaders as his disciples were to him. To illustrate his point, he signaled to two youths high above on one of the towers; both immediately leapt to their deaths on the rocks a thousand feet below.

In the beginning of the fourteenth century, Marco Polo fueled the European fascination with the Assassins when he compiled the ultimate resumé of the scattered Assassin legends to date, embellished with his own contributions. The Venetian traveler had spent twenty-five years in the East, visiting the royal court of China for some seventeen years as well as spending time in Persia. In the classic account of his travels, Polo described legends of a magnificent enclosed garden hidden at Alamut in which all details corresponded to Muhammad's description of Paradise: it contained every variety of fruit, gilded pavilions, exquisite paintings, and silk tapestries. Wine, milk, honey, and water freely flowed throughout. Beautiful women skilled in music, singing, dancing, and the arts of love attended to the every wish of those who were chosen to enter its guarded walls, for the garden was impregnable.

Polo wrote that young disciples, carefully chosen by the Old Man for their martial prowess and personal loyalty to him, were the only people allowed to enter the garden. He would first give them a drugged potion that would cause them to enter a deep sleep. They would awaken to find themselves within the magic garden. These simple youths would spend a period of time in blissful sensuality until the potion was again administered and they would awaken at the castle. Once conducted to the Old Man's presence, they would discuss the experience with the Master. He would then assign one of them a target for assassination. The chosen youth would be promised that upon his return and successful completion of the task he would be readmitted to the garden, or should he die during the mission, the Old Man would send his angels to bear the young man's soul to Paradise.[†]

The word *assassin* entered nearly all medieval European languages to describe a hired or political killer. At first, European popular culture embraced the quality of the disciples' loyalty to the Old Man of the Mountain. Medieval troubadours promised their loved ones the same devotion as the Assassin held toward his mysterious Master. Gradually fear of Assassin skill and cunning spread within the royal courts of European monarchs. Kings began to suspect their enemies had entered

---

[†] Marco Polo's account was so tantalizing that it became the model for an Arabic novel, written in 1430, that has been mistakenly identified as a confirmatory source of Polo's tale. (See Joseph von Hammer-Purgstall, *The History of the Assassins* [1835;

into murderous alliances with the Old Man, who had been persuaded to send his dark minions against them.

To explore this archetypal secret society, we must first focus on the tortuous development of Islam in the four centuries prior to Hasan's birth. For in the boiling cauldron of the numerous factions and schisms that developed since the death of the Prophet Muhammad is to be found the roots of the extraordinary power wielded by Hasan-i-Sabah and his successors. The simple faith of the fierce desert warriors to whom Muhammad preached his message had evolved into a series of complex, sophisticated, and nearly unrecognizable doctrines (discussed in chapter 5) by the time Hasan-i-Sabah added his own contribution to the mix.

reprint, New York: Burt Franklin, 1968], p. 136, and also Farhad Daftary, *The Assassin Legends* [London: I. B. Tauris & Company, 1995], pp. 118–120.) Polo's book remained the most popular European source for the Assassin myth for over four hundred years.

# CHAPTER FOUR

# ISLAMIC ROOTS

## MUHAMMAD AND THE RISE OF ISLAM

The Book of Genesis tells us that the patriarch Abraham was eighty-five years old and childless when God promised him that his descendants would match the number of stars in the heavens. His wife, Sarah, then seventy-six, offered him her handmaid Hagar that she might conceive and bear Abraham a child. Then jealousy arose in Sarah's heart and Hagar was forced to flee. An angel informed Hagar that she was pregnant and should return to inform Abraham and Sarah. Abraham named his son Ishmael. When the boy was thirteen, God spoke again to Abraham. He announced that Sarah would bear him another son who was to be named Isaac, with whom God would establish His covenant. When Isaac was born, Sarah insisted that Hagar and Ishmael be sent away. With heavy heart Abraham complied, after being assured by the Lord that He would protect them and that Ishmael and his seed would be blessed. And so began Western civilization and our three great monotheistic faiths: For Christianity is the child of Judaism as Judaism of Isaac and Islam of Ishmael.

The Prophet Muhammad, may Allah commend and salute him, was born in Mecca about 570 C.E. His birth and entire life were attended with many signs of divine protection and repeated evidence of angelic intervention and guidance. Numerous miracles were ascribed to him or occurred on his behalf. He was said to be handsome, of medium stature, well mannered, and eloquent, with a perfect command of Arabic and possessed of a natural charismatic radiance. His lineage was of the highest Arab tribal nobility, but the death of his father before his birth, and of his mother when he was six, left him an orphan raised in material simplicity by his paternal grandfather. As he grew to young manhood, Muhammad became a merchant renowned for his integrity. At the age of twenty he married Khadijah, his first wife, his business partner, the mother of his children, his friend, and the first Muslim.

Soon after he reached the age of thirty-five, Muhammad began to experience what he called "true visions," which caused him periodically to seek the solitude of a cave for meditation. He began his teachings of submission (*islam*) to Allah in about 613. He was visited by the archangel Gabriel, who announced that Muhammad was the messenger of God, and began to receive the verses of the sacred text known as the Koran. Sometime in 620, Muhammad had a nocturnal vision in which he was transported to Jerusalem, where he mounted a winged steed and ascended to Heaven. In the morning he awoke safely in his bed in Mecca. This experience caused Jerusalem to be regarded as the third holy city of Islam, in addition to Mecca and Medina (where Muhammad had begun the second phase of his teaching in 622). Muslim prayers were originally made while facing Jerusalem. This was changed to Mecca in 624. In 630, Muhammad's army took Mecca, which he declared to be the Holy City of Islam. He cleansed the Kaaba of idols and proclaimed that no unbeliever should again set foot in the city.[†]

Muhammad never claimed to be other than a mortal man, albeit an inspired one. He extended the new religion through conquest in which his armies were often aided by angelic hosts. The martial nature of Islam — with its code of honor and the chivalrous character of its founder — naturally appealed to the warrior culture of the desert tribes of Arabia, who rapidly embraced the new faith. Muhammad stamped out the influence of earlier idolatrous Arab religions, replacing them with his monotheistic Muslim creed, the Shahadah: "There is no god but God, and Muhammad is the messenger of God." Islam introduced a sense of national and racial unity among the scattered tribes of Arabia for the first time. When Muhammad died in 632, the Muslim faith was firmly established.


## MUSLIM CULTURE

At the time of Muhammad's birth, southern Arabia was under the political control of Persia. Minor Arab kings, under the sovereignty of the Byzantine and Persian rulers, held states in northwestern Arabia and Syria from the third to the seventh centuries. These acted as buffer zones against the fierce Arab tribesmen to the east. Some Arabs also

---

[†] This precept is still in force. Describing Muslim leader Osama bin Laden's change of heart toward the United States, reporter James Risen wrote, "Finally he turned completely against the United States with the onset of the Persian Gulf crisis . . . in 1990. He saw the presence of hundreds of thousands of American and other foreign troops on Saudi soil as a deep religious affront — the return of the barbarian Crusaders to defile Islam's holy places" (*New York Times*, September 6, 1998).

lived in Iraq. The basic unit of political organization was the tribe, to whom intense loyalty and devotion were accorded, and among which were frequent conflicts. Arabs were vigorous traders. Records of Arab commerce with Egypt date back five thousand years. Nearly eighty percent of the population were Bedouins, nomadic herdsmen who traveled with their flocks seeking ever-changing seasonal pasture land. They also engaged in the cultivation of orchards, growing dates, peaches, apricots, and other fruits, and produced frankincense and myrrh — commodities as valuable in the ancient world as oil is in the modern. An intense devotion to the arts of music and poetry was characteristic of Arab culture. The religion of these pre-Islamic desert warriors was polytheistic and pantheistic. Insofar as there was a central shrine, it was Mecca, the lively commercial hub of numerous trade routes and home of the Kaaba, in which was housed the sacred Black Stone. This holy object, some seven inches in diameter, was built into the east wall of the Kaaba and was said to have been given to Abraham by an angel. Muhammad taught that it had been pure white when it came to earth but that the sins of mankind turned it black.

*Islam* means "submission" to the will of God. It is an optimistic faith. Adherence to its strict requirements is rewarded in a sensual afterlife whose appeal is universal. The Five Pillars of Islam include belief in Allah and acceptance of Muhammad as Prophet and the four duties — prayer, almsgiving, fasting, and pilgrimage. The Muslim prays five times per day while facing Mecca and follows elaborate purification requirements. Almsgiving includes a tax for the benefit of the poor and generosity toward all as a condition of spiritual well-being. Fasting includes adherence to dietary laws that exclude pork and wine, as well as the annual month-long daylight fast of Ramadan, which honors the reception of the Koran. Pilgrimage includes the duty to travel to Mecca for the elaborately ritualized visit to the Kaaba at least once during the lifetime of a Muslim. The Shariah, or divinely revealed law, is the set of religious commandments by which the Muslim guides his life personally, socially, and politically. The specifics of Shariah were determined by Islamic jurists and religious scholars in accordance with the Koran, and the tradition associated with the Prophet's behavior and sayings recorded during his lifetime in the Sunnah and Hadith. The canon of Shariah was fixed around the ninth century.

Muhammad was deeply concerned with physical cleanliness, and Muslim culture places a high value on bathing, perfumes, and pleasing clothing. Public bathhouses were a feature of every urban community.

Courtesy and honesty were highly prized virtues. Commerce was encouraged and hospitality was universal. Muslim attitudes toward sex were refreshingly relaxed. They shunned celibacy as unnatural. Eroticism was celebrated in literature, dance, and the arts, as well as in the pharmaceutical interest in aphrodisiacs. Men were allowed up to four wives in keeping with the higher male mortality of a warrior culture and the need for population replenishment. Adultery, fornication, and homosexuality were strictly forbidden in theory, less so in practice.

Women were highly regarded in Islam, which prohibited the barbaric cruelties of pre-Islamic Arab tribes — practices such as condoning the burial of infant daughters in order to save food. Women were allowed rights of inheritance and ownership. Any family property received from parents was for a woman's exclusive use; husbands were forbidden to meddle with a wife's private property. The consent of the woman was necessary for marriage, which was encouraged under Islam and based on romantic love. In the upper classes women were often highly educated. The harem (literally, "forbidden," the secluded area in the well-to-do Arabic home or palace reserved exclusively for women) included the gentle arts of dance, poetry, and music. Women were as free to divorce as were men, although they were allowed only one husband at a time.

Slavery was a prominent feature throughout the Near East. While it was gradually giving way to serfdom in medieval Christian lands, slavery had universally been one of the penalties of military defeat for millennia. Additionally, a brisk slave trade moved Blacks from Africa, Turks and Chinese from Turkestan, and Whites from Russia, Italy, and Spain to households and courts throughout the Near East in astonishing numbers. The position of the slave in Islam was, however, less odious than in many other lands. For example, the offspring of a female slave by her master, or of a free woman by her slave, was free from birth. Of the thirty-seven Abbasid caliphs, all but three were the sons of slave mothers.[1]

Muslim civilization was responsible for important contributions in many fields, including science, especially astronomy, chemistry, physics, and botany; literature, especially poetry; philosophy; history; education; mathematics, especially algebra, trigonometry, and in popularizing the use of the number zero; medicine, especially pharmacology, opthamology, and optics; and art, architecture, and music. The works of Aristotle were translated into Arabic in the eighth century and introduced into Moorish Spain at the end of the ninth. (It was not until the twelfth century that the scientific rationalism of this philosopher reached Latin Europe by way of Arab-controlled Spain and Sicily.) The fact that the earth was a sphere was basic to Islamic geography and astronomy. Papermaking came from China to Islam in the eighth century and was the foundation for the Islamic art of manuscript illumination. It was not until the mid–tenth century that papermaking migrated to Moorish Spain, and it was as late as the fourteenth century before it reached England. Coptic printing techniques using inked wooden blocks to print textiles were shared by Egyptian Muslims with the Crusaders, eventually contributing to the development of printing in Europe.

## The First Division: Sunni and Shiite

The transfer of leadership after Muhammad's death was soon to become a problem for his surviving faithful. According to the belief of the majority of Muslims, Muhammad never openly proclaimed his successor. He had chosen his father-in-law and friend, the elderly Abu Bakr, to lead the daily prayers during his last illness. Abu Bakr had been the first nobleman of Mecca to accept Islam and had been responsible for bringing other noble converts to the new faith. A devoted and capable man, Abu Bakr was immediately accepted as Muhammad's successor, or *caliph* (prince of the faithful), by a group of elders in Medina. The caliph was not considered the new Prophet. It is a fundamental tenet of Islam that Muhammad was the Seal of the Prophets — the last of the line that included Adam, Noah, Abraham, Moses, and Jesus before him. Rather, the caliph was the political and religious leader of the Muslim community who would protect the integrity of both the state and the faith. Abu Bakr was the first of the four "Righteous Caliphs," all "Companions of the Prophet," who had accompanied Muhammad on the Hijrah, the historic journey from Mecca to Medina in 622, the event that marks the beginning of the Muslim calendar.

After Abu Bakr's election as caliph, a rival faction asserted that the succession naturally fell to Muhammad's cousin and son-in-law Ali. Supporters of Ali's right to the succession were known as Shiiatu Ali (the party of Ali, later simply Shiites). According to Shiite doctrine, Muhammad declared Ali his successor in 632 at Ghadir Khumm when he took Ali's hand and said to the assembled faithful, "He of whom I am the patron, of him Ali is also the patron."[2] Earlier instances of this apparent designation extended as far back as the beginning of the Prophet's mission. Muhammad had raised Ali since the boy was five years old. At the age of ten, Ali joined Khadijah to become the second Muslim. In the earliest preaching outside the confines of his immediate family, the Prophet designated the young Ali as "my brother, mine executor and my successor among you. Hearken unto him and obey him."[3] Ali was married to Fatima, Muhammad's sole surviving child, and they themselves had two children. On their wedding night, the Prophet had made a special private blessing on the couple and their off-spring.[4] Ali had distinguished himself as a brave and faithful warrior.

Those who supported the succession of Abu Bakr were known as Sunnis. They tended toward a more consensus-driven view of the proper direction for both religion and society, while Shiites believed that a divinely inspired intercessor was required to lead Islam in the true ways of the Prophet and the meaning of the Koran. Thus Sunnis perceived the caliph primarily as an administrator, while Shiites emphasized his functions as a spiritual leader. This Shiite leader would be heir to the *ilm*, the special religious knowledge necessary to guide his flock in the ways of righteousness. As such, he would be the infallible guide of his people, free of both sin and error. Furthermore, they asserted that a leader with the required spiritual authority could come only from the Prophet's bloodline, the *ahl al-bayt*, or "people of the house."

As the caliph is both the religious and secular leader of Islam, the schism between supporters of the caliphate of Abu Bakr and those of the bloodline of Ali was both a political and a religious battle. The ideal form of the Islamic state is a theocracy whose sovereignty is derived from God. The ruler manifests the will of Allah and so directs society as a reflection of the heavenly kingdom. Church and state are one. In a theocratic state, political opposition is apostasy. The Sunni-Shiite split is accordingly far more complex than similar divisions in Western religions.

Abu Bakr's short reign ended with his death in 634. To compound the problem of the young religion, and for unknown reasons, he chose not to appoint Ali as his successor, naming instead Omar, his friend and chief advisor. Thus the chasm was widened between the two factions of Islam, Sunnis and Shiite, a conflict as current as today's headlines.[†]

---

[†] Had Fatima been a man, or Islam willing to accept a female leader, the religion might have been a united world force of even greater power than it is.

During Omar's reign, the entire Arabian peninsula was brought under Muslim control. The desert tribes of Arabia were historically pillagers, but as Islam spread, they were forbidden to steal from fellow Muslims. They therefore turned their sights north to the Palestinian territories controlled by the Christian Roman Empire and the Zoroastrian dominion of Mesopotamia and Iran. Both areas offered little resistance. Each suffered from internal weaknesses that made them appealing targets. Christian passivity had reduced the defensive ability of the Palestinian region, while the Persians suffered from dissension and ennui. In contrast, the fierce Arab tribes celebrated the early stages of religious and political unity. The Muslims were a lean, enthusiastic force whose growing population required territorial expansion.

Muslim armies defeated the Byzantine Greeks in Syria in 634, and that country became the base for future military conquests. Damascus fell in 635, Antioch in 636, and Jerusalem in 638. Caliph Omar traveled to Jerusalem, where he met the Christian patriarch Sophronius and exacted an easy tribute. Arab victories in the Palestinian area encouraged a vast wave of immigration from the Arabian peninsula to the new territories. By 641, Muslims controlled all of Syria, Persia, and Egypt. Alexandria was taken from the Byzantines with the help of a group of Monophysite Christian heretics, who preferred the religiously tolerant Muslims after the emperor Justinian's persecution. While two thirteenth-century historians accused the Muslim conqueror Amr ibn al-As of burning the Alexandrian library and using its invaluable papyri and parchment to fuel the city's baths for six months, this story appears to be a fable. The majority of the library had been destroyed in 391 under Theophilus, the Patriarch of Alexandria.[5]

The rapid spread of Islam was enhanced by its basic tolerance of other faiths and its treatment of occupied populations. Muslim conquerors allowed their subjects to retain lands, customs, and religions. Those who refused to convert were simply taxed at a higher rate than the faithful. The monetary tribute the Muslims demanded, however, was often less than the taxes imposed by previous governments. Thus, they encountered little resistance as they gradually gained control of the entire Near East.

Caliph Omar was fatally wounded in 644 by an enslaved Persian Christian. At this time, the young Muslim empire extended from Arabia in the south to Turkey and Armenia in the north, Iran in the east, and Libya in the west. Within the next sixty years, North Africa would be conquered all the way to the Atlantic coast. As a result, the extensive Christian communities of the Roman period were gradually absorbed into Islam, with the still-surviving Coptic church being a notable exception.

Before his death, Omar named a body of six leaders to elect his successor. Once again Ali was ignored, and Othman was chosen as the third caliph. During his rule, dissension arose because of economic and political conflicts new to the Muslim state. Tribal jealousy was stimulated by Othman's political appointments and distribution of land. The aggressive expansion of Islam had come to an end, leaving behind a group of unemployed and discontented military personnel. Shiites seized this opportunity and began recruiting efforts among the disaffected. In 656, Othman was murdered by a group of mutineers from the Arab army. Muslim had finally shed Muslim blood. The brief period of unity within the new religion was forever destroyed.

Shiites expressed the belief that the Islamic community had taken a wrong turn by focusing its efforts on building an empire. They preached the need to return to the true teachings of the Prophet. They reiterated that the only way to accomplish this was to maintain the succession of leadership within the Prophet's own bloodline so that the spiritual mission of Islam could succeed. They accused the first three caliphs of being guilty of apostasy, a belief that would later stimulate a great deal of enmity from Sunnis. They argued that the evidence of the two decades since the Prophet's death offered bleak testimony in support of their assertion that a formal link to divine wisdom and religious authority was essential.

Ali was finally elected as the fourth caliph in 656. His was a troubled reign during which Islam experienced its first civil war. Aisha, a widow of the Prophet, held a long-standing grudge against Ali.[†] Aisha was joined in her revolt by two influential Companions of the Prophet, Zobeir and Talha. The three rebel leaders raised an army in Iraq, but they were defeated by Ali's forces. Zobeir and Talha were killed in the battle and Aisha was forced to retire to Medina.

Othman's cousin, Muawiya, the governor of Syria, refused to recognize Ali as caliph and declared war against him in 657, ostensibly to avenge Othman's death. Ali's soldiers were winning the battle until

---

[†] During the years after Khadijah's death, Muhammad had taken a number of wives. Aisha, the daughter of Abu Bakr, had long been acknowledged as his favorite. She had once been publicly accused of adultery and believed that Ali was among those who had slandered her.

Muawiya's soldiers placed pages of the Koran on their spears to signal their demand for arbitration rather than battle. Ali's soldiers refused to continue fighting. In the negotiations that followed, Ali's representatives were outwitted by Muawiya. They agreed to accept a new election for caliph and announced that Ali was willing to renounce his title so that the election could proceed. Muawiya's negotiators seized this opportunity to proclaim Muawiya caliph in the face of Ali's abdication. Islam was then split between the caliphates of Muawiya and Ali. In 661, Ali was murdered in Iraq, where he had established his capital. In death he grew in stature. Ali is viewed as a martyr and regarded by Shiites as second in holiness only to the Prophet.

## THE OMAYYAD CALIPHATE AND
## THE MURDER OF THE PROPHET'S GRANDSON

Ali was succeeded by his profligate son Hasan, who resigned in favor of Muawiya in exchange for a large amount of money. (Hasan was murdered in 669 by one of his wives.) Muawiya made Damascus his capital and succeeded in establishing the Omayyad dynasty that would rule Islam for nearly a century. Muawiya instituted the practice of cursing Ali from the pulpit during the Friday prayers, the first official anti-Shiite policy of the Sunnis.

Husayn, the younger son of Ali and Fatima, was approached to lead the Shiites. He stated that he was bound by the terms of his brother's abdication as long as Muawiya was alive. Muawiya died in 680 and was succeeded by his son Yazid. Shortly thereafter, Husayn came to reclaim the caliphate as Ali's rightful successor. In 680, Yazid, with four thousand of his troops, attacked Husayn and his small band of devotees at Karbala. Husayn was slain along with all seventy of the men with whom he traveled. His body was mutilated and desecrated. Only women and some children were spared. Among them was Husayn's young son Ali, who miraculously survived the encounter. The boy had been lying sick in a tent somewhat removed from the main group.

The death of Husayn is regarded as the pivotal event that gave birth to Shiism as a formally separate faith and dogma. The murder of the Prophet's grandson by the reigning political leaders of Islam caused a wave of rage, shame, and self-doubt throughout the entire Muslim world. The followers of Husayn were especially despondent over their inability to support him and prevent his death. The potent religious themes of expiation, suffering, and martyrdom were added to Shiism. Passion plays of the death of Husayn take place to this day and involve the mass self-flagellation familiar to incredulous Western television viewers. Karbala is still considered a holy city of Shiism.

Many contemporaries were unaware that Ali ibn Husayn, Muhammad's great-grandson, had survived, especially since he retired to Medina after the Karbala massacre and remained clear of the political chaos of the period. His cause was eclipsed by developments that temporarily appeared to overshadow his critical role as the sole lineal descendant of the Prophet.

## Muktar and the Rise of Shiism

A new Shiite leader arose named Muktar. He formed what was called the Army of Penitents, composed of Husayn's followers. In 686, Muktar defeated Yazid's Omayyad forces in battle, but he died a year later. While his career was short, Muktar forever changed Islam. He imbued Shiites with an invincible faith in the power of the Imam and the advent of the Mahdi. These two figures are unique to Shiism. The Imams are viewed as the spiritual guides of mankind and temporal rulers of Islam, direct representatives of Allah. The Mahdi is the rightly guided one, the messianic Imam chosen by Allah who will emerge from hiding at the proper time, triumph over his enemies, make the inner doctrine public, and usher in the age of truth, justice, and equality.

Muktar had proclaimed one of Ali's sons, Muhammad ibn al-Hanafiyya, to be the Imam and Mahdi. (Muhammad ibn al-Hanafiyya was not the son of the Prophet's daughter Fatima, who had died within six months of her father's death. After Fatima passed away, Ali had married Khawla, a member of the Prophet's tribe, the Banu Hanifa, and she gave birth to Muhammad ibn al-Hanafiyya. Thus, the new Imam was not a direct lineal descendent of the Prophet.) Muhammad ibn al-Hanafiyya died around 700. Many Shiites believed he had actually gone into hiding in the mountains near Mecca and would return as the Mahdi sometime in the future.

Shiism was widely embraced in Iraq and Iran. Traditionally the semicelestial potentates of the Persian Zoroastrians were regarded in a manner similar to the divine pharaohs of the Egyptians. The Shiite doctrine of the divinely inspired Imam was readily accepted by the Persians. Muktar had also demanded an end to Arab domination of

Islam by demanding full equality for Persian and Iraqi converts to Islam, the *mawali*, or "clients." The fact that their social, political, and religious status was inferior to that of the Arab ruling class had become a source of enormous resentment among converts. Muktar's sensitivity to *mawali* frustration substantially contributed to the growth of the Shiite movement.

Disaffected Arabs were also attracted to the spiritual and political reformist and revolutionary Shiite message. These included pious men unhappy with the worldly concerns of the caliphs, poor Arabs who resented the ostentatious display of wealth by their leaders, nomadic tribes who despised the restrictions on property and travel instituted by the increasingly centralized and arrogant Sunni power structure, and the many other Sunnis sickened and horrified by the murder of the Prophet's grandson Husayn.

Shiism thus became a haven for many forms of political and spiritual dissent. And since Islam grew by conversion, large numbers of new believers brought their Christian, Jewish, and Iranian backgrounds to the sect. Shiism absorbed ideas from the pre-Islamic beliefs of Persian and Babylonian mysticism, Greek religion, Manichaean dualism, and Jewish and Christian Gnosticism. Jewish beliefs about the sanctity of the blood of the House of David, and Christian teachings that the messiah had arisen from that sacred bloodline, contributed to the fervor of Shiism, as did exposure to the Zoroastrian messianic tradition.


## THE ABBASID CALIPHATE BETRAYAL

A major, if short-lived, political success for Shiism was the establishment of the Abbasid caliphate. Descended from al-Abbas, an uncle of the Prophet, the Abbasids claimed the Shiite mantle of leadership in 716 and used the Shiite movement as their political power base. The Abbasids pretended to subscribe to Muktar's designated line of Imams descending from Muhammad ibn al-Hanafiyya. In 716, many Shiites supported the Abbasid claim that the Imamate had been passed to Muhammad ibn Ali, the great grandson of al-Abbas.

The Abbasids next declared that since the Imamate flowed through their bloodline, they satisfied the requirement for Shiite leadership and were fit to challenge the Omayyad caliphate, which had been progressively weakened by endemic factionalism that had degenerated into civil war. In 743, Muhammad ibn Ali died and was succeeded by his son, Ibrahim al-Imam. Ibrahim died in an Omayyad prison in 749, just months before the Abbasid-led victory against the Omayyads at Kufa. In November of 749, Abu al-Abbas, Ibrahim's half-brother, was proclaimed the first Abbasid caliph. In 750, his armies finally defeated the Omayyads in Egypt.[†]

For three decades the Abbasids had preached their belief in the sanctity of the Alid line, that is, of the lineal descendants of Ali. Immediately upon the success of their ambitions, however, they betrayed the Alid faithful who had brought them to victory. First, the Abbasids integrated the *mawali* into a position of political equality. This temporarily solved the problem of *mawali* frustration and weakened their embrace of the Shiite political cause. Next, in order to be accepted by the majority of Muslims, the Abbasids decided to reject their extremist roots. They instituted violent repressive measures against their former Shiite allies, subjecting them to execution, imprisonment, and massacre. Finally the Abbasids declared themselves a Sunni dynasty.

In 762, the Abbasids established their dynastic capital in the newly constructed palaces of Baghdad, the ancient Babylonian city. Here they would serve as the titular leaders of Islam for five centuries, until their defeat by the Mongols in 1258. The final indignity against Shiism took place during the caliphate of Muhammad al-Mahdi (r. 775–85). He declared that the Prophet had never appointed his cousin Ali as his successor but instead had bestowed that role upon his uncle al-Abbas. (In fact, al-Abbas had initially rejected Muhammad's message and been part of the Meccan army sent against the Prophet.) The Abbasid betrayal was complete.

## THE GROWTH OF SHIITE EXTREMISM

The resulting frustration fueled the extremism so natural to the Shiite soul and caused Shiites to withdraw even further from the Islamic mainstream. It also called forth a period of spiritual self-examination and reflection on the development of the Shiite faith to date. As the opposition religious movement, Shiites were subject to more frequent variations in their teachings than the establishment Sunnis. Numerous pretenders to the exalted office of Mahdi or secret Imam appeared from time to time who enriched the description of the power of this hidden

[†] The Omayyads managed to retain Spain and Morocco.

redeemer. There was a growth in the cult of the holy man — the Imams and *dais* (the Imams' direct representatives) were increasingly believed to possess miraculous power.

Illuminist doctrines from various earlier heresies so altered mainstream Islamic beliefs that the resulting cults were nearly independent. Transitions of membership between these different sects were frequent. The eclectic doctrines that grew among the various Shiite groups included beliefs in reincarnation and metempsychosis; deification of Imams and sometimes *dais*; intense speculations on the nature of God; attention to divination and prophesy; doctrines concerning the nature of the soul, death, the afterlife, and immortality; teachings on the cyclical nature of time and history; kabbalistic investigations of the esoteric significance of letters and numbers; and occasionally, the overthrowing of traditional Islamic behavioral restrictions on sexuality, the use of intoxicants, and dietary matters.

The divisions that arose within the Shiite community were often as profound as the basic division between Shiite and Sunni. The political-spiritual program of different factions might include the installation of their chosen Imam as the revolutionary leader who would bring forth universal justice under Allah. Another school of thought regarded the Imams as so engaged in their duties of spiritual leadership that they refrained from any involvement in the political battles to overthrow the Sunni caliphs. Other Shiites believed the Imams were so far beyond the mundane vicissitudes of secular conflict that they were secretly providing spiritual guidance to the Sunni leadership, either directly in a physical manner or covertly through the use of invisible occult powers.

## THE EMBRACE OF THE ALID LINE

The Abbasid betrayal demonstrated the need for standards by which the claims of Shiite leaders could be judged. What were the requirements for the hereditary line of the Shiite Imamate? Who were the legitimate members of the Ahl al-Bayt? Everyone accepted Ali as the first Imam. His two sons with Fatima, Hasan and Husayn, were universally recognized as the next two Imams. Muktar, however, had proclaimed Ali's son of his Hanafite wife an Imam. Other Imams had based their claims to lineage on descent from the Banu Hashim, the Prophet's

tribal clan. After the Abbasid fiasco, Shiites embraced a more restric-
tive definition of the Imamate. Henceforth most Shiites accepted that
the Imamate was to be based solely on descent from the marriage of Ali
and Fatima. Thus, the more limited definition of the Alid line meant
direct descent from the Prophet. Furthermore, most believed that there
was only one active Imam at a time. Husayn's son Ali was recognized by
the vast majority of Shiites (then and today) as the legitimate fourth
Imam. The Alid Imamate descends through him.

Although Ali ibn Husayn was renowned for his piety, his essential
quiescence prevented him from asserting himself as a political leader.
After his death in 714, his son Muhammad al-Baqir became the fifth
Imam. Muhammad is credited with being the first Imam to perform the
charismatic role of authoritative and inspired teacher, firmly establishing the Imamate tradition within Shiism.[6] He introduced the important Shiite survival skill known as taqiyya, which involves dis-
simulation, concealment, or precaution. The doctrine of taqiyya allows
the believer to conceal his true beliefs without entering into a state of
sin, thus preventing martyrdom at the hands of either hostile authorities or the surrounding populace. This practice helped Shiites to spread
their increasingly radical religious beliefs without interference from
more conservative quarters. Concurrently, the political resentments of
a subject people could be effectively stirred by Shiite agents who were
able to lie about their true agenda without the risk of divine disfavor.
Armed revolutionary activities by small independent groups in Persia
were a constant occurrence during the first half of the eighth century,
all of which were defeated by superior forces, first of the Omayyads and
then of Abbasids.

The sixth Imam, Jafar al-Sadiq, succeeded his father in 732 and
became the Shiite rallying point after the Abbasid betrayal. This deeply
spiritual and brilliant Imam was the last to be recognized as such by all
Shiites. His learning and piety were so unique that he was (and continues to be) accepted as an authority by Sunnis. Jafar elaborated on the
doctrine of the nass, or the spiritual designation of his successor by the
reigning Imam. Jafar also taught that the Imam could assume a qui-
escent political stance, freeing the Shiite spiritual leader from the duty
of revolutionary activity directed toward seizing the power of the temporal caliphate. This doctrine allowed the Shiite movement to develop as a faith in circumstances of political powerlessness. Jafar also
expanded on his father's teaching regarding taqiyya. He stated that the

Imam could exercise his rightful spiritual authority in silence. The Imam was not bound to either offend or openly challenge the secular political authority of the reigning Sunni power structure. The true magnitude of the Imam's power could be concealed.

## THE ISMAILI SPLIT

In 765 Shiism gave birth to a new faction that, from the point of view of this history, is decisive. The Ismailis arose from a dispute over succession and the true identity of the seventh Imam.[†] For reasons that are not clear, Jafar al-Sadiq is believed to have disinherited his eldest son, Ismail. Some historians state that Ismail had incurred his father's displeasure by his close relations with extremist groups. Ismail had become associated with Abul-Khattab, a disciple of Jafar's who zealously upheld the authority of the Imam but whose radical religious and political views caused Jafar to publicly curse him. In 756, two years after the Imam's curse, Abul-Khattab was arrested and crucified by the Abbasid authorities. Abul-Khattab preached a kabbalistic doctrine that focused on discovering the esoteric truth behind appearances. His teachings concerned the nature of the spiritual hierarchy, the divinity of the Imam, and the need for initiated interpretation of the inner meaning of the Koran — all themes that were to infuse the later Ismaili movement.

Other historians say that Ismail did not succeed Jafar as the seventh Imam because he died before his father. Jafar was believed to have transferred the succession to Ismail's younger half-brother Musa al-Kazim, who is recognized as the seventh Imam by most Shiites. Musa's line continued through the twelfth Imam, Muhammad al-Mahdi, who disappeared in 873 (or 878). The reappearance of the twelfth Imam at the end of the world, in triumph as the Mahdi, is still awaited by the majority of Shiites, who are known as Twelver Shiites, or Ithna ashariyya. This more moderate branch of Shiism has been the official religion of Iran and Iraq since the sixteenth century.

An opposing Shiite camp supported the succession of Ismail. Some claimed that Jafar had announced Ismail's death merely as a ruse to protect him. Others held that after Ismail's death, Jafar recognized Ismail's son Muhammad as the seventh Imam because he understood that the

[†] To complicate matters even further, different systems are used to number the Imams. See Daftary, The Ismailis, pp. 104–5.

*nass* passed from father to son, not brother to brother. Still others said that before his death, Ismail had formally passed the *nass* to his son, making him the true Imam. Many claimed that Jafar al-Sadiq had no right to withdraw the *nass* succession from Ismail even if he was displeased with his politics.

Those who supported the Imamate of Ismail and his son Muhammad became known as Ismailis, also referred to as Sevener Shiites, or Sabiyya. Muhammad ibn Ismail began a series of travels soon after Musa al-Kazim was generally accepted as Jafar's designated successor. He is believed to have traveled to Persia and then to have disappeared into a period of hiding, isolation, or occultation. A mantle of vagueness covers all further accounts of him.

## THE EARLY WORK OF THE ISMAILI IMAMS

Very little is known of the history and doctrines of the Ismaili Imams from the beginning of the Ismaili movement in 765 until the establishment of the Fatimid Caliphate in 909. By the time the Fatimid Imam revealed himself, however, the Ismaili doctrine he openly proclaimed for the first time was mature. The Ismaili Imams, working in relative secrecy and isolation for over a century, had developed a coherent body of theological teachings that resonated with intellectual and emotional appeal. Beginning after the middle of the ninth century, they began to emerge from their obscurity with an energetic preaching. The Ismaili mission is known as the *dawa*, or "summons," to allegiance to the Imam. The *dawa* is represented by the *dai*, or "summoner," who spreads the teachings of the faith through his propagandizing and missionary efforts.

Philosophically the Ismailis replaced the chaotic speculation and superstitions of earlier Shiite sects with a series of distinguished philosophical doctrines. While scant early Ismaili literature survives, anonymous manuscripts were apparently circulated privately among trusted sectarians. The Ismaili teachings were synthetic, including respect for the Koran combined with an intellectual appreciation for the profundities of Greek Neoplatonic thought and Hindu mysticism. Ismailism's emphasis on the living Imam offered an opportunity for emotional fulfillment by allowing the disciple to direct an intensely spiritualized love toward his or her Master. Finally, Ismailism included a well-organized opposition movement that attracted the politically disaffected.

In Iraq, the leadership of the Ismaili *dawa* had been in the hands of Hamdan Qarmat since 870. His followers were known as "Qarmatis." His energetic preaching efforts had met with great success and the Iraqi mission had become a significant area of Ismaili influence. Hamdan's *dawa* spread through Iraq, Persia, Transoxiana, Syria, Bahrain, Yemen, Sind, and North Africa. This rapid growth led to many late-ninth-century Ismailis also being called Qarmatis, even if they were not specifically Hamdan's followers. His revolutionary political teachings attracted many who were disaffected with Abbasid rule and the lack of any organized opposition among the more numerous Twelver Shiites.

In fact, changing circumstances during the period from 765 to 900 brought a general weakening to both Sunni and Twelver Shiite political and cultural power. From the mid–ninth-century onward, the Turkish palace guards in Baghdad had become the de facto leaders of the Abbasid government. Wine, lechery, pederasty, and love of luxury so weakened the Abbasid dynasty that the empire dwindled, as region after region seceded from their authority. Oppression became common as renegade leaders usurped the power of appointed Abbasid administrators. So severe was Abbasid neglect that the elaborate irrigation systems throughout the Near East — the lifeblood of its food supply — ceased to be maintained.

New social and economic trends included an expansion of industry and trade. Cities were evolving from former garrison towns, and these became centers of economic activity. The Arab tribal nobility was supplanted by a new ruling class composed of landowners, wealthy merchants, military leaders, administrators, religious teachers, and scholars. A conflict of interests developed between city dwellers and the rural population.

Peasant revolts arose among the poor who were attracted to the Ismaili movement through its promise of universal justice under the Mahdi. Ismaili organizing efforts in rural areas were able to proceed effectively, far from the watchful eyes of the urban Abbasid bureaucracy. The Ismaili *dawa* also enjoyed some success in urban centers among the intelligentsia who were attracted by the sophistication of its doctrines. Dissatisfaction with conditions during the eighth and ninth centuries left many prepared once again to listen to the Shiite message that Islam had taken a wrong turn and must correct itself.

## THE PROCLAMATION OF THE FATIMID CALIPHATE
## AND THE QARMATI SCHISM

The Ismailis were prepared to offer the leadership for that correction. In 909, the Ismailis achieved their greatest success, when the Hidden Imam Ubayd Allah proclaimed the Fatimid caliphate in North Africa. His choice of dynastic name expressed the regime's assertion of Alid lineage.

During the century and a half between the death of Jafar al-Sadiq and the caliphate of Ubayd Allah, the Ismailis had enjoyed a period of unity. The Imams who followed the seventh Imam, Muhammad ibn Ismail, consistently kept the fact of their Imamates in occultation. They referred to themselves (under the doctrine of *taqiyya*) merely as *hujjas*, "proofs" or representatives, of Muhammad ibn Ismail the Mahdi, whose reappearance was anticipated as the redemption of humanity. This doctrinal tradition changed abruptly when Ubayd Allah announced himself to be the living Imam and proceeded to trace his lineage back through the Hidden Imams of the last one hundred and fifty years to Jafar al-Sadiq. Of course, a corollary of Ubayd Allah's reform was his rejection of the Mahdiship of Muhammad ibn Ismail.

It should not be surprising that a leader of the stature of Hamdan Qarmat refused to acknowledge Ubayd Allah and his revisionist teachings on the Imamate. In 899, Hamdan had begun to notice a subtle change in the message emanating from the Syrian Ismaili headquarters. He sent his brother Abdan to investigate. Abdan interviewed Ubayd Allah and learned that he considered himself the Imam and no longer acknowledged Muhammad ibn Ismail as the Mahdi. Hamdan assembled his *dais* and announced the heresy of Ubayd Allah. He instructed them to cease their missionary efforts. Soon afterward Hamdan Qarmat disappears from history.

No overall leader of Hamdan's abilities arose to lead the disaffected anti-Fatimid Ismailis, yet dissident groups remained throughout Ismaili territories. The Qarmatis continued to await the reappearance of Muhammad ibn Ismail. Among those accused of being Qarmati agents was the celebrated mystic Mansur al-Hallaj, who had acquired great influence among certain members of the Abbasid royal family. Jealous enemies within the Abbasid court arranged for him to be arrested, tried, and, in 922, tortured, crucified, and dismembered in Baghdad. Mansur al-Hallaj experienced a Gnostic form of union with God during which he was known to cry out, Ana'l-Haqq, "I am the Truth." He was martyred as a heretic, and his disciples were to found a number of mystical Sufi orders.[7]

In Bahrain, the Qarmati dawa continued to thrive as a rival to both Abbasids and Fatimids for nearly two centuries. Here the community developed a particularly hostile and antinomian revolutionary outlook. The Qarmati state was sustained in large measure by frequent raids against caravans and Fatimid and Abbasid towns. The Qarmatis forced Ubayd Allah to flee Syria in 902 and undertake his long and perilous journey to North Africa. Qarmati extremism continued to build to such a fevered pitch that in 930, under the leadership of Abu Tahir, the sect attacked Mecca, massacred some thirty thousand Meccans and Muslim pilgrims, and seized the sacred Black Stone from the Kaaba. The Qarmatis held the stone until 951, when the Abbasids arranged to ransom it in return for a huge sum of money. Sunni polemicists and heresiologists began to lump all Ismailis into the same category, broadly accusing them of the sacrilegious attitudes and behavior of the radical Qarmatis. (They ignored the fact that many of the Qarmati attacks were directed against the Ismaili Fatimids.) The Qarmatis were for all practical purposes absorbed under the Fatimid umbrella by 1077; their Ismaili roots and the bitter memory of Qarmati excesses condemned all Ismailis to guilt by association.

In addition to what might be excused as legitimate misinterpretation of Ismaili belief, an orchestrated campaign of anti-Ismaili propaganda was instituted by the Abbasids. Since the ninth century, Ismailis had been the target of Sunni propagandists who worked for centuries crafting what historian Farhad Daftary calls "the black legend."[8] Twelver Shiites often supported Sunni heresiologists in these attacks, which included elaborate refutations of the Alid descent of the Ismaili Imams. The Imams were portrayed as impostors, proponents of ilhad (the arch-heresy) whose sinister purpose was nothing less than the destruction of Islam from within. The Ismailis were referred to as malahida (heretics) or mulhids (deviators). In 1011, the Abbasid caliph convened a conference of Sunni and Twelver scholars in Baghdad that issued a manifesto condemning the Fatimid Ismailis and refuting their dynastic claims to Alid lineage. These slanders were later repeated by early Western Orientalists of the eighteenth century who encountered them in their studies of medieval Muslim history. Thus, most European scholarship of the eighteenth and nineteenth centuries is replete with misunderstandings of the Ismailis.

## The Classical Fatimid Period

The Fatimid dynasty represented the first successful Shiite state after two and a half centuries of political effort. The classical Fatimid period, called the Golden Age of Ismailism, extended nearly two hundred years — from Ubayd Allah's proclamation in 909 to the death of the eighth Fatimid caliph, al-Mustansir, in 1094 and the subsequent Nizari schism. Fatimid administrators generally provided stable leadership, which encouraged prosperity. Fatimid patronage of the arts and sciences made Cairo a flourishing center of culture and commerce, the chief rival of Baghdad in the eleventh century. This rich period of classical Fatimid literature recorded the immense intellectual and philosophic activities and accomplishments of the Ismailis.

Ubayd Allah spent the years from 902 to 909 organizing among the Ismailis of North Africa. After a brief imprisonment, he was freed by his supporters and proclaimed as caliph in Morocco, after which he established his initial capital in Tunisia. The early decades of his reign were a constant battle for survival. The Fatimids were engaged in open warfare with the Qarmatis and other dissident groups who opposed the rejection of Muhammad ibn Ismail. By the time of the fourth Fatimid caliph, al-Muizz (r. 953–75), the dynasty had sufficiently subdued dissident Ismaili opposition to undertake a policy of territorial expansion. By 969, the Fatimids seized Egypt from the Abbasids and built the city of Cairo (al-Qahirah) as their capital. In 969, Mecca and Medina submitted to al-Muizz in return for substantial economic rewards.

With rare exceptions, the Fatimids respected the religious freedom of the Sunni majority in Egypt and were tolerant of Christians and Jews. Several Christians and Jews were, in fact, placed in positions of authority under Fatimid caliphs. In 988, the Fatimids established the world's first university, the al-Azhar, as a center for the dissemination of Ismaili doctrine. The ultimate goal of the Fatimids was the rulership of all Islam. Throughout the life of the Fatimid state they conducted constant missionary activities, unlike the Abbasids, who ceased such efforts upon attaining political victory.

Al-Muizz died in 975. He had modified the doctrine of the Imamate in an effort to attract dissident Ismailis to the Fatimid fold. Muhammad ibn Ismail was placed within vast cosmological cycles where he held a far more exalted position than Ubayd Allah's doctrine had allowed. Al-Muizz also permitted the incorporation of Ismaili Neoplatonic cosmology within Fatimid cosmology, again welcoming a broader consensus. His efforts helped extend Fatimid influence among the larger Ismaili community.

Under the next caliph, al-Aziz (r. 975–96), the Fatimids reached their greatest territorial extension. At its peak, the empire included Egypt, Syria, North Africa, Sicily, the Red Sea coast of Africa, Yemen, and Hijaz in Arabia, as well as the holy cities of Mecca, Medina, and Jerusalem. By the end of the tenth century, Islam had three separate dynasties in power — the Omayyads in Spain and Morocco, the Fatimids in lands stretching from Algeria to Syria, and the Abbasids in Baghdad. Al-Aziz was also very active in spreading the Fatimid *dawa* to Persia. His was a reign of maximum religious tolerance. In fact, his wife was a Christian, and his vizier was a Jewish convert to Ismailism.

Al-Aziz was succeeded by his eleven-year-old son, al-Hakim (r. 996–1021), a moody and eccentric leader who may have been mentally unbalanced. He took great interest, however, in the arts and sciences and in the activities of the *dawa*. In 1005, he founded the Dar al-Hikma, or House of Wisdom, as a training center for *dais*. Al-Hakim's missionary efforts included an outreach to dissident Qarmatis. Outside of Bahrain, most Qarmatis came to accept the Fatimid Imamate. On the other hand, al-Hakim persecuted both Jews and Christians. In 1009, he ordered the destruction of the Church of the Holy Sepulcher in Jerusalem. This ended the truce his father had negotiated with the Byzantine emperor and was a contributing cause of the Crusades. His intolerance extended to the Sunnis as well. He subscribed to the Shiite practice of cursing the first three caliphs as usurpers of Ali's rights.

The Druze movement arose in 1017 as a dissident Ismaili group, soon to become an altogether different faith. A number of al-Hakim's *dais* began to preach extremist ideas concerning the physical divinity of the Fatimid Imam. The Fatimids recognized the Imam as the divinely appointed, infallible and sinless, sole spiritual leader of mankind — but human. The Druzes carried this a giant step further, thereby incurring Fatimid wrath. The Druze leader was assassinated in 1018, but the movement continued to grow, becoming an ever-threatening source of religious and political dissent. The Druzes stated that al-Hakim was the *Qaim*, the final Imam whose reign heralded the *Qiyama*, the end of Islam and the abrogation of Shariah. (These potent themes of Shiite radicalism would reemerge among the Nizaris a century later. They will be discussed in some detail when examining the reigns of the Assassin leaders Hasan II and his son Muhammad II.) Today there are some three hundred thousand Druzes, living mainly in Syria, Lebanon, and Israel, who continue to await the return of al-Hakim.[9]

Al-Hakim died or disappeared in 1021. He was succeeded by his son al-Zahir, who ruled until his death in 1036. During his short reign, al-Zahir gave permission to the Byzantines to reconstruct the Church of the Holy Sepulcher. He was succeeded by his seven-year-old son, al-Mustansir, who ruled as caliph for nearly sixty years until 1094. For one brief moment during the reign of al-Mustansir, the Fatimids gained titular control of the Abbasids and therefore all Islam. Beginning in 1057, a rebellious Turkish general named al-Busasiri sought al-Mustansir's alliance against the Seljuks and Abbasids. With a substantial gift of arms and money from al-Mustansir, al-Busasiri was able to take Baghdad in 1058. He immediately instituted the Shiite call to prayer and blessed the name of al-Mustansir during the Friday *khutba* prayer for the leader of Islam. Yet, soon he incurred al-Mustansir's displeasure by refusing to deliver the Abbasid caliph to Egypt in person, imprisoning him instead in Baghdad. In 1059, al-Busasiri was defeated and slain by the Seljuk Turks.

## The Fatimid Decline

During al-Mustansir's reign, the state of continuous warfare led to a series of economic crises and encouraged the growth of political power by the military within the civil government. In 1062, open warfare broke out near Cairo between dissident elements in the army. The Turkish commander Nasir al-Dawla became the effective leader of Egypt. He was a vicious and corrupt tyrant. A series of famines and economic distresses between 1065 and 1072 caused further widespread suffering. The caliph himself eventually became a virtual prisoner, while his troops looted his palace. Nasir al-Dawla was assassinated in 1073.

In 1074, al-Mustansir appealed for help against his rebellious troops to Badr al-Jamali, an Armenian general who was the military governor of Acre. Badr acted quickly. His troops suppressed the revolt of the Turks and restored order. He also took control of Egypt. The caliph had traditionally been in charge of the three primary aspects of the realm: the functions of civil government, religious training and missionary work, and the military. Badr al-Jamali took control of all three branches. The post of Commander of the Armies became hereditary, passing to Badr al-Jamali's son and grandson. The Fatimid caliph, like his Abbasid counterpart, had become a mere figurehead. The real power lay with the military, which was under constant threat from the advance of the armies of the Seljuk Turks.

A great famine struck Egypt in 1094, causing widespread suffering and misery. A sense of hopelessness spread among the people, who had seen an idealistic religious revolution evolve into a military dictatorship. One major contributing factor to the decline of the Fatimid Imamate was that the creative, intellectual, and spiritual spark that had inflamed the core of the Ismaili rise to power had long since become burdened by the political responsibility of empire management.

When Caliph al-Mustansir died that year, the succession was decided by Commander of the Armies al-Afdal, who had succeeded his father. Al-Mustansir had two sons. Nizar, the eldest, was approximately fifty years old. He had already been proclaimed as heir, received his father's *nass*, and been accepted as the nineteenth Imam by the Ismaili leadership. His brother, al-Mustali, was a twenty-one-year-old with neither experience nor allies. Al-Afdal arranged for al-Mustali to marry his daughter and, on the day of al-Mustansir's death, appointed him caliph. Al-Mustali's youth and political weakness would make him a dependent tool in al-Afdal's hands.

## THE NIZARI ISMAILI SPLIT

In the final turn of the labyrinth leading to Hasan-i-Sabah, we encounter the last important Ismaili schism, in which Hasan himself was a major player. Nizar had fled to Alexandria to attempt a revolt. After some initial success, he was defeated, captured, and executed. The Fatimid dynasty, however, was fatally weakened. By the time al-Mustali began his caliphate, the territorial holdings of the Fatimid empire had essentially been reduced to Egypt. Many Ismailis refused to accept the Imamate of al-Mustali. Opposition movements arose. The primary leader of the Persian Nizari Ismaili resistance against the Fatimid caliphate was Hasan-i-Sabah. (The Assassins are properly known as Nizari Ismailis.) The revolutionary, mystic, and political visionaries among the Ismailis completely abjured the organized state religion, believing it had become irredeemably corrupt.

Upon the death of Nizar in 1095, his supporters entered into a period of profound creative development that resulted in the *al-dawa al-*

*jadida*, or "New Preaching." Hasan-i-Sabah helped develop and promulgate the doctrine of the Nizari succession. There is no historical record of Nizar transferring his *nass* to any of his sons. However, one tradition that developed held that the mantle of Imam was passed to either Nizar's son or grandson, who was smuggled out of Egypt and secretly raised by Hasan at Alamut. (A variation states that Nizar himself mysteriously survived his execution and journeyed to the safety of Alamut.)

The Fatimid caliphate grew progressively weaker and more isolated throughout the reign of al-Mustali. In 1130, al-Mustali's son and successor, al-Amir, was murdered by Assassins sent from Alamut. The Fatimid Imamate was effectively ended, although it technically endured through four more leaders until the last caliph died in 1171 and Egypt was restored to the Sunni fold by Saladin, whom we shall encounter again. Today, surviving Mustalian Ismailis, known as the Bohras, live in India and Yemen.

## The Rise of the Seljuk Turks

As the Fatimid caliphate was shattered from within, a reinvigoration of the Sunni Abbasids was taking place. When the Seljuk Turks began their conquest of Persia in the initial decades of the eleventh century, they sent a deputation to the caliph in Baghdad announcing their conversion to Islam and their submission to his authority. He welcomed them as an ally against his own waning power, married the niece of the Seljuk sultan Tughril, and appointed Tughril "King of the East and the West" in 1058. Seljuk armies became the protectors of the caliph. Seljuk rulers provided the political strength to thwart the two great dangers threatening to undermine the Sunni establishment: the Fatimid caliph and the invasion of the European Crusaders.

The downside of this alliance was that the Seljuk Turks became the true power behind the Abbasid throne. They caused enormous resentment among the local populace of each region they entered. The new ruling class were foreigners. Turkish soldiers and political appointees were not acculturated. While they provided strength and order in a weakened realm, the cost included subjugation to their militancy. The Seljuks themselves experienced internal factional rivalry whose net effect was to further destabilize the population.

## The Sufis

The other singular development that contributed to a renewal of Sunni energy was the growth of the Sufi movement. Formed around independent spiritual teachers, various Sufi groups sought to explore the esoteric meaning of Islam and worked to develop and practice exercises to increase mystical awareness. The Sufis were allowed to pursue their religious explorations by the Abbasids. While the tolerance they extended to the Sufis helped to strengthen the Sunni revival, Sufi emphasis on spirituality could only have served to highlight Abbasid spiritual bankruptcy. The fervor with which the Ismailis approached their religious goals, on the other hand, compared favorably to the spiritual characteristics of the Sufi movement.

Thus, inadvertently, the two developments that contributed to a Sunni political and spiritual revival simultaneously helped to strengthen the Ismailis as an opposition movement. Shiism, most at home in turbulence, and with its rebellious Ismaili offspring, was about to find itself again the parent of revolutionary genius.

# CHAPTER FIVE

# Teachings of Ismailism

## Mahdi, Imam, and *Dai*

The anticipated Shiite redeemer, the Mahdi, patiently awaits the divinely ordained moment for his final appearance on earth. He is the *Qaim* (the last one), who will establish the ideal Islamic state. He is the seventh Prophet-Hierophant, who will inaugurate the seventh epoch of humanity as Muhammad had opened the sixth. As the final Imam, he will reveal the esoteric meaning of all preceding history and usher in a period of pure spiritual knowledge, in which truth will take precedence in all areas of human behavior.

In the meantime, the community is guided in righteousness toward that sublime moment by the Imam, heir to the Prophet, the chosen of God, and the sole leader of mankind. Descended from the bloodline of Ali and Fatima, the Imam carries a genetic link to the spiritual stature and mission of the Prophet. He is infallible and without sin. The Ismailis view the world as ruled by a succession of Speaking and Hidden Imams who, by Allah's grace, are present in each generation. The Imam is a personification of the metaphysical soul of the universe, and thus divine. His command of esoteric truth demands obedience from his followers. He alone can interpret the hidden meaning of the Koran and reveal the truth within the profane religious practices of unenlightened orthodoxy. The Imam and his knowledge are superior even to the Koran. For the Koran alone reveals the letter of the Law, the *zahir*, or outward teaching, while the Imam is needed to open its *batin*, or inner meaning. (The Ismailis were sometimes called Batinis.) The Imam is often referred to as the "speaking Koran."[1]

The Ismailis carried the doctrine of the Imam to the greatest heights of any Shiite sect. The Imam alone can guide the seeker through the practices necessary to attain the knowledge of God and provide him with the means to reach salvation. The Imam enjoys the highest form of *ilm*, or gnosis, direct spiritual wisdom bestowed by Allah and transmitted through the Imam to the community of believers. While only one Imam can be incarnate on earth at any one time, his silent successor, *samit* or *hujja*, may also be present in anticipation of his future role. The Imamate is passed along by the bestowal of the *nass* upon the designated successor, the process by which the current Imam transfers his *ilm* to the next Imam.

The Imam's spiritual function of interpreting and distinguishing the inner meaning (*batin*) from the outer teaching (*zahir*) is known as *tawil*. The ability to receive *tawil* is transmitted through initiation, in which the spiritual comprehension of the candidate is gradually prepared for the realization of esoteric truth. The *tawil* interpretation often makes use of kabbalistic exegesis to explain the journey from appearance to reality. For example, the conjoining of the male and female principles — represented by the letters kaf and nun in the word *kun*, "be" — is acknowledged as the original means by which God created the universe.[2] Every appearance implies an inner truth, or *haqiqa*. The *batin*, which embodies the *haqiqa*, can be communicated to the disciple only after an oath of secrecy is taken and an initiation into the sect is undergone. Initiation requires the payment of dues. "The early Ismailis held that while the religious laws were announced by the Prophets, it was the function of the Imams . . . to interpret and explain their true meaning to the worthy few, those who were initiated and acknowledged the Imams."[3]

The Imam works through his chosen priesthood of teachers, the *dais*, whose role is to bring the inner teaching of the Imam to the greatest number of seekers through the activities of the *dawa*, or teaching mission. The function of the *dai* is to complete the spiritual circuitry between the Imam and the pupil. The inner spiritual vision of the hidden essence of the Imam as the embodiment of *nur*, the mystical radiance of divine light, is regarded as the highest goal, and the necessary prelude to the disciple being flooded with divine grace. In addition to his religious duties of conversion and instruction, the *dai* has a political duty to establish the Imam's kingdom on earth. The *dai* is described as "charged with hastening not only the establishment of an Ismaili state but also articulating the fundamental doctrine and moral ends that state was meant to serve."[4]

The hierarchy of *dais* operated under a chief *dai* who worked immediately under the Imam. The *dais*, though often compared by Western scholars to missionaries, were highly trained and educated philosophers and theologians, as well as disciplined mystics. They were schooled in the language and religious beliefs of their potential converts in order to excel in the arts of persuasion. The *dai* sought to cultivate a personal relationship with his intended convert in order to be able to achieve the deepest level of communication. Mass proselytizing was never the strategy. The individual was always recognized as such and treated as unique. The guiding principle was gnosis, or knowledge, attained through illumination.

The individual's impassioned search for truth is a recurrent Ismaili theme as the disciple seeks the acceptance of the Imam after persevering through the necessary trials. His goal is to escape the limitations of the human condition and attain the liberation of spiritual return. The devotee expresses through his own spiritual journey the cosmic desire of the *nafs al-kull* (the principle of universal animation, symbolized in humanity as the Imam Ali) to return to its origin, the *aql al-kull* (the principle of universal reason, symbolized in humanity as the Prophet Muhammad).[5] Thus the Ismailis enjoyed a hierarchy of living truth — a community united under the supreme wisdom of the Imam, who shared his divinely revealed knowledge through a chain of *dais* directly to the body of the faithful, each of whom individually sought God through the adventure of his personal search for truth.

The elaborate hierarchical nature of Ismailism, with its emphasis on the uniqueness of the individual quest for enlightenment, was in stark contrast to the impersonal egalitarianism of the traditional Sunni model. From the Sunni point of view, the universal requirements of the Shariah blur the concept of spiritual distinctions because they are applicable to every Muslim.

The Ismailis controlled a vast network of *dais* and their followers throughout the Sunni territories. Caliph al-Hakim's training school for Ismaili missionaries, the Dar al-Hikma, housed a library of some two hundred thousand books on theology, astronomy, and medicine. Upon completion of their novitiates, the *dais* would be sent throughout the greater Islamic world clandestinely seeking converts and preaching the revolutionary teachings of the Ismaili Imam. As a persecuted sect, the Ismailis were required to cloak their religious practices and conversion efforts in the utmost secrecy. The *dai* risked execution should a student panic and betray his teacher to the authorities. The dangerous process of conversion involved a gradual breakdown of reverence for established Sunni religious doctrine and the political authority of the Sunni caliph under which the student had been raised.

The medieval Ismaili doctrine included an eclectic mix: it combined advanced philosophical speculation with Persian, Jewish, and

Christian esotericism; Gnostic, Neoplatonic, and Hindu mysticism; and elements of Sufi and Islamic occultism. It included kabbalistic techniques for the investigation of creation through the analysis of words and numbers. It held cyclical views of history based on seven cosmic eras and the seven Prophet-Hierophants charged with guiding humanity during these epochs. A variable list of these teachers would include Adam, Noah, Abraham, Moses, Jesus, Muhammad, and Muhammad ibn Ismail. Adam was replaced by Ali in some versions, and the Fatimids were forced to make major modifications in order to accommodate their teachings on the seventh Imam. The Ismailis incorporated eschatological doctrines on resurrection and believed in a final judgment, when the redeemed would be separated from the unredeemed. Ismaili views on salvation included the idea that the perfectibility of the human soul was necessary to achieve perfection of the universal soul.

Neoplatonism was introduced into Ismailism around the time of the founding of the Fatimid dynasty. The elaborate emanationist doctrines contained in the writings of the third-to-fifth-century Greek philosophers Plotinus, Porphyry, Iamblichus, and Proclus had been translated into Arabic during the ninth century. Several hundred years earlier, the Sassanian dynasty of Persia restored the sovereignty of the Zoroastrian religion of the Magi and offered a haven for pagan philosophers and scholars uprooted by the upheavals taking place in the Roman Empire after its embrace of Christianity. After Justinian closed the Neoplatonic academy in Athens in 529, the college of Jund-i-Shapur (or Gondeshapur), founded by Khosrow I in southwest Iran, became a great educational center, attracting Jews, Christians, and Neoplatonists, who infused Persian culture with Western spirituality and philosophy. Neoplatonism begins with the concept of an absolutely transcendent, supreme, and incomprehensible God. "The basic tenet of Neoplatonism could thus find ready acceptance in Ismaili theology, which adhered to strict monotheism and at its core was revelational rather than rational."[6]

An interesting manifestation of these beliefs was a group who appeared in Basra at the end of the tenth century and called themselves the Ikhwan al-Safa, or Brethren of Sincerity. Their revolutionary Gnostic teachings were preserved in the anonymous and encyclopedic *Rasail Ikhwan al-Safa*, a collection of fifty-two epistles divided into four sections that discusses all known science of the time, including astronomy, mathematics, music, and geometry, in addition to philosophical and religious speculation on cosmology, theology, and eschatology. The goal of the teachings is to help the reader purify his soul and achieve salvation through a blending of Greek philosophy, Christian ethics, Sufi mysticism, and Muslim law. It "exercised a profound influence on Muslim intellectual life from Persia to Spain."[7] The *Rasail* may also have been raised as an anti-Fatimid banner under which to unite Ismaili dissidents, because its teachings support Muhammad ibn Ismail. (The *Rasail* was known to have been studied by the charismatic Syrian Assassin leader Rashid al-Din Sinan, and by his friend and fellow student, the fourth chief of Alamut, Hasan II. It may also have been familiar to Hasan-i-Sabah.[8])

One model of the Ismaili wisdom teaching that has proven to be both controversial and long-lived is the system of initiatory grades referred to as the Nine Degrees of Wisdom, which dates back at least to the tenth century. A tract from that period, *The Book of the Highest Initiation* (*Kitab al-halagh al-alhar*), assumes familiarity with the degrees on the part of the reader. Recent scholarship has identified this writing as an anti-Ismaili forgery whose purpose was to slander and discredit the sect.[9] The book purported to be a cynical, secret Ismaili indoctrination manual for *dais*, designed to bring the innocent and unwary into a cult of lawless atheism and amorality. *The Book of the Highest Initiation* is reminiscent of that modern anti-Semitic forgery, *The Protocols of the Learned Elders of Zion*, or the prophetic *Report from Iron Mountain*, detailing the creation of an eco-socialist model as the organizing principle of the modern state. "It is, however, inherent in the nature of such libelous products to be travesties rather than mere phantasies; they would miss the greater part of their effect if the object of their caricature were unrecognizable."[10]

What is abundantly clear (and undisputed by modern scholarship) is that something secret, mysterious, and progressive did take place in the conversion and initiation process administered by the *dais*, and in the training program by which the *dais* were educated. "In form, the Ismailis were a secret society with a system of oaths and initiations and a graded hierarchy of rank and knowledge. These secrets were well kept, and information about them is fragmentary and confused."[11] Samuel M. Stern, writing about the degree structure of *The Book of the Highest Initiation*, also acknowledges that a progressive system of initiation took place: "It is, therefore, undeniable that Ismailism knew the idea of gradual initiation. . . . The author of our pamphlet did not invent anything in the framework he used. . . . [W]hat is to be put down to his malevolent invention is the *contents* he attributed to the doctrines taught on the different stages of the initiation."[12]

The nine-degree model has a fascinating symmetry that has enabled it to survive as an intimation of the hierarchical teachings of the Ismaili secret society for a thousand years. In deference to modern Ismaili scholarship, with a sincere desire not to propagate anti-Ismaili disinformation, and in view of the fact that much speculation will be involved, further discussion and a modern assessment of the nine-degree system can be found in appendix 1.

CHAPTER SIX

# Enter Hasan

## The Early Years

Hasan-i-Sabah was born around 1055 in Qum, about seventy-five miles southwest of Tehran in Persia (modern Iran), to a Twelver Shiite family. When Hasan was quite young, the family traveled northeast and settled in the nearby city of Rayy, which had been a center of *dai* activity since the ninth-century mission of Hamdan Qarmat. Hasan developed a love for religious teaching from the age of seven and kept strictly to the Twelver Shiite doctrines of his father until the age of seventeen.

Then he met a teacher named Amira Darrab, known as a comrade, or *rafiq*, who introduced him to the Sevener or Ismaili doctrines of the Fatimid caliphate. (The *rafiq* was the first level of instructor below the rank of *dai*.) Initially Hasan was resistant to the Ismaili teachings. He tells us, in his surviving autobiographical fragment, that he denigrated the Ismaili doctrine as "philosophy," that is, of far less value than the pure Islamic religious teachings of the Shia of which he was a fervent believer. In time, however, his respect for Amira Darrab caused him to probe deeper. He immersed himself in study. A severe illness was the final step in his conversion. He became fearful that he would die without attaining the truth. Upon his recovery, he continued his instruction with another Ismaili, Abu Najam Sarraj. He eventually swore the oath of allegiance to the Fatimid caliph al-Mustansir through a third *dai* named Mumin. In May or June 1072, Abd al-Malik ibn Attash, chief of the Ismaili *dawa* in western Persia and Iraq, visited Rayy and met Hasan. Impressed with the young man, he elevated him to the position of deputy *dai* and instructed him to travel to Egypt and present himself at the caliph's court. It took Hasan several years to fulfill this command.

The circumstances of Hasan's departure from Rayy have been the subject of dispute by historians. A contemporary story is attributed to Nizam al-Mulk, the powerful vizier to the Turkish Seljuk sultan Malik-shah. Although his authorship of the book is disputed, in his *Wasiyat*, or Testament, a guide to future statesmen, Nizam writes that he, Hasan, and the poet Omar Khayyam were students together of the Imam Mowaffek. The three friends made a pact that whoever succeeded first in life would share the bounty of his success with the other two. Nizam was the first to achieve worldly success, and Omar Khayyam presented himself at the court to remind him of his pledge. Nizam arranged for an annual pension that allowed Khayyam to write and meditate as he had requested. Hasan also sought Nizam's adherence to his pledge. According to the story, Nizam elevated the ambitious Hasan to a position of responsibility within the sultan's court, whereupon Hasan began to plot ways to discredit Nizam and supplant him as vizier. Nizam, learning of his friend's treachery, plotted against Hasan in return and ultimately succeeded in disgracing him. Hasan fled to Egypt to plan his revenge. This story is disputed by later scholars because of the age differences between the three men. Some historians have suggested that Hasan was accused of harboring agents of the Fatimid caliph in Rayy and escaped arrest as a political agitator by fleeing to Egypt in 1076.

Nizam, while remaining Hasan's lifelong enemy, was a brilliant and capable administrator. His thirty years of service brought many improvements to the Seljuk empire. He encouraged industry, trade, and finance; improved roads and bridges; and undertook educational, cultural, and architectural projects. He was committed to a policy of religious orthodoxy as an administrative prerequisite to a secure and well-run state. Although his implacable hostility to the Ismailis was particularly noteworthy, his intolerance was extended to Christians, Jews, and Shiites as well. Omar Khayyam, known to the West chiefly for his exquisite poetry, was one of the greatest mathematicians of medieval times. He reformed the Persian calendar, making it slightly more accurate than our present one. This calendar was never used, however, because it conflicted with the orthodox lunar calendar specified by Muhammad.

## HASAN'S JOURNEY

Hasan's two-year journey to Egypt was circuitous. First he traveled several hundred miles south to Isfahan. Here he stayed with Resi Abufasl, under whom he continued his studies of Ismaili doctrine. He shocked Abufasl one day by saying that if he had just two devoted friends, he could overpower both the sultan and his vizier and turn the Seljuk realm upside down. Abufasl was so stunned, he decided Hasan was suffering from insanity and offered him aromatic drinks and dishes prepared with saffron to help heal the brain. (Twenty years later, Hasan's

Assassins had felled the immensely powerful Nizam al-Mulk. Sultan Malikshah died soon after. At Alamut, Resi Abufasl had become one of Hasan's devoted disciples. Hasan is said to have teased him for his earlier suspicions, saying, "Resi, which of us two was out of his senses . . . and which would the aromatic drinks and dishes dressed with saffron . . . have best suited, thee or me?"[1])

Continuing his journey, Hasan traveled several hundred miles north to Adharbayjan (modern Azerbaijan) in southern Russia. He continued west toward Turkey to just north of the origin of the Tigris River at Mayyafarikin. He was driven out of town for denying the authority of the Sunni *ulema* to interpret Islam, a right he asserted was reserved to the Imam. He then traveled south through modern Iraq and Syria. At Damascus he learned that military disturbances had closed the overland route to Egypt, so he traveled to the coast and set sail from Palestine.

Hasan arrived in Cairo on August 30, 1078, and remained for two to three years. He completed the required course of study and was elevated to the full rank of *dai*. Historian Enno Franzius describes the Ismaili doctrine to which Hasan devoted himself: "It was at one and the same time a Shiite sect combining Islamic with pre-Islamic Greek, Persian, Syrian, and Babylonian concepts; an Alid secret society dedicated to the overthrow of the Sunni Abbasids; and a revolutionary social movement pledged to improve the lot of the depressed."[2] The weakened and threatened condition in which Hasan would find Caliph al-Mustansir may have inspired in him a sense of his own mission in the future survival of Ismailism.

Hasan fell afoul of Commander of the Armies Badr al-Jamali, de facto ruler of Fatimid Egypt. The precise reason is not clear. One apocryphal account states the problem was Hasan's Nizari leanings. This cannot be accurate because the dispute over Nizar's succession had not yet taken place. Hasan's Persian biographer, Rashid al-Din Tabib, writing in 1310, reported that Hasan was caught in the midst of the tension between Badr and Caliph al-Mustansir. Badr forbade a meeting between Hasan and the Imam despite al-Mustansir's desire to meet the young traveler from the north. Badr caused Hasan to be briefly imprisoned. Legend has it that a minaret collapsed at the prison. This was interpreted as an omen, and Hasan was released and deported from Egypt. The ship on which he traveled was wrecked by a storm of which Hasan had been forewarned by the Imam. Hasan's imperturbable calm in the midst of the storm was said to have resulted in conversions among his fellow passengers. He was rescued and taken to Syria. He traveled to Aleppo and Baghdad and finally reached Isfahan in 1081.

## Hasan's *Dawa*

Hasan traveled extensively through Persia as a *dai* for the next nine years. He eventually focused his *dawa* in the mountainous region of Northern Persia on the Caspian Sea, particularly the highlands known as Daylam. This area was the home of a fierce and independent mountain people much isolated from their fellow Iranians living on the plateau. The area had resisted conquest since ancient times. Daylam had also been a center of Shiism since the end of the eighth century. In the tenth century Daylami power briefly extended through most of Persia and Iraq, until the coming of the Seljuk Turks.

Daylam was a fertile region for Hasan's preaching, and he worked tirelessly. He was eventually appointed by ibn Attash to the position of chief *dai* of Daylam, and he dispatched his personally trained *dais* throughout the region. Nizam al-Mulk, Hasan's old rival, learned of Hasan's preaching efforts and commanded the governor of Rayy to capture him. Hasan eluded them and traveled deeper into Daylam.

## Alamut

Throughout his revolutionary and missionary travels, Hasan was searching for an impregnable fortress from which to conduct his resistance to the Seljuk empire. In about 1088, he finally chose the castle of Alamut, built on a narrow ridge on a high rock in the heart of the Elburz Mountains in a region known as the Rudbar. The castle dominated an enclosed cultivated valley thirty miles long and three miles across at its widest, approximately six thousand feet above sea level. Several villages dotted the valley, and their inhabitants were particularly receptive to the ascetic piety of Hasan. The castle was accessible only with the greatest difficulty through a narrow gorge of the Alamut River. It had been built by the Daylamese king Wah Sudan ibn Marzuban in about 860. The king was hunting one day and released an eagle, which then perched on a rock that rose another six hundred feet above the valley. Immediately recognizing the strategic value of the bird's choice, the king built a castle on the rock and named it *Aluh amut*, which means "eagle's teaching" in the Daylami language.[3]

Hasan employed a careful strategy to take over the castle, which had been granted to its current Shiite owner, named Mahdi, by the Seljuk sultan Malikshah. First, Hasan sent his trusted *dai* Husayn Qaini and two others to win converts in the neighboring villages. Next, many of the residents and soldiers of Alamut were secretly converted to Ismailism. Finally, in September 1090, Hasan himself was secretly smuggled into the castle. When Mahdi realized that Hasan had in fact quietly taken over his fortress, he left peacefully. Hasan gave him a draft for 3000 gold dinars in payment. Hasan, it is said, had offered this sum for the amount of land an ox's hide could contain. He then cut the hide into fine strips and strung them together to encompass the entire area of the Alamut rock. Hasan directed Mahdi to the home of a wealthy noble who was to pay the draft. Mahdhi had little faith in the validity of the document; however, he eventually presented it to the nobleman, who, when he saw Hasan's signature, immediately kissed the paper and paid out the gold.

The acquisition of the Assassin fortress of Alamut marked the foundation of the Nizari state and the proclamation of their open revolt against the Seljuk empire. From the moment of his entry into the castle in 1090 until his death thirty-five years later, Hasan-i-Sabah never left the rock. He is said to have left the seclusion of his house on only two occasions, when he went up to the roof. He devoted his time to prayer and fasting, reading, recording the teachings, developing the strategy for his revolutionary campaign, administering the affairs and strategic necessities of his realm, and doing his utmost to extend the Nizari New Preaching. He was reputed to be deeply versed in mathematics, astronomy, magic, and alchemy.

His was an extremely ascetic and pious life. When some of his followers drew up an elegant genealogy for him, he threw it in the water, declaring he would rather be the Imam's favored servant than his degenerate (or illegitimate) son. A musician at Alamut once played a flute at the castle and was forever expelled, since music was considered a sign of dissoluteness to Muslim purists. In fact, so abstemious was Hasan that he had one of his own sons, Muhammad, executed for drinking wine, thus disobeying the Islamic prohibition against alcohol, which was strictly enforced at Alamut. Another son, Ustad Husain, was executed for his part in an alleged conspiracy to murder Husayn

Qaini (a charge later determined to be false). During a famine caused by a Seljuk siege of Alamut, Hasan sent his wife and daughters to the safety of Girdkuh, a neighboring Ismaili community. He never brought them back, thus establishing a tradition among the chiefs of Alamut, who henceforth never allowed their women at the fortress while engaged in military campaigns.

## THE ASSASSINS UNDER HASAN

Once his base at Alamut was secured, Hasan was entirely free of constraints and diversions, and his entire will was able to focus on the task at hand. This meant the consolidation of his existing power; the fortification of Alamut; the acquisition of more castles; and the continuation of proselytizing efforts. To increase his holdings, Hasan made use of a variety of techniques, from sending missionaries and using persuasion to purchase, guile, and armed attack. Soon after the death of the Fatimid caliph al-Mustansir in 1094, Hasan succeeded ibn Attash as the chief *dai* of Persia and was acknowledged as the supreme head of the Nizari movement. The Nizaris were now a fully independent sect within Islam, free of any outside allegiance.

Success greeted Hasan's efforts. The mountainous and isolated area around Alamut was ripe for organizing because of the general Shiite susceptibility to Ismaili religious fervor, the negative effects of the oppressive Seljuk regime, and the fact that the Elburz region had never been known for religious orthodoxy. The strategically important castle of Lammassar, some thirty miles west of Alamut, was taken by Kiya Buzurgumid in 1096 or 1102. A secondary regional outpost was established at Quhistan in southeast Persia, to which Hasan sent Husayn Qaini. Conditions in Quhistan were favorable for Nizari organizing, since the Seljuk governor of the region was abusing the Ismaili populace. A third regional center was established in the mountainous region in southwestern Iran near Khuzistan by Abu Hamza, a *dai* who had been trained in Egypt before joining Hasan. The fourth Nizari area of great importance was Syria. Hasan sent missionaries to Aleppo in the very beginning of the twelfth century.

In 1092, the Seljuk sultan Malikshah decided to attack Alamut and rid his kingdom of the growing Nizari menace. Under the strategic direction of Nizam al-Mulk, the Seljuks launched simultaneous attacks against Alamut and Quhistan. Both Seljuk forces were defeated by the small Assassin garrisons and the reinforcements they were able to raise among the indigenous populace of each area. Later that year, the Assassins achieved their first great success in the art of political murder, their victim being Hasan's early friend and later nemesis Nizam al-Mulk. Disguised as a Sufi, Bu Tahir Arrani, the *fidai* (meaning "faithful"), approached Nizam al-Mulk's litter and plunged his dagger home. The death of the sultan Malikshah within weeks of Nizam's assassination effectively ended the first Seljuk campaign against Alamut.

The Seljuk empire was plunged into chaos and civil war for the next decade. Rival claims to succession and internecine warfare created wide avenues of weaknesses through which both the Nizaris and the Crusaders entered. Although Sultan Berkyaruq succeeded his father, he was fully occupied with the struggle against his half-brother Muhammad Tapar, who was allied with his full brother Sanjar. In addition to the Seljuk rulers and their agents of occupation, independent Seljuk warlords were given control of their own territorial domains as central Seljuk power weakened.

The Nizaris, in contrast, were blessed with a unified central command run by a strategic genius. Hasan handpicked a group of loyal semiautonomous leaders to form a decentralized network of Nizari power. The Assassins were a formidable opposition force within the fragmented Seljuk domains. Each Nizari stronghold functioned as its own headquarters for local military operations and was capable of providing safe haven for those seeking refuge from Seljuk forces. The Nizari revolutionaries could be flexible in their overall tactical methods — making alliances here or initiating military attacks there as the individual case required.

The patriotism and religious fervor of the average Nizari soldier made him a fierce and enthusiastic warrior. The tradition that the glorious death in battle was a direct means of entering Paradise had been a tenet of Islam since the military campaigns of the Prophet. The natural hierarchical obedience of the Nizaris allowed their armies to develop a high level of military prowess throughout all their scattered territories. An idea of the scope of some of these military efforts is conveyed by the battle outside Rayy in 1093, in which the Nizaris defeated a Sunni army of ten thousand men.

The pattern of Nizari expansion continued to aggravate the Seljuks. The Assassins seized fortresses scattered over ever greater areas. The acquisition of Girdkuh in the eastern Elburz region in 1096 bore the classic Assassin signature. The Seljuk governor Muzaffar was a secret Ismaili. Concluding that the castle was strategically ideal for the Nizaris, he persuaded the Seljuk emir to request the sultan appoint him commander. Muzaffar then stocked and fortified Girdkuh at Seljuk expense, after which he declared himself a disciple of Hasan-i-Sabah. He continued to rule the castle for forty years.

Attempts were made to expand into Isfahan beginning as early as 1093. Shahdiz had earlier been an important Seljuk stronghold. Ahmad ibn Attash, the son of the head of the Persian *dawa*, succeeded his father as the *dai* of Isfahan. He quietly began his conversion activities among the children of the garrison of Shahdiz. He was said to have converted some thirty thousand people in the area. By 1100, he had seized Shahdiz. The Nizari presence in Isfahan represented a major inroad into the heart of Seljuk power. Other fortresses followed. Attacks against the Assassin community were countered with assassinations against their instigators.

To the Seljuks, Assassin power grew to unacceptable levels. For example, Nizari leaders in Quhistan and Isfahan began to levy taxes on residents of these Seljuk domains. Berkyaruq's court and army were infiltrated by Ismaili agents. Officers who refused to cooperate with the Nizaris were forced to remain continuously armed for their personal protection. By 1101, Seljuk rivals Berkyaruq and Sanjar determined to join together and focus their energies against the Assassins in Quhistan and Isfahan as well as against suspected clandestine converts within the Seljuk power structure. A well-armed force was sent to Quhistan. After a successful initial attack, the emir leading Sanjar's forces was bribed to leave the area. Three years later, another attack was launched against the Ismailis; it also was victorious but settled on very generous terms from the Nizari point of view. Berkyaruq's efforts were criticized as half-hearted. In order to appease his critics, he allowed for a massacre of Ismailis in Isfahan, to be followed by widespread massacres throughout Iraq.

Order was restored to the Seljuk empire when Muhammad Tapar succeeded Berkyaruq in 1105. Muhammad Tapar ruled as the undisputed supreme Seljuk sultan until his death in 1118. He initiated campaigns against the Nizaris throughout the Persian territories. He personally led an attack against Shahdiz in 1107. When Muhammad Tapar attacked Shahdiz, Ahmad ibn Attash held out gallantly until he was betrayed. Ahmad's wife bedecked herself in jewels and leapt to her death from the castle wall. Ahmad was paraded through the streets of

Isfahan and then flayed alive. His skin was stuffed with straw and sent, along with his head and that of his son, to Baghdad.

A second Seljuk expedition was launched against Alamut in 1107, led by the son of Nizam al-Mulk, Ahmad, who had succeeded his father as the Seljuk vizier. Ahmad's brother had also been felled by Assassin daggers the previous year. Ahmad inflicted great hardships on Alamut, including a hideous famine. But despite the virulence of his hatred, Ahmad was defeated and the siege lifted.

Two years later, a third Seljuk effort against Alamut was commanded by Anushtagin Shirgir, who decided that a direct attack was inefficient. Instead, he undertook a siege that was to last eight years. He began by destroying crops in the region, plunging Alamut into renewed conditions of famine. This was the campaign in which Hasan and many others sent their wives and daughters out of Alamut. Shirgir continued the siege until 1118, when he learned of the weakness of his victims. He then decided to launch a concerted attack. With the Assassins on the verge of defeat, Shirgir's assault was interrupted by news of the death of Muhammad Tapar.

The Seljuk empire weakened once again after the death of Muhammad Tapar. He was officially succeeded by one of his sons, Mahmud, but the actual position of Seljuk sultan was assumed by Muhammad Tapar's younger brother Sanjar, who ruled until his death in 1157.

An amusing story illustrates the creativity Hasan could bring to diplomacy during this period. Attempting to make peace with Sanjar in the beginning of his sultanate, Hasan sent his ambassadors to the young leader. The ambassadors were rebuffed. One morning the sultan awoke to find a dagger stuck in the ground beside his bed. Alarmed, he chose to keep the matter secret. A messenger arrived from Hasan who stated, "Did I not wish the Sultan well that dagger which was struck in the hard ground would have been planted in his soft breast."[4]

For the next several decades there ensued a basic cease-fire between the Nizaris and Seljuks. Sanjar allowed the Assassins a pension from the taxes collected on lands they owned; he allowed them to collect tolls from travelers; and he gifted them with other grants and licenses. The Assassins became an established and stable political force in their numerous far-flung centers of power and remained in a relatively comfortable relationship with the Sunni majority. While occasionally there would arise the need for activities against one or another individual or group, the period of Nizari open revolt against the Seljuks was over. At one critical moment of Seljuk civil war, Sanjar's army battled that of his nephew Mahmud with a force that included Nizari soldiers.

In 1121, Hasan's *fidais* traveled from Syria to Cairo to kill al-Afdal, the vizier and commander of the armies who had deprived Nizar of the caliphate. Caliph al-Amir rejoiced over al-Afdal's death because he resented the usurpation of Fatimid power by the military, as discussed earlier. He gladly seized his late vizier's substantial property and treasure. It now seemed appropriate to heal relations with Alamut. The caliph wrote to Hasan and begged him to renounce his Nizari beliefs. But the new vizier, al-Mamun, a Twelver Shiite, was very unhappy with the caliph's rapprochement efforts toward the Assassins. He suspected that Hasan's plans included eliminating both himself and the Imam. He ordered the borders tightened and instituted internal security precautions that would be the envy of modern statists; these included citizen registration, strict identification requirements, travel restrictions, and mass arrests of suspected Assassin terrorists and their allies. In 1122, he arranged an assembly of supporters of the Mustalian succession to refute the Nizari claims, which resulted in an epistle read from the pulpits of all Egyptian and Syrian mosques. The relations between Cairo and Alamut continued to deteriorate.

In May 1124 Hasan became ill and appointed his successor. He died on May 23, 1124.[5] Hasan-i-Sabah is revered by Ismailis today as the principal force in the promulgation of the Nizari movement. His grave at Alamut was a pilgrimage site for Nizari faithful until it was destroyed by the Mongols in 1256. Hasan never claimed to be the Hidden Imam, but he was acknowledged as the *hujja,* the proof, the source of knowledge and authorized teaching, the immediate representative of the concealed Imam, and the custodian of the Nizari *dawa* until the Imam chose to reveal himself.

For more than nine centuries, Hasan's political and religious enemies have ascribed the basest motivations to his efforts. Extraordinary methods of manipulative mind control have been posited to explain the fanatical love and devotion accorded him by his *fidais*. The true explanation of his power is far simpler: Hasan-i-Sabah successfully convinced his disciples by the sanctity of his behavior and the force of his personality that he was the purest and closest link to the Hidden Imam to whom their aspiration was devoted.

# CHAPTER SEVEN

# AN OVERVIEW OF HASAN'S ASSASSINS

## THE ASSASSINS WITHIN THE LARGER ISLAMIC COMMUNITY

The establishment of a successful independent state in the midst of a hostile environment was the singular accomplishment of Hasan-i-Sabah. As we have seen, the Assassins faced both the religious antagonism of the Sunni majority and the military might of the great Seljuk empire. The success of the Nizari state was fueled by ideology — the Ismaili belief that conversion and military domination of those less pure were conditions of jihad (the spiritual duty to make war against the unbeliever, imposed upon Muslim faithful by the teachings of the Prophet). Nizaris further believed it was their duty to the Imam to provide the military and political might by which he might establish his rule of righteousness on earth.

Prior to the Seljuk attack against Shahdiz in 1107, there was a great debate in the court of Muhammad Tapar concerning the relationship between the Ismailis and Islam. The Nizaris and their supporters had appealed to the Sunni legists to forbear against attacking them as they were Muslims who subscribed to the Islamic creed of the oneness of God and prophethood of Muhammad, practiced Shariah, and were prepared to recognize Seljuk authority. The only difference they claimed was that they recognized a spiritual Imam. This assertion of Muslim orthodoxy on the part of the Nizari Ismailis was rejected by certain of the Sunni fundamentalists. The hostile theologians asked the Nizaris what their response would be if their Imam allowed what the Holy Law of Islam forbade, or if he forbade what the Holy Law demanded. While some of these same theologians soon fell victim to Nizari daggers, their argument would prove prophetic when the Qiyama proclamation was issued by Hasan II in 1164.

The Assassin war against the Sunnis engendered complex social relations with the majority Shiites. Although the Twelver Shiite would naturally tend toward an anti-Turkish, anti-Sunni stance, especially in the early years of Assassin organizing, the Ismaili belief was a heresy from the Twelver point of view. Furthermore, Nizari use of assassination often led the Sunnis to violent acts of retaliatory revenge, including massive generalized assaults against suspected Ismailis and their sympathizers. Thus, the entire Shiite community frequently fell victim to indiscriminate Sunni attacks directed against the Nizaris. These massacres at first created sympathy among non-Nizari Ismailis and Twelver Shiites. Yet over time, sentiment hardened against the Assassins, and they began to be blamed as troublemakers. Eventually most Shiites became as fiercely opposed to the Assassins as were the Sunnis. Anti-Nizari literature of Twelver Shiite origin began to appear in ever increasing quantity.

Nizari secrecy led to widespread accusations against them that rose to whatever level of imagination the accuser could summon. Like modern urban legends of Satanic cults and antigovernment extremist bogeymen, the Assassins became the dark embodiment of the shadow-self of Islam. They were accused of drug taking and licentious sexual orgies. Unlimited powers of mind control were ascribed to Assassin leaders, whose zombielike disciples were considered either too stupid, too brainwashed, or too drug-addled to resist the manipulative, charismatic power of sect leaders. Nizari leaders were said to follow no law but their own and to be willing to stoop to any depth, including witchcraft, to mislead their flock. The Sunni establishment accused them of plotting to undermine Islamic law and renew the ancient pagan faith of Persia — the dualist doctrines of Zoroaster. The tenth-century "black legends" of criminal blasphemy that had been directed against the earlier Ismailis were resurrected and attained their apotheosis during the Alamut period of Nizari Ismailism, and have lived long after.

Abul-Mahasin Ruyani, a famed Sunni teacher, was assassinated in 1108 because of the vehemence of his anti-Nizari preaching. He claimed the Nizaris were so far afield of Islam they should be killed as non-Muslims, despite the traditional Sunni tolerance applied to all who uttered the formula of faith, the Shahadah: "There is no god but God, and Muhammad is His Prophet." Feelings continued to rise against the Nizaris throughout the century and a half of their political power. Only when they were completely destroyed as a political force were they grudgingly accepted again as part of Islam. Marshall Hodgson states that the Nizari Ismailis so challenged the inclusive tolerance of the Sunni community as to determine the future character of the Muslim faith, ". . . preparing the way for the relative intolerance of later Islam against deviation."[1]

## The Policy of Selective Political Murder

Assassination in Muslim culture is said to be traced to the Prophet, who was known to state his dissatisfaction with an enemy and then to express his appreciation when one of his men was able to kill the designated foe.[2] One of the first Muslims to heed the Prophet's call to assassination was Abd Allah ibn Unays, who killed the chief of a hostile tribe and thereby saved the Islamic community of Medina from a powerful and dangerous enemy.[3] Of the four "Righteous Caliphs" who succeeded Muhammad, three were murdered. The application of jihad to individual killings, however, was an early Shiite development.

It was Hasan-i-Sabah who turned assassination into an art form — maximizing the political benefit of minimum loss of life and offering a more humane method of resolving political differences than the carnage and suffering of the traditional battlefield. Assassination has the unusual effect of entering directly into the halls of power and touching the decision makers themselves rather than the average citizen, the age-old victim of the political adventurism of his leaders.

Since Islamic culture placed a high premium on individual excellence, the leader who was able to rise up and survive his acquisition of power was a tested and unusual individual. Thus his death was often sufficient to alter substantially the balance of power. On the other hand, the Assassins were generally uninterested in pursuing the same techniques against the Christian military orders such as the Hospitallers and Knights Templar. They reasoned that these orders were so structured that assassination of leaders would only lead to competent replacement from within the ranks.

Islamic historian Bernard Lewis cites the roll of honor at Alamut as containing the names of fifty assassinations performed during the thirty-five-year reign of Hasan-i-Sabah.[4] Rashid al-Din Tabib, Hasan's early Persian biographer, stated that, in total, seventy-five people were assassinated by Hasan and his two successors.[5] In fact, most assassinations occurred within these first decades of the Nizari struggle and became less frequent thereafter. The practice of assassination caused an unprecedented hatred to be directed at the Assassins. Marshall Hodgson points out the correlation between assassinations and retaliatory massacres against the Nizaris; as assassinations declined, so did the indiscriminate massacres.[6]

For the devoted *fidai*, the act of murder was a genuine religious sacrament. Lewis writes, "For their victims, the assassins were criminal fanatics, engaged in a murderous conspiracy against religion and society. For the Ismailis, they were a corps d'élite in the war against the enemies of the Imam; by striking down oppressors and usurpers, they gave the ultimate proof of their faith and loyalty, and earned immediate and eternal bliss."[7] One story that illustrates the role of assassination and the cultural values of the medieval Nizari Ismaili community concerns the mother of a Syrian *fidai*. Upon learning of the death of her son during a successful mission of political murder, she rejoiced and adorned herself in celebratory garb; upon the unexpected safe return of the young man, however, she entered into a state of mourning.[8]

No Assassin *fidai* is known to have attempted to evade capture, nor to use any weapon other than a handheld dagger for his kills. Most Assassin victims were heavily guarded men of state — emirs, sultans, and military leaders — whose assassinations were almost always carried out in public places in broad daylight. Local Sunni religious teachers who preached against Ismaili beliefs were targeted, as were presumed converts who recanted after having been exposed to the true revolutionary nature of the faith. The intention of assassination was to create maximum intimidation and a psychological pattern of chronic fear and anticipation among Nizari enemies.

Assassination was also sometimes used against the enemies of Nizari allies. This led to accusations of mercenary behavior. These accusations were largely untrue with the following exceptions: If an assassination was suggested that fit their overall plan, the Assassins might certainly be willing to accept money if it was offered; and, grateful allies might provide gifts to them upon the elimination of enemies. The idea that the Assassins worked for other political leaders surely would have been an effective means of sowing suspicion and discord among their enemies. Thus the "confessions" extracted from some *fidais* may have been prearranged disinformation designed to serve their inexorable campaign against the established order. In the end, after the destruction of the Nizari political state in the second half of the thirteenth century, individual Assassin chieftains in Syria were willing to allow their *fidais* to be hired out for pay.

## Drugs and Apostasy

Sunni historians have tended to characterize the Assassins as a degenerate band of *malahida*, heretics whose religious philosophy was a cover for criminal activity and whose sectarians were duped by the sinister manipulations of their apostate leaders. In contrast, many Ismaili chroniclers regard the Assassins as the guardians of sacred mysteries progressively revealed through hierarchical initiation.

The Assassins were known to both Sunnis and hostile Shiites as *hashishim*. The first known use of the term *hashishiyya* was in an anti-Nizari tract issued in 1123, prepared during the reign of the Fatimid caliph al-Amir, son and successor of al-Mustali. No explanation was given for the use of the term.[9] It has long been thought that the name was a reference to legends of Assassin chiefs administering that drug to disciples during their sojourn in the Garden of Pleasure. But even the most hostile contemporary Islamic writers, both Sunni and Shiite, nowhere accuse the sect of drug use.

The greatest European Arabic scholar of his day, Silvestre de Sacy, demonstrated in 1809 that the word *assassin* was derived from the Arabic word *hashish*.[10] Although de Sacy rejected the notion that the *fidais* were a group of drug addicts under the sinister power of their ruthless and scheming chief, he believed that a potion composed of hashish, perhaps mixed with other substances such as opium, was initially administered to the *fidais* to induce a definitive ecstatic experience. Despite his speculation, there is no historical evidence that any *fidai* was ever given any drug or intoxicant.

From the eleventh century until at least the late fourteenth, hashish use was frowned upon by the Muslim majority, who associated it with the lower classes and believed it was inevitably accompanied by the moral ennui symptomatic of social outcasts.[11] Most probably the name *hashishiyya* was a term of abuse, a pejorative label of derision used by Sunni writers in describing the fallacious beliefs and wild behavior of the sect, contemptuously associating them with drunkards and drug addicts.[12] That which may have been intended as a moral criticism by Muslims was seized upon by Westerners as a ready explanation for the self-sacrificing behavior and willingness to accept martyrdom of the *fidais*, which they otherwise found irrational and alien.[13]

## HASAN'S CONTRIBUTION TO ISMAILI DOCTRINE

A mere fragment of Hasan's writings survived the destruction of the library at Alamut by the Mongols in 1256. The most important work with which we are familiar is Hasan's critique of the doctrine of *talim* (authoritative teaching), preserved by being carefully summarized and commented upon by the twelfth-century Sunni heresiologist Shahrastani. The fundamental Shia doctrine of *talim* essentially states that as human beings we are incapable of determining religious truth for ourselves; we do not possess the required expertise with which to judge. Thus, God needed to send the Prophet to mankind in order that he might teach truth. God continues to lead humanity through His Imams, each of whom appoints his successor in an unbroken chain.

Hasan elaborated upon this with a carefully reasoned theological argument for the necessity of the Imam, and the nature of the Imam's truth as the direct representative of both God and Muhammad. Under the terms of Hasan's discourse, Muhammad and the chain of Imams were proof of the existence of God, while the existence of the Imam himself was dependent on the disciple's search for God. The unity of God, *tawhid*, is the key to the discovery of truth in doctrine, for the sign of truth is unity, and the sign of error is multiplicity. Hasan's Imam is singular and his authority is absolute. Both the Sunnis and the Shiites were liable to error because of their misunderstanding of the true nature of the Imam. The Nizaris were the only Islamic sect free from error and were therefore in a position to lead the larger Muslim body.

The key to *talim* is the community of those who subject themselves to the Imam. As *talim* was the organizing principle of Nizari society, it served to enhance cohesiveness and discipline among the warriors of Alamut. Hasan demanded unconditional loyalty from the Nizari devotee as a direct duty to God — going far beyond the traditional Shia requirements of allegiance to hierarchical authority. "From the very beginning, the principle of *talim* was given the greatest importance. This was, of course, a fundamental principle of Ismailism, but its relevance was naturally even greater now that discipline and obedience became indispensable values in the conditions in which settlements like those of Alamut had to be maintained."[14]

As we have seen, Hasan's ambitions reached far beyond the isolated confines of Alamut. "[He] sought for universal validity in the authority of an Imam whose claims were validated by a devastating scepticism of any more conditional claims. . . . Nothing was left any independent meaning save the power drive of the one community which dared to accept so ultimate a position."[15]

# CHAPTER EIGHT

# AFTER HASAN

As is the case with any number of spiritual movements following the death of the inspired and charismatic founder, the subsequent history of the Persian Assassins is one of progressive devolution with rare interludes of creativity. After the death of Hasan, a series of seven leaders of the Nizari state followed. With one outstanding exception, none of the remaining lords of Alamut approached the state of illumined spiritual fervor, nor the revolutionary sense of limitless possibility, incarnated by Hasan-i-Sabah.

Nevertheless, the Lord of Alamut always remained the undisputed leader of the far-flung Nizari territories, in which decentralized and semiautonomous local command was the rule. The Nizari succession was unusually stable in comparison with that of other Muslim dynasties. Despite the many differences in the policies and individual spiritual stature of the heads of Alamut during the next century and a half of its existence, the Assassin dynasty maintained its unique identity, strong sense of community, and consciousness of its divine mission until the end. The 166 years of the Alamut state may be divided into three periods: the first is the Revolutionary, beginning with Hasan in 1090 and extending through his successors, Buzurgumid and Muhammad; the next is the Qiyama period, beginning during the reign of Hasan II in 1164 and continuing through his successor Muhammad II; and last is the Satr period of rapprochement with the Sunni world that began in 1210 under the leadership of Hasan III and was continued by Muhammad III and his short-lived successor, Khurshah, who was defeated by the Mongols in 1256.

## HASAN'S SUCCESSORS OF THE REVOLUTIONARY PERIOD

### Buzurgumid (r. 1124–38)

Buzurgumid was one of Hasan's most trusted generals; he had commanded the castle of Lammassar, the second most important Assassin fortress, for over two decades. During the last months of his fatal illness, Hasan summoned Buzurgumid to Alamut and appointed him his successor. Hassan is said to have whispered to Buzurgumid that as long as

he remained worthy, Hasan's spirit would counsel him. Buzurgumid inherited the large Nizari Persian territories, composed of three regional
centers some fifteen hundred miles apart: the first at Alamut; the second to the southeast in Girdkuh; the third in Quhistan farther to the
southeast in central Persia. The fledgling Syrian branch of the Nizaris
was also under his command. Confounding the expectations of his enemies, Buzurgumid provided strong unopposed leadership and continued the strategic policies of his predecessor. Although he was not a
creative political revolutionary like Hasan, Buzurgumid was an able
administrator and a courageous leader.

He faced immediate tests of his leadership. In 1124, a brutal massacre of some seven hundred Ismailis took place at Amid in southern
Armenia. In 1126, Buzurgumid successfully resisted a major Seljuk
offensive launched by Sanjar, whose behavior was uncharacteristic in
view of his friendship with the Assassins during Hasan's lifetime. A mis-
judgment of the newly ascended Buzurgumid's weakness must have
weighed in Sanjar's decision to attack. Two *fidais* later murdered Sanjar's vizier, who had counseled this course of action.

In 1129 an Assassin diplomat was invited to discuss peace terms by
Mahmud, the Seljuk regional sultan in Isfahan. The Nizari envoy and
his colleague were lynched by a mob. Mahmud apologized to Buzurgumid but refused to punish the murderers. In retaliation, the Assassins
murdered four hundred citizens of Qazwin. Mahmud's retaliatory attack
against Alamut failed.

In 1130, Buzurgumid's *fidais* traveled to Egypt and slew the Fatimid
caliph al-Amir, who had succeeded his father al-Mustali as Imam. Al-
Amir had unsuccessfully sought to end the Nizari schism during the
reign of Hasan, as mentioned earlier. He had reigned for twenty-nine
years. His death plunged the Mustalian dynasty into a new schism based
on a dispute about whether he had or had not produced a son to succeed him.

In 1135, twenty-four *fidais* murdered the Abbasid caliph al-
Mustarshid, who had been defeated in battle, captured, and imprisoned
by the Seljuk sultan Masud, Mahmud's successor in Isfahan. Although
al-Mustarshid was treated with respect during his confinement, accusations persisted that both Masud and the supreme Seljuk leader Sanjar
were involved in his assassination. The death of the powerful Abbasid
caliph, titular chief of the entire Sunni empire, occasioned great rejoicing and a seven-day celebration at Alamut.

The political and religious isolation of the Nizari community made their continued survival and expansion all the more unexpected. Under Buzurgumid's leadership, Alamut even operated its own mint. Buzurgumid remained a powerful force with which to be reckoned by both Sunni and Shiite powers, and he expanded the Nizari state to its ultimate territorial limits.

## Muhammad (r. 1138–62)

Just days before his death, Buzurgumid passed the leadership to his son Muhammad, a conservative man whose ascension to power indicated a new phase for the Nizari state. For one thing, the succession to the Master of Alamut would henceforth be passed from father to son. For another, Muhammad's overall ambition for expansion was limited. His military activity, for example, was considerably more provincial than his father's. Fourteen assassinations were recorded during his twenty-four-year reign, most taking place during his first five years. No significant military operations were undertaken outside the region of Alamut and the other established Nizari centers, although some of his local campaigns were quite aggressive.

For example, in 1138, Nizari *fidais* slew the new Abbasid caliph al-Rashid, son and successor to al-Mustarshid, while he too was staying in Isfahan. Although the Assassins again celebrated his death at Alamut, a horrible massacre of Ismailis took place in Isfahan in retribution. A series of local assassinations followed, culminating in the murder of the son of Shah Ghazi Rustam in 1142, which turned the shah into a bitter and powerful foe of the Nizaris. In his rage, the shah attacked the Ismailis wherever he found them and built towers of their severed heads. In 1143, Muhammad's *fidais* slew the Seljuk sultan Daud, who had also persecuted the sectarians. This led a Seljuk official in Rayy, named Abbas, to order another massacre in which severed Ismaili heads were again piled into towers. The Nizaris sent an emissary to Sanjar seeking protection from their persecutor. Soon after, the head of Abbas was sent to Alamut, beginning a renewed, but brief, period of alliance with Sanjar.

During Muhammad's reign, Seljuk power continued to weaken. In 1141, Sanjar faced the Mongols near Samarkand and barely managed to survive the encounter. In 1153, he faced the wild and rebellious Turkoman tribes, who defeated his army, captured him, and pillaged and plundered the area. Sanjar's death in 1157 further weakened the Seljuk empire.

An increasing number of Nizaris at Alamut began to feel frustrated that the fire had gone out of their movement. The limit of Muhammad's quest for territorial expansion seemed to be his mission to Afghanistan. To many it seemed that the grand vision of world conquest and domination had become trivialized into local raids and cattle theft. A nostalgia for the spiritual frenzy that had animated the community in earlier times became pronounced. People were impatient for the promised appearance of the long-awaited Imam.

Many young people in particular turned their attentions toward Muhammad's son Hasan. Born in 1126, he was a radical and brilliant young man. Hasan was devoted to the teachings of Hasan-i-Sabah, the occultism of earlier Ismaili philosophers, and the mysticism of the Sufis. He developed his own following at Alamut and throughout the Rudbar. Intimations of an extraordinary character were hinted at. It was said that he secretly drank wine, a behavior he was able to conceal from his father. It was rumored that his heretical acts were possible only because he was the Hidden Imam and therefore above the Law. His father adamantly opposed this movement. Muhammad publicly insisted that Hasan could not be an Imam because Hasan was his son and he was merely a *dai*. He punished Hasan's devotees in a particularly bizarre fashion — he first killed 250 of Hasan's supporters and then bound their corpses to the backs of another 250, whom he then banished from Alamut. Hasan retreated from his energetic preaching activities and worked patiently to regain his father's trust so that he would not be disinherited from the succession.

## THE PROCLAMATION OF QIYAMA

### Hasan II (r. 1162–66)

Prior to his death, Muhammad did in fact appoint Hasan as his successor. Hasan was then thirty-five years old. The first two and a half years of his reign were uneventful, although he showed leadership skill in continuing to define the position of the Lord of Alamut as the spiritual head of the far-flung Nizari state.

On August 8, 1164, Hasan II proclaimed the advent of the millennium, the Resurrection, or Qiyama, to the assembled representatives from the various Persian Nizari territories. His announcement was made in the middle of the holy month-long fast of Ramadan, on a day in which Shiites commemorate the death and martyrdom of Ali. At noon, clad in white and wearing a white turban, Hasan mounted a pulpit whose four corners were covered with white, red, green, and yellow banners and began praying toward the west with his back to Mecca. While holding aloft his sword, he is reported to have announced that the Hidden Imam had proclaimed a New Dispensation and freed his faithful from the Shariah practices of Islam. He declared that the Hidden Imam had appointed him chief vicar, and that those who believed in his truth and followed his instructions would experience immortal life upon the death of their bodies. In fact, he proclaimed that those who believed in the Imam had already entered a state of Paradise while in the physical body. At the conclusion of this breathtaking speech, he descended from the pulpit and held a banquet, stating that the Ramadan fast was at its end. This supreme act of blasphemy was reportedly accompanied by wine drinking, pork eating, and sensual indulgences.[†]

The proclamation of Qiyama implied that the Last Day, the Day of Judgment, had arrived. Those who accepted the Nizari Imam and his representative Hasan had been judged and entered Paradise at that moment. All others had been condemned to Hell. The culmination of all the historical and religious cycles had come at last. The holy practices prescribed by Muhammad as Shariah were merely outward symbols of inner spiritual truths. Outward symbols were now profanations of inner truth. Under the terms of religious freedom and evolution following the New Dispensation, one was to experience inner spiritual union with Allah directly. One no longer prostrated oneself and prayed to Allah five times per day in an act of symbolic union with God. Under the New Dispensation, one maintained a state of continuous prayer and union.

Those Nizaris who persisted in the traditional practices of Islam and refused to follow the New Dispensation were chastised, stoned, and killed as blasphemers — exactly as those who had previously been found guilty of breaking the Shariah were treated. Only the Nizari

---

[†] In deference to the opinion of some modern Ismaili scholars regarding Hasan II's proclamation, we quote the following, "However, the current view among some historians that the proclamation [of Qiyama] involved an abrogation of Sharia has never been substantiated." "The Ismailis in History" by Aziz Esmail and Azim Nanji in Nasr, Seyyed Hossein, ed. Ismaili Contributions to Islamic Culture, p. 249.

faithful were able to receive and comprehend spiritual truth. All others, including non-Nizari Muslims as well as all non-Muslims, "were henceforth cast into eternal Hell which was in effect a state of spiritual nonexistence."[1]

Ten weeks after the proclamation at Alamut, a similar pronouncement was made in Quhistan by Hasan's representative, who read aloud a formal message from the Lord of Alamut, God's direct representative on earth, Caliph of the Nizari Ismailis. Hasan's statement that he was the divinely appointed ruler (caliph) of the Ismailis involved another massive break with tradition. Previously all Shiite caliphs had claimed a bloodline to Ali (no matter how tortuous). The Qiyama proclamation was later repeated in Syria by Hasan's representative Sinan.

It is not clear whether Hasan ever publicly claimed to be the Imam. He called himself teacher (dai), proof (hujja), and divinely appointed ruler (caliph), all positions that imply the representation of the Imam. The medieval historian Rashid al-Din stated that Hasan sent out secret letters after his public announcement in which he proclaimed that he was the inward Imam, if not so in the flesh. His son and successor, Muhammad II, however, erected his own teaching on the premise that his father was the literal Imam and physically descended from Nizar, a position accepted by Nizari Ismailis since. Beginning with the Qiyama proclamation of Hasan II, the Lord of Alamut was recognized by the Nizaris as the Imam rather than his chief dai or hujja.

Marshall Hodgson explores an even deeper dimension concerning the radical depth of Hasan's proclamation of Qiyama and his suggestion (and his son's assertion) that he was the Imam. The Imam who would announce the Resurrection was a figure already known to the Ismailis as the Judge of the Resurrection, the Qaim of the Qiyama. His special role was to be the consummation of the teachings of the Prophet at the end of time. All Islamic doctrine points to him. The Prophet Muhammad is one of six prophets of mankind who precede the Qaim (Adam, Noah, Abraham, Moses, and Jesus were the first five). Therefore, in a very real sense, the Qaim is greater than even Muhammad himself. This is the Imam whom Hasan II proclaimed at the Ramadan feast. It was the function of Hasan-i-Sabah to prepare the way for his advent.[2]

The blasphemous proclamation by Hasan II, and the embrace of the doctrine by his son Muhammad II, severed any remaining Nizari ties with both Sunnis and Shiites. By their own efforts, the Assassins had fully attained the uncontested status of malahida, or heretics. No longer was the argument centered around simple issues like acceptance or rejection of this or that Imam. With Qiyama, the Nizaris had declared their ultimate independence from the larger Islamic community. "In sum, the Nizaris were now collectively introduced into Paradise on earth, while the rest of mankind was made non-existent and irrelevant."[3] "But at the same time it was an admission of defeat in the attempt to take over Islam at large."[4] One indication of this was the change in the *dawa* efforts of the post-Qiyama Alamut period. More emphasis was devoted to teaching the new doctrine to members of the Nizari community than to spreading the faith through proselytizing and conversion.

Hasan II was murdered a year and a half after his proclamation, stabbed to death by his brother-in-law, who vigorously refused to follow the Qiyama teachings and apparently hoped to return the Nizari community to its pre-Qiyama faith. Despite the intense controversy surrounding Hasan's religious activities, he is held in veneration by Ismailis today and is always referred to as Hasan *ala dhikrhi al salam* (upon whose mention be peace).

## Muhammad II (r. 1166–1210)

Hasan II was succeeded by his son Muhammad II. Muhammad was a young man of nineteen at the time. He was a powerful personality who immediately caused his father's murderer to be executed along with the rest of his family. He declared his father to have been the spiritual and physical Imam, and thus, as his son, Muhammad proclaimed himself Imam. He continued the Qiyama revelation of Hasan II and devoted considerable personal energy for the rest of his long life to a careful and sophisticated elaboration of its doctrine.

Muhammad first undertook to provide a proper Alid lineage for his father. He stated that Hasan II was not the son of the third Lord of Alamut, Muhammad, son of Buzurgumid, after all, but that he was secretly the son of the Hidden Imam. Some believed that Hasan had been surreptitiously switched as an infant with the son of Muhammad, others that Muhammad had unwittingly taken a pregnant woman to wife, still others that Hasan's mother had an adulterous liaison with the secret Imam who lived at the foot of the mountainous rock upon which stood Alamut. Eventually, Hasan II's genealogy was traced to the grandson of Nizar, who had been secretly raised by Hasan-i-Sabah and had grown to be either the father or grandfather of Hasan II. "Thus, after a period of some seventy years following Nizar's death, the line of the Nizari Imams emerged openly. . . . "[5]

The theological contribution of Muhammad II elevated the concept of the Nizari Imam far higher than it had been within earlier Shiite theology. The Qiyama brought Paradise directly to earth, and therefore God was manifest in all His magnificence *through* the Imam. The Imam became the very form of God, his attributes were the attributes by which God revealed Himself to the people of the time. The Imam was to be the spiritual center and focus of each Nizari's life. Through the practice of holy awareness upon the limitless virtue of the Imam, the disciple would be liberated from error and prepared for the personal attainment of Godhead. Achieving the true inner spiritual vision of the Imam was the gateway to the ultimate reality — Paradise — for the Nizari disciple. This belief is not dissimilar to the higher reaches of mystical Christianity or to the practices of *guru bhakti* within Indian and Sufi traditions. In fact, it is one of the reasons the Nizaris were able to blend so successfully into the Sufi movement nearly a century later.

Muhammad II was a competent leader in the best tradition of Alamut. One interesting tale concerns his treatment of a Sunni scholar named Fakhr ad-Din al-Razi who had begun a vigorous lecture campaign against the Nizari doctrine. Muhammad sent a disciple to attend the scholar's lectures in Rayy. After some months, the *fidai* threatened the scholar at dagger point and extracted an oath from him to cease his teachings against the Assassins. He then conveyed Muhammad's invitation to visit Alamut and passed along the Imam's gifts of gold and beautiful garments. When another student later asked al-Razi why he no longer attacked the Assassins, he responded that their arguments were both too pointed and too weighty!

From a political perspective, the first part of Muhammad's reign was uneventful. Only one assassination is recorded outside Syria during the first twenty-six years of his leadership. The preoccupation of Islamic rulers with their battles against the Crusaders left little room for concern with the Nizaris.

As time went on, however, the political situation became more complicated. The Seljuk empire began to experience its death throes. By 1194, Seljuk control of the various warlords of Persia was at an end, and former Seljuk generals battled among themselves. The Nizaris occasionally became allied with one or another depending on the concerns of the moment.

Some five hundred miles northeast of Alamut, in the isolated region of Khwarazm in the upper Oxus River (mod. Amu Darya) area south of the Aral Sea, grew a new military threat to fill the void left by the Seljuk decline. Originally vassals of Sanjar, the Turkish Khwarazmians were rapidly expanding into a regional power. They killed the last Seljuk sultan, Tughril III, in Rayy in 1194. They raided Alamut in 1198, employing a ruse in which they momentarily sought Assassin protection and then betrayed their benefactors. During one Khwarazmian attack against Qazwin in 1199, the Assassins outwitted their numerically superior enemy by agreeing to yield the fortress and leave in peace. They stipulated that they would split into two groups. If the first group was allowed to leave unmolested, the second would surrender the fortress. The first group left and the Khwarazmians waited for the second party to surrender. Eventually they realized that the entire Assassin garrison had escaped in the first group.

The Khwarazmians were themselves under assault from the Ghurids, a tribe from the Hindu Kush who had converted to Islam and gained control of Afghanistan. The Ghurids also battled the Nizaris in Quhistan. The superior Ghurid force rapidly subdued any opposition. Shihab al-Din, the local Ghurid leader, was assassinated in 1206. The Nizaris took credit for the deed, although it is not clear whether they were responsible. They claimed they had acted on behalf of the Khwarazmians, which led to negotiations between the Khwarazmians and the Ghurids.

Another contemporary development confronting Muhammad was the renewed power of the Abbasid caliphate of Baghdad. This established icon of Sunni orthodoxy had undergone a new revitalization under the leadership of Caliph al-Nasir al-Din Allah (1180–1225). Curiously, he was a Shiite, but he used the traditional Sunni seat of power in an effort to unite Islam. He promulgated a chivalrous ceremonial order of which he had become Grand Master. The order had originated among the Sufis and grown among the artisan class. The order was devoted to the practice of *futuwwa*, the way of *fata*, meaning in Arabic "a handsome brave youth." "After the enlightenment of Islam, following the use of the word in the Holy Koran, [it] came to mean the ideal, noble and perfect man whose hospitality and generosity would extend until he had nothing left for himself; a man who would give all, including his life, for the sake of his friends."[6] Each new initiate pledged his loyalty to the Master who brought him into the order, wore special vestments, drank from the cup of knighthood, and added the order's heraldry to his personal coat of arms. Al-Nasir spread the order to the rulers of Islamic territories. Thus each Islamic leader would receive the spiritual imprimatur of the Abbasid caliph. The devotion to the high ideals of honor and fidelity imbued Sunnism with a romantic glamour that had long been absent.

Undoubtedly, the most troubling factor claiming the attention of Muhammad II was the state of mind of his son and heir, Hasan III, who dreamed of amalgamating the Nizaris within the larger body of Islam. This caused a great deal of tension between father and son, reminiscent of the earlier struggle between Muhammad I and Hasan II. The problem was exacerbated by the importance Muhammad II had placed on the Imamate and its irrevocable mantle of succession — Hasan III had already been proclaimed as the next Imam. Both men feared the other would kill him, and each went about Alamut fully armed at all times.

## THE PERIOD OF SATR (CONCEALMENT)

### Hasan III (r. 1210–21)

Eventually Muhammad II passed away (from natural causes) and the mantle of leadership fell to his son Jalal al-Din Hasan. His mother was a Sunni. As Grand Master of Alamut, Hasan III caused the Assassins to embrace Sunni orthodoxy. He became known as Hasan Nawmusulman, the "new Muslim." His mother went on a pilgrimage to Mecca, where she was graciously welcomed by Caliph al-Nasir. Hasan III informed the Khwarazmian shah and other Muslim rulers that he had embraced Sunnism and reintroduced adherence to the Shariah among the Nizaris. He invited Sunni scholars to instruct his followers and arranged for them to inspect the books of the renowned Alamut library. He burned those books of which they disapproved. He built mosques and bathhouses in his various territories. He publicly and ceremonially cursed his forefathers for their sins.

His leadership seems to have been accepted at Alamut without dissent. The more subtle Nizaris would have considered his rejection of Qiyama a practical application of the doctrine of *taqiyya*, concealment of the Imam's true beliefs for the physical safety and survival of his community. On the other hand, the spiritual responsibility and isolation imposed by the exalted demands of the Qiyama were undoubtedly beyond the capability and ambition of most to fulfill. A longing for simplicity is common to a populace that has come to enjoy the material rewards won by the fiery struggles of their ancestors. Acceptance of Shariah would place the Assassins in the position of being immune from attack by fellow Muslims. For the first time, the Nizari state was recognized by the Sunnis as a legitimate government within the greater Islamic whole.

Hasan undertook military campaigns in alliance with the Abbasid caliph during a two-year period. Religious conversion was no longer the rationale for Nizari military expeditions; rather, the goal became collecting material tribute from the vanquished. Hasan III and al-Nasir appear to have established a personal friendship, and Hasan was undoubtedly initiated into al-Nasir's chivalric order. Al-Nasir extended the Abbasid imprimatur to Hasan and even helped arrange for him to receive four noble Sunni wives, one of whom would become the mother of the next Assassin Imam. Eventually his friendship with al-Nasir led to a break with the Khwarazmian shah with whom Hasan III had also formed an alliance.

Hasan III is believed to have secretly offered his allegiance to the great Mongol chieftain Genghis Khan. Upon the arrival of the Khan's armies in the area in 1219, Hasan was the first Islamic ruler to send ambassadors.

Hasan III died in 1221, apparently of dysentery. He had appointed his vizier to act as regent for his young heir. The vizier accused Hasan's wives and sister of poisoning Hasan and caused them and other intimates to be executed.

## Muhammad III (r. 1221–55)

Hasan III was succeeded by his nine-year-old son Muhammad III, also known as Aladdin, the penultimate Nizari leader. As he matured, he quietly returned Alamut to the Shiite fold, announcing that his father's Imamate was to be viewed as a period of occultation. Muhammad's reign witnessed a great deal of intellectual activity as he consciously embraced the traditional Muslim leader's role of patron of the arts and sciences. The Ismaili respect for learning, which led Hasan-i-Sabah to establish the renowned library of Alamut, had long acted as a magnet to scholars and scientists, including Sunnis, Twelver Shiites, and even Jewish intellectuals.

The Nizaris developed a new doctrinal turn in order to reconcile the Qiyama teachings with the behavior of Hasan III. It was said that Qiyama was a time of the outward revelation of the true spiritual identity of the Imam in all his glory to the community, during which direct communication with God was possible. In periods of the radiant presence of the Imam, concepts like Shariah become meaningless, if not blasphemous. On the other hand, there are also periods of occultation, when the Imam chooses to conceal his true self from the community, even when he is physically present. During these times, the outward observance of Shariah is required to maintain the purity of the Law. This phase of allegiance to the Shariah was designated as Satr, the period during which the Imam hides his true spiritual status by appearing to act merely as the worldly ruler of the Nizaris, rather than as the Qaim of the Qiyama, which is the true potential of every Nizari Imam. The alternation between the open and hidden phases of the Imam, between Qiyama and Satr, takes place at his discretion. Thus, under the reign of Muhammad III, as in pre-Qiyama Alamut, there was an observance of the Shariah, although not so strictly enforced as under his father's rule.

These complex philosophical doctrines were largely conceived by the great Islamic philosopher Nasir ad-Din Tusi, who wrote at Alamut as the guest of Aladdin. Tusi may have temporarily converted to Ismailism while at Alamut, although it is not certain that he did. His teachings, however, may be understood as the philosophical lifeline that allowed the Nizaris to maintain their own identity after the Imamate of Hasan III, who left them with a difficult choice. On the one hand, they could accept amalgamation within the Sunni community if they followed the teachings of Hasan III. On the other, they could reject his embrace of Sunnism and become merely another Shiite sect by foregoing the Qiyama glories preached by Hasan II and Muhammad II. Tusi offered a third doctrinal alternative.

But Tusi's elaborate and skillful intellectual efforts, and the apparent return to the spiritual purity of the Nizari Ismaili belief, might be characterized, in retrospect, as too little too late. For according to the earliest Persian historian, Juvayni, who hated the Assassins, Muhammad III was a degenerate leader whose personal weakness mirrored the waning powers of the Alamut community. Juvayni claimed that in his youth, Aladdin had suffered brain damage from a doctor's incompetence in excessively bleeding him during an illness. Whatever the cause, Muhammad III may have been mentally defective if not insane. As he grew older his behavior was reportedly that of a madman —

cruel, imperious, sadistic, alcoholic, and unpredictable. The end of the Nizari state was approaching.

The last decades of Assassin political independence remain a fascinating story. Hasan III's alliance with the larger Muslim community had enlarged the boundaries of Nizari political aspirations. The grand vision of world domination returned for a time. Purely local squabbles were replaced by ambitious diplomatic activities to lands as far away as Europe and Mongolia, while a Nizari religious mission was firmly established in India. Financial tribute for their safety was received from political leaders as distant as Germany, Aragon, and Yemen.

Among the Sunnis, a love of luxury acquired through contact with the Abbasids began to undermine the characteristic ferocity of the remaining Seljuks, Khwarazmians, and Ghurids. In the familiar historical pattern, the lean nomadic tribes of northwest Asia moved west to fill the vacuum left by the decreased political will of a complacent populace. The Mongols — descendents of the Huns who had attacked self-indulgent Rome eight hundred years earlier — began their conquest of Central Asia under Genghis Khan in the twelfth century. By 1219, angered by insults from the Khwarazmian shah, the Mongol invasion of Islamic territories began. In 1221, the year Muhammad III assumed the Imamate, the Khwarazmian empire fell to the Mongol armies.

The Mongols presented a more dangerous threat. Although an uneasy truce had existed between the Assassins and the Mongols since the diplomatic mission of Hasan III to Genghis Khan, the inevitable conflict between the two antagonists approached. The widespread Nizari ambitions placed them in direct opposition to similar aspirations of the Mongols. Muhammad III inherited the multiple alliances his father had made, but they were crumbling because of the rapidly shifting and turbulent political situation brought about by the escalation of Mongol aggression. The Ismailis were becoming an increasingly solitary force in the region again, just as the Mongols were settings their sights on Persia.

The great Mongol armies had first reached the Jaxartes River (modern Syr Darya) in 1218 during the reign of Genghis Khan. In 1238, the Assassins sent envoys to France and England in a joint effort with ambassadors from the Abbasid caliph to enlist Christian rulers Louis IX of France and Henry III of England against the Mongols. Unfortunately, the Europeans were at this moment seeking an alliance with the Mongols against the Muslims. By 1240, the Mongol assault had reached as far as western Iran and would soon progress to Georgia,

Armenia, and northern Mesopotamia. In 1248, an Ismaili delegation to a Mongol assembly was turned away.

In 1252, Mangu, the grandson of Genghis Khan, was elevated as supreme Khan of the Mongols at Karakoram. He immediately ordered his younger brother Huelgu to set out against the Nizaris and destroy them utterly. In 1254, Mangu received William of Rudrick, the Franciscan friar and ambassador of Louis IX. Louis wished to enlist Mongol support for the Christian armies of the Seventh Crusade. William learned that the great Khan was in fear for his life because he had heard that upward of forty Assassins in various disguises had been sent after him in retaliation for his campaign against them. Although Huelgu would not arrive in Iran until 1256, advance armies preceded him and battled their way through Ismaili territories. The Mongols attacked the Nizaris of Quhistan, then marched against Girdkuh and sent raiding parties to the Rudbar valley. Meanwhile Huelgu continued his inexorable approach.

Many at Alamut were terrified by the ferocity of the Mongol hordes. Muhammad III maintained his defiant (perhaps irrational) courage against the Mongols until the end. But he also developed an obsession against his eldest son and heir, Khurshah. In 1255, Assassin leaders decided that the Imam's mental deterioration was so alarming that they must supplant him with his son. The plan was to elevate Khurshah to regent and, without harming him, to restrain Aladdin from further decision making, particularly regarding the Mongol menace. This plan proved unnecessary, however; as if in final testimony to his degeneracy, Aladdin, while in a drunken stupor, was slain with an ax blow delivered by his homosexual lover, Hasan Mazandarani, whom he had mutilated years earlier during their sadistic love play. Hasan's wife, who was Aladdin's mistress, reported her husband's confession to Khurshah, who executed Hasan Mazandarani along with three of his children.

## Khurshah (r. 1255–56)

The final act of Alamut began when Khurshah succeeded his father as the twenty-seventh Nizari Imam. Recognizing the inevitability of capitulation to the Mongol power, Khurshah wrote to offer his submission to Yasur, the Mongol commander in Iraq. The general replied that Khurshah must appear before Huelgu himself. Khurshah instead sent his younger brother Shahanshah to Huelgu's camp in Khurasan. Yasur meanwhile invaded the Alamut area in June 1256. Khurshah's soldiers held out against the attack. Huelgu sent word that he would accept Khurshah's surrender and hold him guiltless for his father's crimes, if he would destroy his fortresses and surrender in person before the Mongol leader. Yasur's army moved on.

Khurshah requested a year's grace before presenting himself to Huelgu so that he might personally supervise the dismantling of his fortresses. He also asked that Alamut and Lammassar be spared in view of their antiquity. Huelgu responded that if Khurshah was unable to come, he should send his son as a mark of good faith. Huelgu had by now advanced to Rayy. Khurshah sent the boy to him. Although Huelgu suspected he was not the true heir, Nizari historians maintain that he was. Huelgu continued his advance as Khurshah sent another of his brothers along with a group of three hundred Nizaris as pledges to the Mongol chieftain. In November 1256, Khurshah was at the castle of Maymundiz. Huelgu's army advanced upon the fortress and demanded that Khurshah surrender himself within five days. On November 19, 1256, Khurshah entered Huelgu's camp to surrender, accompanied by his family, his entourage, and his treasure. The remaining Assassins within the castle refused to surrender and were killed by the Mongols.

Huelgu received Khurshah graciously, distributing the Assassin treasure to his Mongol warriors, but gifting the Imam with a hundred camels and a beautiful Mongol bride. He then asked the Imam to accompany him so he might personally appeal for the surrender of the remaining Assassin castles. Approximately one hundred Nizari castles are said to have surrendered to the Mongol armies at the request of the weakened Imam. Each fortress was evacuated and then destroyed. The commanders of Alamut and Lammassar initially refused to surrender, but Alamut capitulated in December 1256.

The Mongols were rapt in amazement at the marvels of Alamut. Huelgu himself climbed to the fortress to observe the carefully crafted brilliance of its design. Water ran through solid rock channels and was stored in enormous tanks hollowed out from the massive rock. Food and weapons were stored in subterranean chambers also cut from solid rock. The impregnable fortress still contained viable supplies from the time of Hasan-i-Sabah. Hasan had also planted many trees in the Alamut valley and developed irrigation systems to increase the productivity of the soil. Alamut had been designed to sustain the community during military conditions of long-term siege. With much labor, the Mongols destroyed it all.

The Persian historian Juvayni accompanied Huelgu's army. He personally oversaw the burning of most of the remaining books in the

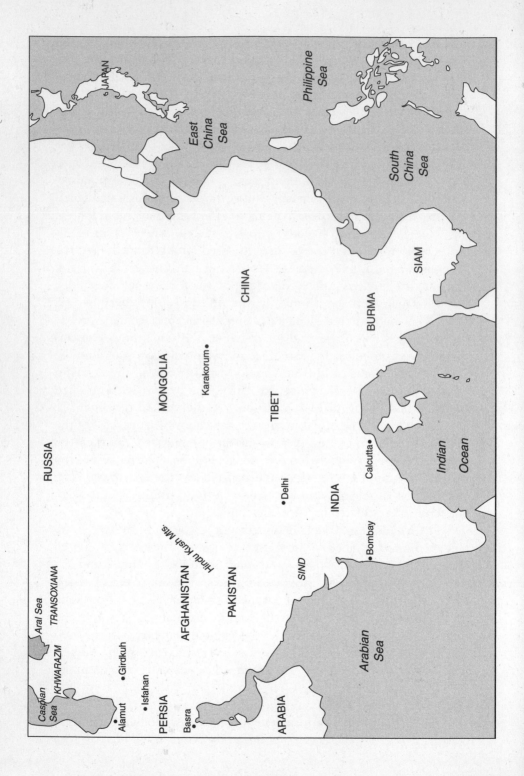

RUSSIA

JAPAN

East China Sea

Philippine Sea

South China Sea

CHINA

MONGOLIA

Karakorum•

TIBET

SIAM

BURMA

Aral Sea

TRANSOXIANA

KHWARAZM

Caspian Sea

•Girdkuh

•Isfahan

Alamut•

AFGHANISTAN

Hindu Kush Mts.

PAKISTAN

SIND

PERSIA

Basra•

ARABIA

•Delhi

INDIA

•Bombay

•Calcutta

Indian Ocean

Arabian Sea

Alamut library, including works of Nizari history and theology as well as non-Ismaili mathematical, philosophical, and scientific writings. The destruction of the central library is one factor accounting for the lack of surviving Assassin literature from the Alamut period. The other is that the continual state of military preparedness inclined the Nizaris more to active conversion efforts than to either literary pursuits or philosophical speculation.

The garrison at Lammassar held out for a year longer. Huelgu and Khurshah departed for Qazwin, where Khurshah wrote to the Syrian Assassins commanding them to surrender to the Mongols. Meanwhile, he requested a meeting with the great Mangu Khan himself. In 1257, Khurshah, accompanied by Mongolian troops, embarked on the long journey to Karakoram. When he arrived, the great Khan refused him audience because Lammassar and Girdkuh still held out against the Mongolian army. On his return journey, the disappointed Khurshah was beaten, kicked, and stabbed to death by his Mongolian guards.

The main concern of the Ismailis was smuggling Khurshah's son Shams al-Din Muhammad to safety. (The modern Aga Khan is descended from this surviving child Imam.) The Mongols began a ruthless campaign to wipe out all memory of the Assassins, which included their efforts to kill every man, woman, and child, particularly anyone related to Khurshah. One of the worst massacres took place in Quhistan, where some eighty thousand Ismailis were slaughtered in one day. Many were sold into slavery. The defenders of Lammassar and Girdkuh were obliterated when their castles fell, although the garrison in Girdkuh managed to hold out until 1270. In 1275, an Assassin force recaptured Alamut, but the Mongolian military reclaimed the castle within a year.

The Mongolian army had gone on to attack the Abbasids at Baghdad in 1258. The Abbasid caliph al-Mustasim Billah surrendered as abjectly as Khurshah. After revealing the hiding place of the Abbasid fortune, he was put to death. The dynasty that had ruled Islam (at least in name) for half a millennium was crushed. The Mongolian army pillaged Baghdad for forty days, during which an estimated eight hundred thousand Muslims were massacred. In 1260, Huelgu seized the Ayyubid cities of Damascus and Aleppo. Soon after, Baybars, the Mameluke sultan of Egypt, decisively defeated the Mongols and expelled them from Syria. The devastation wrought throughout Islam by the Mongol slaughter is perceptible to this day.

# CHAPTER NINE

# The Syrian Assassins

Hasan-i-Sabah's mission to the Ismailis of Syria resulted in the early European contact with the Assassins during the Crusades. The mythical Old Man of the Mountain, celebrated by troubadours and feared by kings, was the Syrian chief of the Order.

Like Iran, Syria has a varied topography that includes mountainous regions ideal for the strategic fortress concept employed by the Nizaris. The mountains, valleys, and deserts of Syria also played host to a diverse and fragmented populace with strong traditions of political independence and religious diversity, including various heretical sects. Among these were the Druzes, the Fatimid Ismaili splinter group mentioned earlier. Another radical Syrian sect were the Nusayris, Twelver Shiite extremists who believed that Ali was God and Muhammad his Prophet. Valentinian and Manichaean Gnostic beliefs were also incorporated in the Nusayri faith. This sect was founded in the ninth century, and Nusayris still exist in Syria.

Politically, Syria was ripe for Nizari organizing. By the time Hasan sent his missionaries some time after 1090, the Seljuk Turks had spent several decades battling the Fatimid empire and had gained control of the majority of the country. The Hidden Imam, it will be remembered, had arisen from his occultation in Syria to proclaim himself and establish the Fatimid dynasty in 909 — which points to a strong and enduring Ismaili presence in Syria. The arrival of the Turkish forces can only have disrupted the area in a manner similar to what we have observed in Persia, where local hatred seethed under the perceived injustice of rule by foreign conquerors.

In 1095, the death of the Syrian Seljuk overlord Tutush, brother of Malikshah, left the region divided into several rival states ruled by different Seljuk princes. The most important principalities were governed by the two sons of Tutush: Ridwan in Aleppo, and Duqaq in Damascus. The Nizari organizing efforts began in Aleppo. The initial success of the Syrian mission was greatly facilitated by Ridwan's support. Aleppo had a large Shiite population, divided into various sects, that collectively outnumbered the Sunnis. Ridwan had originally supported the Fatimid Imam al-Mustali before switching his support to the Nizaris.

In 1097, the Christian Crusaders burst upon the scene. The barbaric armies of European infidels swept through Palestine like an invincible horde. The Syrian Assassins were aided in their missionary activities by the weakness of the Mustalian Fatimids and their failure in repelling both the Seljuk Turks and the Crusaders. The arrival of the latter can only have encouraged popular willingness to hear the messianic message of the hidden Nizari Imam.

At the same time, however, the Alamut mission suffered a profound disadvantage. Nizari missionaries in Syria, like the Seljuks and the Crusaders, were foreigners, imported from Persia under the command of the Lord of Alamut. Throughout the life of the Syrian Assassin community, its leaders were appointed by the successive heads of Alamut. Nizari progress in Syria was slow in coming and accompanied by many setbacks, requiring half a century before a secure base of operations was established.

The onslaught of the Crusaders caused the Seljuk governors to dispute among themselves for whatever territory they were able to retain against the invaders. Ridwan's alliance with the Nizaris aided him against his rivals. For example, in 1103, under the leadership of al-Hakim al-Munajjim, known as the "Physician-Astrologer," the Assassins were accused of murdering Ridwan's rival Janah al-Dawla, the ruler of Homs.

The first documented contact between the Assassins and the Crusaders took place in September 1106. Tancred, prince of Antioch, attacked the newly acquired Nizari castle of Apace outside of Aleppo. The Christians defeated the Nizaris and leveled a tribute against the sect. Tancred captured the new Syrian chief *dai*, Abu Tahir, "the Goldsmith," and forced him to ransom himself. In 1110, the Nizaris lost a second piece of territory to Tancred. Despite these losses, the Syrian Assassins were able to assist Ridwan in expelling Crusader troops from various strongholds, a feat that other Seljuk princes had been unable to accomplish.

After Ridwan's death in 1113, his son Alp Arslan came to power. Bowing to pressure from the overall Seljuk sultan Muhammad Tapar, as well as from popular anti-Ismaili sentiment that had developed in Aleppo, he sanctioned the destruction of the Aleppine Nizari community. He was responsible for the execution of Abu Tahir, and he caused over two hundred Ismailis to be imprisoned or murdered and then seized their properties. By 1124, any remaining Nizaris who had managed to remain in Aleppo were expelled.

The second Ismaili attempt to establish a Syrian base took place in

Damascus. The sect was never able to take root there. In 1125, however, under the leadership of the Syrian chief *dai*, Bahram, Nizari soldiers provided critically needed military support against the Franks. Bahram was given the Syrian frontier fortress of Baniyas by the Seljuk Damascene ruler Tughitigin, whose chief vizier, al-Mazdaqani, was partial to the Nizaris. Bahram was also given a mission house in Damascus to serve as his urban headquarters. Bahram began to fortify the castle at Baniyas, send out missionaries, and conduct military operations throughout Syria. During one of these he was killed; his head and hands were taken to Cairo, where they earned a large reward from the Fatimid caliph.

In 1128, Tughitigin died and an anti-Ismaili wave arose in Damascus reminiscent of the persecutions in Aleppo. Tughitigin's son Buri began the attack by murdering the vizier al-Mazdaqani and publicly exposing his severed head. This gave the signal for a general massacre of some six thousand Ismailis in Damascus. Rumor spread that the Assassins had made an alliance with the Franks to betray Damascus in return for Tyre. While this was untrue, Bahram's successor, al-Ajami, had written to Baldwin II, king of Jerusalem, with an offer to surrender Baniyas in exchange for safe haven from his Sunni persecutors. Al-Ajami, died in exile among the Franks in 1130. In 1131, two Nizaris sent from Alamut assassinated Buri. It was during this period (1130s) that Buzurgumid succeeded in assassinating the Fatimid caliph al-Amir, virtually ending Mustalian Ismailism in Syria.

After the Nizaris failed to secure a base in the urban centers of Aleppo and Damascus, they purchased the important fortress of Qadamus in the Jabal Bahra mountain range in 1132 under the leadership of Abul Fath. Over the next seven years they successfully acquired eight or ten more castles in the area.

In 1140 they took the important fortress at Masyaf. In 1142, the Hospitallers received the nearby castle of Krak des Chevaliers, becoming hostile neighbors of the Nizaris. In 1149, the Assassins cooperated with Raymond of Antioch in an unsuccessful battle against the Turkish Zangids, during which both Raymond and the Assassin leader Alf ibn Wafa were killed. The alliance with Raymond was motivated by Nizari perception of Raymond's strength against the Zangids, who had just taken Aleppo. The Zangids will be further discussed in part 3 as enemies of the Knights Templar, but they also represented a twofold threat to the Nizaris: they were frequently allied with the Seljuks; and they championed the Sunni cause to the point of declaring Shiites to be heretics. The shifting alliances of the period are well illustrated by the fact that in 1151, the Assassins battled the Franks over Maniqa, and in 1152 they assassinated their first Frankish victim, Count Raymond II of Tripoli. This shocking murder led to a Templar attack against the Nizaris and the imposition of an annual tribute of some two thousand gold pieces payable to the Templars.

## RASHID AL-DIN SINAN

The most famous of the Syrian Assassin chiefs, the quintessential Old Man of the Mountain, was Sinan ibn Salman ibn Muhammad, also known as Rashid al-Din Sinan (r. 1162–92). In Sinan is found another legendary Nizari spiritual leader. Like Hasan-i-Sabah, the revolutionary founder, and his spiritual heir, the short-lived Hasan II who burst the chains of Islamic orthodoxy, Sinan was a charismatic and powerful man who changed history.

Sinan was born near Basra in southern Iraq to a well-to-do family and fled to Alamut while a young man after an argument with his brothers. At Alamut he befriended the young Hasan II, his fellow student. Upon Hasan's accession to the position of Imam, he sent Sinan to Syria. Sinan traveled to Kahf, where he worked quietly to develop a following. When the aged chief *dai* Abu Muhammad died, Sinan succeeded to the leadership of the Syrian Assassins after a brief succession struggle was resolved by decrees from Hasan II.

The Syrian Nizaris were in a precarious position because of the immediacy of the Crusader invasion. Tensions were high and alliances fluid. In addition to the Crusaders, Sinan faced four threats from within Islam. Two new forces appeared among the Sunnis during his reign. Both exerted their efforts to bring together the various splintered factions of the Muslim community against their common Christian enemy.

The first was the great Zangid general Nur al-Din, headquartered in Aleppo. In addition to his political and military activities, he set up a system of *madrasa* schools throughout the Holy Land, designed to foster a unified approach to the Sunni faith. Nur al-Din had sent his general Shirkuh to Egypt to battle the remains of the Fatimid state. Shirkuh became the vizier of the titular Fatimid caliph. When Shirkuh died, his nephew Saladin succeeded him.

Saladin was the second major Sunni threat to Sinan. Saladin proclaimed the end of the Fatimid caliphate in 1171, and he declared

Sunnism the religion of Egypt. He became the greatest proponent of Muslim unity since the Prophet himself. Saladin dreamed of a single Islamic society governed by the purest religious principles. Both Nur al-Din and Saladin regarded the Frankish Christians as their most dangerous enemies, but the Ismaili heretics were of deep concern to both as well.

The third Islamic threat came from the hostility of the neighboring Nusayri tribes, who had lived in the Jabal Bahra mountain region long before the Ismailis arrived. The fourth Islamic threat was also localized. Sunni vigilante groups, called Nubuwwiyya, had been organized and roamed the countryside in search of Shiite groups they could attack.

Sinan thus faced a complex series of challenges. On the diplomatic front, he needed to form skillful alliances so that he did not fall victim to a unified Muslim attack. This, at first, inclined him to support Nur al-Din as the lesser of two evils, Saladin being recognized as the more implacable foe. He also needed to cultivate a successful relationship with the Crusaders, with whom he, as a Muslim, was technically at war. The Assassins were already paying a tribute to the Knights Templar by the time Sinan took charge. He must have considered this money a reasonable investment to prevent open warfare. Finally, he needed to establish and fortify more defensive strongholds to maintain himself against attack from any of several different potential sources of aggression, including hostile neighbors.

In 1173, Sinan sent an ambassador to King Amalric I of Jerusalem proposing an alliance. He asked for a relaxation of the tribute he was paying to the Templars as his only condition. It is commonly believed that Amalric agreed to Sinan's terms, and that the Assassin ambassador was murdered by the Templars during his return journey in order to prevent their losing the tribute. It is also generally accepted that the murder prevented further progress regarding an alliance, despite Amalric's apology to Sinan and his imprisonment of the responsible knight. The potential for additional discussion was obviated by Amalric's death soon after in 1174.

Archbishop William of Tyre, a contemporary historian, wrote that Sinan had expressed, through his ambassador, the willingness of the Assassins to convert to Christianity in furtherance of such an alliance. Farhad Daftary suggests this was a gross misinterpretation of Sinan's offer.[1] The sophistication of Sinan's theological interests and his ecumenical viewpoint would naturally incline him to learn more of the religious doctrines of his potential allies. The Qiyama doctrine was misinterpreted by more than one medieval historian as a distorted acceptance of Christianity and a rejection of Islam, which raises the important point that certain elements of the Qiyama doctrine are not incompatible with aspects of Christianity. The revolutionary stance taken by Jesus in rejecting much of the outward observance of Jewish law certainly finds an echo in the Qiyama teachings.

It is believed that at the time of his death in 1174, Nur al-Din was planning an expedition against the Ismailis in retaliation for their suspected arson of a mosque in Aleppo. Upon learning of Nur al-Din's passing, Saladin proclaimed his independence from the Zangid dynasty and established himself as the first ruler of the Ayyubid dynasty. Saladin was a threat to Nur al-Din's young son and heir, al-Malik al-Salih. The regent who ruled in the boy's name sought the help of Sinan in stopping Saladin by assassination. One reason for Sinan's cooperation was the hatred the Assassins had developed for Saladin. In 1174–75, Nubuwwiyya vigilantes had raided two Ismaili centers, killing some thirteen thousand people. Saladin was passing by at the time. He learned of the massacres and took advantage of the situation to attack other Nizari strongholds before moving on.

Sinan sent some *fidais* against the Ayyubid sultan in 1175. A local ruler with whom Saladin was visiting recognized them and thwarted the attempt. A second effort was made in 1176. Saladin was slightly wounded, but he was saved by his quick reaction and the chain mail armor he wore at all times. In August 1176, Saladin attacked Masyaf and laid siege to this central Nizari fortress. Without warning, he ended the siege and departed. Various explanations have been given, including the following reliable account from Sinan's biographer. One day a messenger from Sinan approached Saladin. He stated that the message was personal and must be delivered only in privacy. Saladin progressively emptied his court until only two Mameluke attendants were left. Sinan's messenger asked Saladin why he would not order the Mamelukes to depart so he could deliver his message in private. Saladin replied, "I regard these two as my own sons. They and I are one." The messenger then turned to the Mamelukes and said, "If I ordered you in the name of my Master to kill this Sultan, would you do so?" They drew their swords together and replied, "Command us as you wish."[2]

This incident seems to have henceforth allied the two leaders.

There are no more records of conflict between Saladin and Sinan. An important consequence of their alliance may have been the assassination of the Frankish king of Jerusalem, Conrad of Montferrat, in 1192, shortly before Sinan's own death. Two *fidais* disguised as Christian monks were responsible for Conrad's murder. Besides an alliance with Saladin, numerous motives have been suggested for this most crucial assassination, including that it was done at the behest of King Richard I, "the Lionhearted." The simplest explanation, however, may be that there had been problems between the Assassins and the Franks during the previous several years. Conrad's recent seizure of a Nizari ship and its cargo, and his murder of the crew, could of themselves have been sufficient motivation for Sinan's vengeance. In any case, the death of Conrad aided Saladin in his efforts to conclude a truce with Richard. The Nizaris were included in the treaty at Saladin's request. Sinan and Saladin died within months of each other, while Richard left the Holy Land for Europe.

Sinan was a nearly mythological religious figure among the Syrian Nizaris. He had no bodyguards to protect him, ruling through the sheer force of his personality. He traveled from fortress to fortress, with no permanent base or established bureaucracy. Because of his continual movement, the network of Ismaili fortresses was both close-knit and ever alert. William of Tyre, writing during Sinan's reign, estimates that there were some sixty thousand Syrian followers of the Assassin chief. Sinan was described by another historian as a tender and gentle ruler.

Sinan was reputed to be an advanced astrologer and alchemist, as well as adept in the arts of magic, telepathy, and clairvoyance. His numerous feats of clairvoyance included his making precise and accurate predictions for each of forty Damascene Sunni legists who had tried to best him in religious argument and lost to his eloquence, intelligence, and piety. He was never seen to eat or drink. He was credited with healing powers. He was twice said to have prevented great rocks from crushing people by the use of psychokinetic powers. He was reputed to have psychically repelled an attack by Saladin's soldiers by holding them immobile and beyond striking distance of Nizari troops.

Sinan's courtesy was as much a part of his legend as his clairvoyance. One anecdote tells of his visit to a village in which he was honored by the local leader, who brought him a covered plate of food specially prepared by his wife. Sinan gently had the plate moved to one side. The official was disappointed at this apparent rejection of his hospitality and asked Sinan the reason. Sinan quietly took him aside and explained that, in her excitement, the village chief's wife had forgotten to properly clean the insides of the chickens. If the plate were uncovered, the chief would have been embarrassed before his people. On checking beneath the cover, he discovered that Sinan was correct.

A less benign tale demonstrates Sinan's capacity for cunning and ruthlessness. He was said to have brought a number of *fidais* into his chamber. On the floor was the bloody head of one of their fellows resting on a plate, apparently decapitated after successfully completing a mission of assassination. Addressing the head Sinan asked it to describe Paradise. The head proceeded to wax rhapsodic about the joys found there. The assembled youths were duly impressed. When they left, Sinan had the plate uncoupled from the hapless devotee who was actually standing in a pit dug under the floor for the performance. Sinan then swung his scimitar and in a single stroke dispatched the youth to the afterlife he had so well described to his companions.

On several occasions Sinan was known to have expressed a belief in the doctrine of metempsychosis. The transmigration of souls was a tenet of the Nusayri faith. Sinan's embrace of this unusual doctrine may have contributed to his ability to make allies and converts among the Nusayris. Sinan also appears to have accepted the model of reincarnation in which the perfectibility of the soul is both the goal and the solution.

Sinan subscribed to Hasan II's Qiyama proclamation and was charged with promulgating the doctrine in Syria. He held the Qiyama feast of Ramadan soon after his arrival. He seems to have accepted Hasan II as a legitimate spiritual Master; however, he was unwilling or unable to transfer his allegiance to Hasan's son and heir, Muhammad II. Thus the Syrian Assassins became independent of Alamut from the death of Hasan II until the death of Sinan. This was unacceptable to Muhammad II, who sent several different groups of *fidais* against Sinan. But Sinan is said to have either killed or won over each of his would-be Persian assailants.

One unanticipated consequence of Sinan's Qiyama proclamation involved some Ismailis in the Jazr region, the desert area between the Jabal Bahra mountains and Aleppo. In 1176 or 1177, these Nizaris, who called themselves the "Pure" or Sufat, embraced antinomian practices consisting of licentious and drunken orgies that they believed were a concomitant of the Qiyama. Sinan managed to save some of them from punishment by the Aleppine authorities, stating that he was the correct authority to discipline them. He was, however, unable to prevent a massacre outside Aleppo by a group of Sunnis who managed to slaughter an entire Sufat community. Other authorities say that it was Sinan himself who attacked and destroyed the sect. Bernard Lewis suggests these Qiyama excesses in Syria were a source of the myth of the Garden of Paradise.[3]

Many Syrians believed Sinan was the divinely ordained Imam or at least his *hujja*. Some even regarded him as an incarnate deity. He appears to have viewed himself as a divinely chosen instrument on a level with the most advanced souls of history, such as Adam and Jesus. One story has him discovered by his disciples in a nocturnal conversation with a green bird glowing with light. Sinan explained that this was the soul of Hasan II come to request the help of the Syrian Imam. Sinan was honored beyond precedent by a Syrian shrine built in his honor.[4] Like the Mahdi, he was said not to have died but to have entered a state of occultation from which he will one day emerge.

## The Syrian Ismailis after Sinan

Sinan left his people well situated in a relatively independent and peaceful relationship with both Franks and Sunnis. The Syrian Nizaris continued in active relation with both groups during the remaining near century of the crusading period, functioning as a distinct third center of power in the Holy Land. They formed a series of temporary alliances with various Christian factions and various Sunni leaders, remaining an unknown factor within a region particularly susceptible to political instability.

Absent Sinan's powerful leadership, the Syrian Ismailis renewed their dependence on Alamut. In 1211, Hasan III mandated the return to Shariah practices and entered into a political alliance with the Abbasid caliph. No further assassinations of Muslims are recorded after this date. In 1213, however, Syrian *fidais* assassinated Raymond of Antioch, son of Bohemond IV. The enraged Bohemond launched an attack in revenge. The newfound orthodoxy of the Nizaris allowed them to appeal for help to the Sunni Ayyubid rulers of Aleppo and Damascus, which forced the Franks to suspend their attack.

Although the Syrian Nizaris were able to make whatever decisions were necessary in their day-to-day lives, they could claim dependence on Alamut when it served their purpose. For example, during the Cru-

sade of Frederick II, launched in 1228, Frederick attempted to negotiate directly with the Assassins. He brought valuable gifts. The Syrians
replied tactfully that although they were honored by his attentions, the
embassy would have to make the long and dangerous journey to Alamut in order to obtain the authority for Frederick's request. (Despite
their caution in this instance, they were raided by the Franks for negotiating with Frederick and ultimately forced to pay tribute to the Hospitallers in addition to their continuing financial obligation to the
Templars.)

In 1230, the Nizaris assisted the Hospitallers in their military
efforts against Bohemond IV. His successor, Bohemond V, wrote to
Pope Gregory IX complaining of the alliance between the Hospitallers
and Assassins. Gregory sent letters to the archbishop of Tyre and the
bishops of Sidon and Beirut demanding that both the Templars and
Hospitallers cease any alliances with the Assassins.

In 1250, the Nizaris sent a mission to King Louis IX of France, who
was in Syria on a crusade. They requested that he lift the tributes they
were paying to the military orders. Although the mission was unsuccessful (as discussed in more detail in part 3), an Arabic-speaking friar
named Yves the Breton returned with the Assassin ambassadors to
Masyaf. Here he was the guest of the Ismaili chief, probably Taj al-Din,
with whom he discussed biblical and other religious matters. Yves later
reported that his host was friendly, intelligent, and learned, and that he
kept a Christian book by his bedside. Yves also explained the Syrian
Ismaili doctrine that a favorable reincarnation would accrue to one
who died in service to his lord.

With the fall of Alamut to the Mongols in 1256, the decline of the
Syrian Nizaris was a forgone conclusion. Syrian Assassin power was ter-
minated — first by the Mongols, then by the rise to power of the
Mameluke dynasty in Egypt. In 1259, the great Mangu Khan died.
Upon learning of this, his brother Huelgu returned to Persia, leaving
Ket-Buqa in charge of his Syrian forces. The ruthless and extraordinary
Mameluke military leader Baybars defeated Ket-Buqa in 1260 and at
last drove the hated Mongol army from Syria. The Syrian Nizaris, along
with other Muslim forces, came to the aid of the Mamelukes in this
decisive campaign.

The Mamelukes ("owned") were former white slaves, generally
Turkish and Mongol, who had been the palace guards of the Ayyubids.
When al-Salih, the last sultan of the Ayyubid dynasty, died in 1249, his

widow, a former slave named Shajar-al-Durr, arranged the murder of her stepson and proclaimed herself queen. The nobility of Cairo insisted she take a husband and chose another former slave named Aybeg as her royal consort. In 1257, Shajar-al-Durr murdered Aybeg, after which she was beaten to death by his slaves. Their heir, Qutuz, ruled as the Mameluke sultan until he was murdered by Baybars in 1260. The Mameluke dynasty ruled Egypt until their defeat by the Ottoman Turks in 1517.

Baybars was born a Turkish slave. He rose to become a general in the Egyptian army. Now he ruled Egypt as sultan and was the undisputed power in Syria. In 1265 he began collecting taxes from the Assassins on tributes paid to them by others. They also paid over to him the tribute they had formerly paid to the Hospitallers, as that Order also fell to Baybars's conquests. By 1270, Baybars began to appoint his own representative as the Assassin chief. In 1271, he learned of a Nizari plot to assassinate him, which ended any tolerance he may have extended toward them. He methodically conquered each Assassin stronghold in turn. By 1273, every Nizari fortress in Syria was controlled by one of Baybars's lieutenants.

The Syrian Order of Assassins had finally been crushed. Unlike the Mongol extermination of the Persian Assassins that followed their defeat, however, Baybars allowed the Syrian Assassins to survive as his loyal subjects. Henceforth they often functioned as the paid hirelings of their Egyptian masters — in a cruel display of historical irony, finally performing assassinations for hire. Slander had become reality. Baybars was also responsible for the final defeat of the European Crusaders, including the Knights Templar, and we shall meet him again in part 3.

# CHAPTER TEN

# The Nizari Ismailis Today

The surviving Nizaris from both Persia and Syria abruptly entered a stateless reality after their respective defeats at the hands of the Mongols and the Mamelukes. The Persian Nizaris, unlike the Syrians, could not maintain even the illusion of political independence. Their faith may have been stronger, however, because of the presence of the child Imam Shams al-Din Muhammad, the son of Khurshah who had been carried to the safety of the Adharbayjan region northwest of Alamut. Fortunately as well, just before the fall of Alamut, a Nizari community had developed in the remote upper Oxus region that remained unaffected by the Mongol invasion. This group preserved the bulk of the medieval Persian-language Ismaili literature available to modern scholars.

The post-Alamut period extends for over seven centuries. Only certain high points will be mentioned here. The interested reader is referred to Farhad Daftary's encyclopedic study, *The Ismailis*, which presents an extensive discussion of the subject as well as many references for further research. Following Vladimir Ivanow, the early twentieth-century pioneer in the study of Ismailism, Daftary divides the post-Alamut Nizari history into three broad periods. The first lasted some two centuries and might be called the aftermath of the destruction of their state. The second lasted another two centuries and is known as the Anjudan revival. The modern period began in the mid–nineteenth century with the relocation of the Imamate to India under the first Aga Khan.

Any discussion of Nizari survival must begin with the observation that despite the loss of many sectarians by immersion in the greater Islamic mass, the Nizari Ismailis have been able to maintain their unique perspective and traditional loyalty to their Imams, and to resist cultural dispersion during the centuries following the loss of Alamut and Masyaf.

For two centuries after the fall of Alamut, the Imams concealed their identity from even their followers, living under intense conditions of *taqiyya* in an extremely hostile environment. During this overtly leaderless phase, assimilation, the gradual but peaceful scourge of cultural identity, succeeded in reducing the Nizari population more effectively than any armed attack ever had. Many Persian and Syrian survivors, however, still managed to retain their religious and cultural identity under the most trying of circumstances. Their training in the disciplines of a secret society no doubt saved many lives.

The Nizaris were separated from the mountain strongholds in which they had grown for over a century and a half. Disoriented and confused by the Mongol military devastation and subsequent persecution, the sect became fragmented and dispersed, developing into a profusion of separate communities without central leadership. As individuals arose to fill a teaching or leadership role, the unified doctrine characteristic of the Alamut period became fragmented.

Many Persian Nizari survivors were able to gracefully conceal themselves within the esoteric currents of Iranian Sufism. The common elements shared by Sufism and Ismailism — mysticism, gnosticism, speculative philosophy, techniques of self-development, and loyalty to a central teacher, *pir*, or *shaykh* — encouraged mutual interaction. Assumption of the Sufi mantle would later allow the Imams to cloak themselves as *shaykhs* who taught the esoteric meaning, or *batin*, to their disciples, or *murids*. One Alamut survivor was the immortal Shams-i-Tabriz, famed spiritual Master of the Persian poet Jalal al-Din Rumi, founder of the Mevlevi Sufi Order, the Whirling Dervishes. Shams-i-Tabriz may have been a son of Hasan III, or even one of the Ismaili Imams.[1] The confluence of Ismaili and Sufi traditions has led to Nizari assertions that such well-known Sufi poets as Sanai, Farid al-Din Attar, and Rumi and the renowned Sufi Master Ibn al-Arabi were all Ismailis.[2]

The Imam Shams al-Din Muhammad died in 1310–11 in Adharbayjan. Although the details are obscure, there was a dispute among members of his family over the succession, resulting in the first Nizari schism. Two separate lines of Imams arose — the Muhammad-Shahi and the Qasim-Shahi. The Muhammad-Shahi line was more popular in Syria, although it had a large following in Persia until the second half of the fifteenth century. The last Imam of this line died in India in the late nineteenth century without a successor. In 1887, a delegation of Syrian sectarians who had journeyed in search of the new Imam returned to Syria with this announcement. The majority of Syrians transferred their allegiance to the Qasim-Shahi Imam, Aga Khan III.

In the beginning of the fifteenth century, the Mongol Ilkhanid dynasty, established by Huelgu, collapsed in Persia. Following the Ilkhanid disintegration, Persia remained politically fragmented for the

better part of the next century. The Nizaris were able to take advantage
of the more relaxed religious and political environment to expand their
activities.

The period known as the Anjudan revival extended from the latter half of the fifteenth century when the Qasim-Shahi Imam Mustan-
sir Billah II relocated to Anjudan in central Persia and emerged from
his concealment to proclaim the continuation of the Alamut Imamate.
This inaugurated a renaissance in Nizari thought and philosophy as
well as a revival of Nizari literary efforts. Succeeding Imams worked
diligently to reassert their control of the far-flung and fractured Nizari
population scattered throughout Persia, Syria, and India.

The steadily increasing influence of the Sufi *tariqas*, or orders, and
the reemergence of Shiism were important developments during the
fifteenth century. The Safawi Sufi *tariqa* worked steadily to extend its
political control throughout Persia. In 1501, they succeeded in
installing their *shaykh* as the ruler of Persia and founder of the Safawid
dynasty, which governed the country for over two centuries. The
Safawids established Twelver Shiism as the state religion. Soon after
their accession to the throne, they began to suppress some of the more
popular rival Sufi groups, as well as the more extreme Shiites. While the
Nizaris did suffer some persecution, overall they seem to have fared well
under the Safawids, attesting to the success of their *taqiyya* practices.

Both the Nurbakshiyya and Nimat Allahi Sufi orders were influential in the rise of the Safawids and the spread of Sufism through
Persia. The long-lived founder of the Nimat Allahi *tariqa*, Shah Nimat
Allah (1330–1431), traced his lineage through the Fatimids to
Muhammad ibn Ismail. Thus it was natural for the Nizaris to form an
alliance with the Nimat Allahi Order, through which they could conduct their renewed *dawa* activities, cloaked in the language of Alid Shiite Sufism. This reduced level of *taqiyya* allowed them to fit comfortably
within the Persian cultural landscape of the time while maintaining
their security in the midst of the ever-present danger of renewed
persecution.

Another important development during the Anjudan revival was
the Imam's emphasis on the importance of tithing, collecting one-tenth
of the annual income of sectarians throughout the scattered Nizari territories. Tithing served a twofold purpose: it helped finance the Imam's
activities, and, equally important, it helped reestablish central control
over the disparate groups that had developed during the diaspora following Alamut. The Imam was able to install his own representatives in

each Nizari community, or, in the more remote areas, to conduct collections and inspections through a handpicked network of traveling representatives.

In Syria, the rivalry between the Muhammad-Shahi Imams and Qasim-Shahi Imams was more protracted than in Persia, and this internecine dissension had a negative effect on the Nizari community. In addition, an ongoing state of warfare with the Nusayris (which continued into the twentieth century) further weakened the Syrian Nizaris. When the Ottomans succeeded the Mamelukes as the rulers of the region, any renewal of Syrian Nizari political ambitions was prevented.

The third, or modern, post-Alamut period begins with the relocation of the Nizari Imam to India in the mid–nineteenth century. The Nizari *dawa* in India had begun in the early thirteenth century during the later Alamut period. Pir Sadr al-Din was the most successful *dai* in India, converting large numbers of Hindus to the Ismaili faith during the fourteenth century. He chose the name *khojas*, which means "lords" or "masters," for the Indian Nizaris. One reason for the success of the *dawa* in India was the characteristic respect shown by the *dais* or *pirs* for the beliefs and traditions of their Hindu converts. Thus Indian Nizarism has been enriched by its contact with Hindu religion and mythology.

By the mid–eighteenth century, the Nizari Imam moved his headquarters from Anjudan to Kirman in southeast Persia, closer to the Indian border. This allowed for safer travel by the Nizari pilgrims visiting their Imam from India, as well as for the uninterrupted flow of Indian tithes into Persia. When the Qajar dynasty established itself in Persia in 1794, the Nizaris were well treated. The forty-fifth Nizari Imam, Shah Khalil Allah, married the daughter of a prominent Nimat Allahi Sufi. She would become the mother of his successor, Hasan Ali Shah, born in 1804. Khalil Allah was murdered by a Twelver Shiite mob in Yazd in 1817. In response to the murder, the Qajar ruler Fath Ali Shah gave the young Imam Hasan Ali Shah a grant of additional lands, as well as the hand of one of his daughters in marriage. He also bestowed on him the honorific title of Aga Khan, "Chief Commander."

Fath Ali Shah was succeeded by his grandson, whose ill treatment of the Nizaris caused Hasan Ali Shah (Aga Khan I) to organize an unsuccessful rebellion. Hasan tried again some years later and again faced defeat. He then traveled to Afghanistan in 1841, ending the eight centuries of the Persian Imamate. He befriended the British in Afghanistan and came under their protection. In 1842, he continued

on to India, where he again allied himself with British interests, apparently hoping they would help him return safely to Persia one day.
The British did attempt to negotiate with the Persian Qajar rulers but
were unable to assist the Imam in returning to the traditional Nizari
homeland.

In 1844, Aga Khan I traveled on to Bombay. Most of the Indian
Khojas enthusiastically welcomed their Imam. Aga Khan I flourished in
Bombay. For example, he received the Prince of Wales at his home during a state visit to India by the future English monarch. Aga Khan I was
a strong, effective, and well-organized administrator who strengthened
his people. A group of dissident Khojas, who resented his efforts to cen-
tralize the Imamate, eventually brought suit against him in 1866 to prevent him from interfering in their affairs. A hearing was held before the
British High Court of Bombay that lasted twenty-five days. Massive
amounts of historical documents, genealogical data, and religious doctrines were examined. The Aga Khan was declared by Chief Justice Sir
Joseph Arnould to be the legitimate descendent and heir of the Alamut
Imams — and thus of the Fatimid Caliphate, and thus of the Prophet
Muhammad — and to be entitled to the customary dues and tithes collected from the Khojas. The Imam's final years were spent in Bombay,
where he indulged his love of horse racing, maintaining excellent
stables.

With the successful establishment of the Imamate in India, and its
legal recognition accomplished, Aga Khan I passed the Imamate to his
son, Aqa Ali Shah, in 1881. Aga Khan II was particularly concerned
with establishing a modern school system for Nizari children. He continued his father's policy of good relations with the British. He reached
out to the Nizari communities in the upper Oxus and in Burma and
East Africa. He also continued close relations with the Nimat Allahi
Sufis. He was a renowned hunter and shared his father's passion for racing and breeding thoroughbred horses. After a brief Imamate, he was
succeeded in 1885 by his eight-year-old son, Muhammad Shah.

Aga Khan III was raised and educated in the most modern and cultivated social circles by his mother, a Qajar princess, who took an
active role in the leadership of the Nizari community during the Imam's
youth. Aga Khan III visited the courts of Europe as part of his education. He developed a friendship with King Edward VII and was
appointed the British viceroy of India. He enjoyed relationships with
most of the royal families of Europe, and he established primary
residences in Switzerland and the French Riviera. He aided the British

in both World Wars and urged his followers to do the same. He led the Muslim delegation to the Round Table Conference in London in 1930, which discussed the future of India. In 1937 he was elected president of the League of Nations for a session. He secured recognition of his leadership of the East African Nizaris and opened relations with Burmese Nizaris.

Aga Khan III instituted administrative reforms that included providing written constitutions and establishing administrative councils to govern his followers. He regularized Nizari religious practices regarding marriage, divorce, inheritance, guardianship, and burial. He worked tirelessly in support of education, welfare, and health care for the Nizaris. Aga Khan III utilized much of the tithes he collected for investments to provide business opportunities for his people, including construction of housing, schools, mosques, libraries, sports and recreational facilities, banks, and hospitals. In Syria, primarily an agrarian economy, he established an agricultural institution that greatly improved crop yield and the subsequent standard of living.

Aga Khan III died in 1957 after a reign of seventy-two years. He passed the *nass* to his grandson, the forty-ninth and present Nizari Imam, Karim al-Husayni, Aga Khan IV. Educated in the best European schools, Aga Khan IV completed his undergraduate studies at Harvard, majoring in Islamic studies. He has pursued his grandfather's ambitious plans to improve the quality of life for his people. He has provided numerous scholarships to eligible Nizari students to attend Western institutions of learning. He has also expanded the indigenous educational opportunities for the Nizaris to some three hundred institutions worldwide, ranging from day-care centers and elementary schools to a medical college and nursing school in Pakistan. He has built six hospitals. Both the Nizari schools and health services are open to people of all races and religions.

In 1984, the Imam established the Aga Khan Fund for Economic Development as the umbrella organization for his third-world community self-development projects. He has instituted programs for promoting Islamic religion, architecture, and civilization among Western students by providing scholarships at such prestigious American universities as Harvard and MIT. Aga Khan IV has also encouraged the growth of worldwide Ismaili scholarly research by founding the Institute of Ismaili Studies in London in 1977.

Aga Khan IV is recognized as the head of several million Nizari Ismailis, scattered in more than twenty-five countries, who constitute the majority of Ismailis in the world today. Shiite Muslims account for approximately ten percent of the total Muslim community, which now numbers approximately one billion.

Each of the Aga Khans has been concerned with improving the socioeconomic status of his people in the modern world, raising the Nizaris from the third-world status of the countries in which they live. The Nizari Imams have made intelligent objective judgments of the achievements of Western civilization, while many other Muslim leaders have affected a jingoistic rejection of Western culture. Standing apart from the poverty, illiteracy, and religious intolerance of much of the Islamic world, the success of the modern Nizaris may serve as an object lesson for collectivists, statists, and special-interest ethnic pleaders the world over of the continued merit of hard work and strongly held moral values. Despite the loss of their state and their failure to attain world conquest and control of Islam, the modern Nizaris have accomplished much of the miracle envisioned by their illustrious chief *dai* at Alamut ten centuries ago.

# CHAPTER ELEVEN

# REFLECTIONS ON THE ASSASSIN ORDER

The end of the Nizari state is in many ways bleak testimony to the ever-present reality of the stultification of creativity and the continuous displacement of revolutionary fervor and patriotic idealism by the grinding mill of Molochian cosmic indifference.[†] An eloquent modern children's tale, *The Neverending Story* by Michael Ende, paints an imaginative world threatened by a death-dealing force called the "Nothing," which will inevitably destroy hope unless people are courageous enough to seize their dreams. From Hasan-i-Sabah grasping the sword of Shiite purity against the encroaching insolence of the military takeover of the Fatimid Imamate, to Thomas Jefferson declaring the God-given sacred supremacy of the individual against the pretensions of the British monarch — may visionaries forever arise to keep alive the flame of the human spirit.

While the Assassins have been identified as the world's first organized band of terrorists, their methods were far different from those of today's indiscriminate bomb-wielding kamikazes. The warrior tradition of Islam frequently justifies killing, as do the sacred scriptures of many world religions — from the Old and New Testaments to the Hindu *Bhagavad Gita*. The Islamic concept of jīhād, or holy war, applies equally against Muslim usurpers of the Law of God as it does against the non-Muslim infidel. The Assassins served the greater glory of God through their practice.

Early nineteenth-century European Orientalists such as Joseph von Hammer-Purgstall (the first popular European chronicler of the Assassins), many historians after him, and even some modern commentators virtually fume with anger against the Assassins. The intensity of their emotional paroxysms has been fueled by the hostile bias of Sunni historians, medieval Christian propagandists, and their own righteous indignation at such a *peculiar* group of people.

Hasan-i-Sabah is still vilified as a murderer and described as a heinous criminal, while the record indicates he was responsible for

---

[†] It must be acknowledged that Hasan-i-Sabah could as easily be painted as an intolerant religious partisan, the successful establishment of whose ideal would have forced religious creativity into the dark crevices of yet a new underground.

some fifty handpicked political slayings over a thirty-five-year reign. By way of contemporary comparison, we have witnessed the Mongol massacre of eighty thousand Ismaili men, women, and children in a single afternoon in Quhistan.

The Ismailis were innovators who expanded the hierarchical mystical secret society model (composed of religious ideology, hidden wisdom, special bonds of loyalty, and elaborate ceremonial procedures) and directed it against the established religious and political world order of Sunni Islam. They were religious revolutionaries, true subversives and conspirators upon whose secret whisperings kingdoms actually did rise and fall. For over a century and a half, the Assassins managed to turn the tables on the victimization and powerlessness characteristic of the Shiite experience in Islam.

The Order of Assassins was reflected in European culture by the Knights Templar. The Templars were similarly hierarchically structured. Their raison d'être also involved armed struggle in the name of the highest religious aspirations. A rich tradition of historical supposition maintains that contact with the sophisticated religious teachings of the Assassin Order was a primary influence in the development of the secret Templar heresy that is said to have led the Knights Templar far afield from their Christian roots. As this look at the Assassins should have made clear, there was a great deal of documented historical contact in the Holy Land between the Templars and the Assassins. The religious ideals that returned to Europe with the Crusaders are believed by many to have become the basis for the European occult revival, which continues to the present day. Thus the hand of Hasan-i-Sabah seems to stretch far beyond the confines of the Persian and Syrian mountains, and well past the early years of the first millennium.

PART THREE

# The Knights Templar

✠

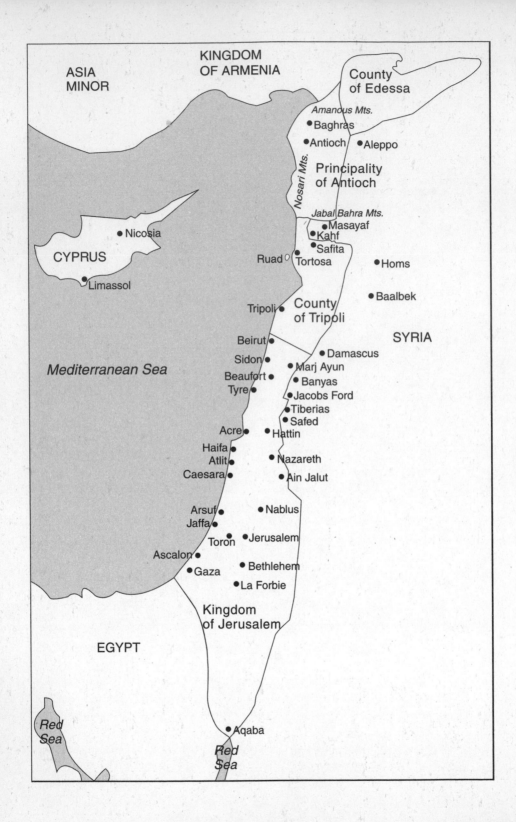

ASIA
MINOR

KINGDOM
OF ARMENIA

County
of Edessa

*Amanous Mts.*
● Baghras

● Antioch      ● Aleppo

*Nosari Mts.*

Principality
of Antioch

*Jabal Bahra Mts.*
● Masayaf
● Kahf
● Safita
Ruad ○ ● Tortosa        ● Homs

● Nicosia

CYPRUS

● Limassol

● Baalbek

Tripoli ●   County
of Tripoli

*Mediterranean Sea*

Beirut ●

Sidon ●           ● Damascus

Beaufort ●   ● Marj Ayun

Tyre ●       ● Banyas

● Jacobs Ford

● Tiberias
● Safed

Acre ●   ● Hattin

Haifa ●

Atlit ●    ● Nazareth

Caesara ●   ● Ain Jalut

SYRIA

Arsuf ●   ● Nablus
Jaffa ●

Toron ●   ● Jerusalem

Ascalon ●   ● Bethlehem
● Gaza
● La Forbie

Kingdom
of Jerusalem

EGYPT

*Red
Sea*

● Aqaba

*Red
Sea*

# CHAPTER TWELVE

# THE FIRST CRUSADE

From Freemasonry to the Ordo Templi Orientis, hierarchical Western secret societies claim derivation from the Knights Templar. This religious order of crusading warrior-monks was originally established in 1118–20 to protect Christian pilgrims as they expressed their devotions with visits to the birthplace of their savior and their faith. The Order was for many years an enormously successful and respected part of European culture, enjoying the singular patronage of Saint Bernard of Clairvaux, medieval Christianity's most famous and powerful religious leader. The Knights Templar constituted the pope's private army; for this and many other reasons these elite warriors enjoyed the protection and support of most of the popes to whom they were ultimately responsible. Yet within two hundred years of its founding, the Order was ruthlessly crushed — its leaders tortured and burned at the stake; its members accused of magic, heresy, sexual perversion, and treason; its vast wealth and holdings seized. What happened? And why has their legend persisted so strongly ever since? To begin to answer these questions, a few words on the First Crusade, undertaken some twenty-five years before the Templars' founding, are necessary.

Urban II assumed the papacy in 1088. His first concern was to reunite Roman Catholicism. The antipope Guibert, Clement III, still reigned in Rome, although his influence was limited. Urban had won the allegiance of the majority of Europe. In March 1095, at the Council of Piacenza, Urban felt his position was strong enough to excommunicate both Guibert and his followers. He also made overtures to the Eastern Church. One of his first acts as pope had been to lift the excommunication of the Byzantine emperor. Representatives of Alexius Comnenus were in attendance at the Council of Piacenza to plead for Western assistance in their decade-long battle against the Seljuk Turks.

Urban could see many benefits to this course of action. The opportunity to strengthen the Church and promote a greater alliance with Constantinople was certainly alluring. The chance finally to put the many disruptive and warlike knights to a useful purpose would be salutary. The possibility that a united Christianity might develop the political will and military capability to eradicate the infidel from the

Holy Land appeared to Urban's understanding to be aligned with the divine plan. The merciful God who had allowed humanity to survive the millennium would certainly desire His Church to reclaim Christ's homeland.

Urban traveled through France amid rumors of celestial signs such as the aurora borealis, comets, and star showers. In November 1095 he convened the Council of Clermont and issued his call for the First Crusade. This was one of history's inexplicably perfect moments when an idea can inflame an entire population. Europe's cultural stagnation is best illustrated by the eagerness with which vast numbers heeded Urban's call. Nobles and knights at once began to lay plans for a crusade to begin after the harvest in August 1096. This was too long a wait for the masses. A mob of over twenty thousand souls, led by Peter the Hermit, began the long journey to the Holy Land after first attacking neighboring Jews in their own communities. Six months later, after many thousands of deaths, those who had survived were wiped out by the Turks after journeying beyond Constantinople.

The organized armies were slower and more meticulous in their progress, departing in four separate groups between August and October 1096. The first was led by Godfrey de Bouillon, duke of Lower Lorraine, and his younger brother Baldwin. The second army was led by Bohemond, Norman prince of Taranto in Italy, and his nephew Tancred. The third was led by Raymond, count of Toulouse and St. Gilles. The fourth was led by Robert of Normandy, the son of William the Conqueror; Robert of Flanders; and Stephen of Blois, William's son-in-law. An estimated thirty-five thousand soldiers participated.[1]

The first battle of the Crusades was fought at Nicaea in Turkey. The Turks were overly confident after their effortless victory against the People's Crusade and were defeated by the disciplined European forces. By the conclusion of this siege, all four Crusader armies had made their rendezvous. They continued a unified march across Turkey, battling the infidel while facing harsh conditions of hunger and thirst. They reached the northern region of Palestine and the city of Antioch in October 1097. (Baldwin's army had separated from the conjoined forces and continued to eastern Turkey, where he succeeded in establishing himself as prince of Edessa.)

The main force laid siege to Antioch. The strength of the city's fortifications, the poor weather conditions, and the lack of food contributed to a long and painful siege. One-seventh of the army died of hunger. Finally, in June 1098, the Crusaders were able to take Antioch, aided by the treachery of some Muslim guards who allowed the Christians to enter the walls. The Crusaders came into possession of what many believed to be the lance that pierced the side of Christ as he hung upon the cross. A meteorite fell from the sky, injuring the Turkish forces. Angels clad in white mantles, carrying a white banner, and mounted on white horses were said to have aided the Christian army.

In June 1099, the Crusaders began the siege of Jerusalem after defeating the Fatimid military commander al-Afdal near Ascalon. (Al-Afdal will be remembered as having denied the proper succession of the Fatimid Imamate to Nizar.) The siege of Jerusalem lasted only five weeks, until Friday, June 15, at midday, the hour of the Crucifixion. A contemporary Crusader reported that soldiers were wading up to their ankles in the blood of the enemy. Urban died just two weeks before Jerusalem was taken. The leaders of the four armies all survived the campaign. Some returned to Europe; others remained and divided the territory in the following manner: Baldwin was established in Edessa; Bohemond became prince of Antioch; Tancred became prince of Galilee; and Godfrey de Bouillon was elected Advocate of the Holy Sepulcher in Jerusalem. Godfrey felt it wrong to wear a royal crown in the city where Christ had worn the Crown of Thorns and so refused the title of King of Jerusalem.

Godfrey died within a year. His brother Baldwin traveled from Edessa and was crowned King Baldwin I of Jerusalem on November 11, 1100. Baldwin consistently strengthened and extended European power throughout his reign. Upon his death on April 2, 1118, the succession passed in an orderly manner to his cousin, who was crowned as Baldwin II.

# CHAPTER THIRTEEN

# An Overview of the Order

## The Founding

The Knights Templar, or Poor Knights of the Temple of Solomon, or Poor Fellow-Soldiers of Jesus Christ, were founded by Hughes de Payens, a French knight who had taken religious vows upon the death of his wife. He is known to have been an austere man of deeply held spiritual values, humility, and uncompromising valor. He was nearly fifty when he founded the Order, a veteran of the First Crusade who had spent the previous twenty-two years of his life east of Europe.[1]

The most widespread accounts of the Order's founding are based on three historians, writing within fifty to seventy-five years of the event. Two agree that in 1118 or 1119, Hughes, along with eight other knights, took vows of obedience to Warmund of Picquigny, the Patriarch of Jerusalem, resolving to live in holy poverty and chastity, and to devote themselves to the care and protection of Christian pilgrims traveling through the Holy Land. King Baldwin II awarded them lodging in the al-Aqsa mosque near the Dome of the Rock, the original site of the Temple of Solomon. The third historian wrote that Hughes de Payens was in Jerusalem at the beginning of Baldwin II's reign after having taken an oath never to return to Europe. He had fought in the Holy Land for three years until he and thirty fellow knights sought to renounce warfare and take holy orders. Their skill in battle and loyalty to Christ attracted the attention of the king, who persuaded them they could better serve Christianity by pursuing their martial expertise and protecting pilgrims.[2]

The timing of the founding of the Knights Templar was more critical than the questions of whether nine or thirty men were initially involved, or if the knights themselves or King Baldwin first suggested the conceptual basis for the Order. A group of seven hundred pilgrims had been attacked on the eve of Easter 1119. Three hundred were brutally massacred. Sixty more were taken prisoner, and all the possessions of the group were seized as booty. Despair swept through Jerusalem. Whether the Templars were founded in 1118, immediately after the 1119 massacre, or even in 1120, as Malcolm Barber suggests,[†] the

---

[†] See Barber, *The New Knighthood*, pp. 8–9, for a discussion of the dating-system

development of the Order was a prerequisite for the continued survival of Christendom in the Holy Land.

The Order of the Hospital of Saint John of Jerusalem (now the Knights of Malta) had been established around 1080 as a charitable group to provide medical care and shelter for pilgrims and had received papal recognition in 1113. The model of an order dedicated to the needs of pilgrims in the Holy Land was undoubtedly an influence on the knights who joined together as the Templars. During the 1130s, the Hospitallers, reciprocally influenced by the Templars, became involved in military activities, although militarism was never the exclusive province of the Hospital as it was of the Temple.

Jerusalem was virtually isolated from the rest of the European holdings in Palestine. Though symbolically and emotionally of the greatest importance to Crusaders, the city was surrounded by Muslims and in constant danger of attack. It was ruled jointly by the Christian patriarch, the Latin king, and whichever particularly powerful crusading feudal lord might be in the area, a politically unstable situation that often led to breakdowns in communication and conflicts of interest.

The dangers to pilgrims were manifold as there was little control of the route between the port of Jaffa (modern Tel Aviv) and Jerusalem, some thirty-five miles as the crow flies — a two-day journey along a dangerous mountain road through fierce desert heat and arid terrain, surrounded by brigands, Muslim armies, and wild animals such as lions. The Holy Land endured a chronic shortage of stable military manpower.

The port cities of Palestine were the only real centers of economic activity. Merchants from the Italian cities of Genoa, Pisa, and Venice conducted a brisk Mediterranean trade. The desire of King Baldwin I to build up the Western population of Jerusalem as a safeguard against the surrounding Muslim enemies had motivated him to provide economic incentives to encourage people to move there. These included lowering certain duties and taxes, providing land grants, and making cheap housing available. Employment was offered by public construction projects undertaken to fortify the city. While these programs enjoyed some success, the continued isolation of Jerusalem and its lack of economic vibrancy were directly attributable to the dangers of the overland route from Jaffa. The partnership between the king and patriarch as generous

---

problems of the medieval calendar; see also J. M. Upton-Ward, *The Rule of the Templars*, (Suffolk: The Boydell Press, 1992), p. 2. In the twelfth century, many areas of France began the new year on March 25.

sponsors and supporters of the Knights Templar as a regional standing army is perfectly understandable.

## SAINT BERNARD OF CLAIRVAUX AND THE GROWTH OF THE ORDER

The young Order was particularly vulnerable to any number of problems in its infancy. With no Rule, no financial resources, and no official standing, it required the determination of its original members to keep it alive, along perhaps with the exigencies of fate. The knights, having pledged themselves to poverty, wore secular clothing donated by the faithful. Their seal shows two knights riding a single horse, emblematic of the vow of poverty and their humble origins. Their quarters were described as somewhat dilapidated by a contemporary historian. Yet they were growing. For example, Count Fulk V of Anjou (who was later to succeed Baldwin II as king of Jerusalem) stayed at the Temple during a visit in 1120–21. He is the first European noble known to have provided an annual subsidy to the Order.[3] It is generally accepted that Fulk was admitted as an associate or lay member.

Another prominent figure in the early years of the Templars was Count Hugh of Champagne, a great French landowner and feudal lord, the liege lord of Hughes de Payens. Count Hugh officially joined the Order in 1125. Some years later, he provided the site on which the Council of Troyes was held, convened by the pope to recognize the Templars as an ecclesiastical body of the Church. He also donated land to the Cistercian Order for the Abbey of Clairvaux. Saint Bernard was chosen to be its first abbot. Bernard was the nephew of another of Count Hugh's vassals, André de Montbard, one of the original knights of the Temple and later a Grand Master. Saint Bernard rose to become the most influential and politically powerful Catholic theologian of his time.

In 1126, André de Montbard and a Templar named Gondemar left Jerusalem for Europe. Baldwin II had written to Bernard, asking for his help in getting papal approval for the Order and crafting a Rule to guide Templar conduct. Hughes de Payens traveled to Europe shortly thereafter to recruit new knights, solicit donations of land and money, and spread the word of the Order's works.

Bernard was of enormous help to the Templars. He was uniquely qualified to synthesize the concept of a knightly religious order. Born in 1090, he had grown up intending to become a knight until he experienced a religious conversion at the age of twenty that forever changed his life. At age thirty-six, Bernard was approaching the height of his power. While chronic ill health made him physically frail, he radiated an immense spiritual vitality. His personal influence on the twelfth-century Church is incalculable by modern standards. He literally functioned as the conscience of Christianity. That which he supported flourished, that which he condemned withered. His energetic support of the Templars practically guaranteed their success.

Bernard had become a Cistercian monk in 1112, when the brotherhood was on the verge of failure. In 1115, at the age of twenty-five, he was chosen to become the superior of Clairvaux. Under his leadership the Cistercians grew from 7 abbeys in 1118 to 328 in 1152. He was an extremely talented organizer who had a particular skill for hierarchical organization and the efficient structuring of power. He applied this skill to the Templars.

Bernard was also a highly developed mystic. He was a leading exponent of the cult of the Virgin Mary that began to flourish in the twelfth century. The ideal of the Virgin as mother and intercessor would inform the Templar Order. Bernard realized the tremendous emotional potential offered by the worship of the mother of Christ. He taught that a sincere, ardent, and sustained aspiration on the part of the seeker would result in a "sweet inpouring of the Divine Love."[4]

In January 1128 (or 1129),[†] the papal council, convened at Bernard's request, assembled at Troyes, some ninety miles southeast of Paris. The purpose of the Council of Troyes was to discuss the Templar question as it had been advanced by Hughes, Baldwin II, and Bernard. Numerous archbishops, bishops, and abbots attended. Pope Honorius II was represented by his legate. At the command of the pope and of Stephen, the Patriarch of Jerusalem, a Rule was written for the Order. The pope also awarded the Templars their own distinctive dress, a plain white robe, to which a red cross would be affixed in 1147.

## THE TEMPLAR RULE

Bernard presided over the writing of the Rule that dictated the behavior of the members of the Order. Bernard's Latin Rule consisted of 72

---

[†] See note on pages 156–57. January 1128 would probably be January 1129 by modern reckoning. See also Upton-Ward, *The Rule of the Templars*, p. 2, and Barber, *The New Knighthood*, pp. 13–14.

paragraphs. A major enlargement of the Rule took place under Hughes's successor, Robert de Craon, who arranged for a French translation around 1139. Military functions, organizational hierarchy, and the practical conduct of members were the primary topics addressed by the expanded Rule. It continued to be updated over the years, eventually growing to 686 paragraphs. The care with which the Rule was written and continually enlarged, and its translation from Latin into the more accessible French language, tend to belie the idea that there was a heretical doctrine at the Templar core.[†]

J. M. Upton-Ward has recently (1992) provided an English translation of the complete Rule. She summarizes its seven main sections as follows: "The Primitive (or Latin) Rule," written by and under the supervision of Bernard after the Council of Troyes in 1129; "The Hierarchical Statutes," dated around 1165, in which the structure of the Order is delineated; "Penances," which summarizes discipline and the consequences of infractions thereof and offers details about the chaplain brothers; "Conventual Life," which details daily life in practical terms such as prayer, meals, sleeping, and so on; "The Holding of Ordinary Chapters," which explains the functions and operation of a chapter "established so that the brothers could confess their faults and make amends;"[5] "Further Details on Penances," probably written around 1260, which provides anecdotal examples of Order discipline to help guide future chapters; and "Reception into the Order," which explains the membership ceremony.[6]

"We speak firstly to all those who secretly despise their own will and desire with a pure heart to serve the sovereign king as a knight and with studious care desire to wear, and wear permanently, the very noble armour of obedience."[7] In the opening sentences of the Latin Rule, Bernard weaves a tapestry in which he celebrates the ideal of pure knighthood and perfect chivalry and exposes the failing of then-modern secular knights to live up to that high standard. "In this religious order has flourished and is revitalized the order of knighthood.

---

[†] In 1877, a forged "Secret Rule" of the Templars was published by the German Mason Merzdorf. He pretended it was a recently discovered thirteenth-century manuscript that proved the Templar heresy in detail, including their alliance with the Cathars and other dualist sects, their defiling of the cross, the worship of Baphomet, the obscene kiss, the ceremonial readings from the Koran, and so on. See Partner, *The Murdered Magicians: The Templars and Their Myth* (Oxford: Oxford University Press, 1981), pp. 161–63.

This knighthood despised the love of justice that constitutes its duties and did not do what it should, that is, defend the poor, widows, orphans and churches, but strove to plunder despoil and kill."[8] Edward Burman remarks, "The Templars themselves already looked back to an imagined ideal knighthood as later sects and secret societies dreamed back to the Templars."[9]

Among the Rule's provisions are the following: The Master of the Order was all-powerful, so powerful that the final paragraph of the Latin Rule stated that all the specific instructions contained therein were to be followed or not at the discretion of the Master. His term of office was for life. His death was celebrated with great dignity and many prayers. His successor was chosen by an electoral college of thirteen members — eight knights and four sergeants representing the twelve apostles, plus a chaplain brother symbolizing Jesus Christ. They would ideally be chosen from representatives of the many countries from which Templar membership was drawn.

The responsibilities of the elite corps of knights were strict. The daily religious lifestyle of the Templar house was based on that of the Benedictine monk, including extensive prayer and attendance at Mass. This was, of course, counterbalanced by the necessity to attend to weapons, armor, horses, and the other tools of the warrior trade. The knights were to wear the white habit at all times except when in the hospital. No decorations were allowed on weapons or armor. They were to say 26 Paternosters upon rising and 60 more before eating; in all the prayer was to be repeated 148 times each day. Meals were to be taken together in silence, with neither wine nor water present at the table. Meals were to be accompanied by scripture reading. Leftovers were to be distributed to servants and the poor. One-tenth of all bread was to be given as alms. Meat was allowed three days per week. A light was to burn in Templar dormitories all night.

Templars observed two seasons of Lent each year, at Easter and at Christmas, with forty days of partial fasting prescribed for each. On the other hand, the traditional monastic fast common to religious brotherhoods was forbidden to the Templars, as it was essential they maintain physical fitness for battle. Knights were to wear the tonsure and live amid the simplest of all furnishings as further signs of poverty and humility. The Master, in commemoration of Christ's humility, was obliged to wash the feet of thirteen paupers on Maundy Thursday (the Thursday before Good Friday). He was then to distribute clothing, food, and alms. The knights were also directed to perform this annual ceremonial oblation and almsgiving. Hunting was forbidden, except of lions, identified by Saint Peter as a form of the devil (1 Peter 5:8). All property was held in common. Even a personal letter was to be read aloud in the presence of the Master. Provisions were made for the care of elderly, pensioned, and sick members.

The Order was open to men only. The knights were under strict vows of celibacy and were forbidden to marry or remain married upon joining. Wives of men who became Templars were expected to join other religious orders as nuns. Templars were forbidden to kiss their mothers, wives, sisters, or any woman. They were warned against even looking upon women. Knights were forbidden to act as godparents. While the Rule may have had an almost misogynistic quality, it also makes especially clear the role of the Virgin Mary: "Our Lady was the beginning of our Order, and in her and in her honour, if we please God, will be the end of our lives and the end of our Order, whenever God wishes it to be."[10]

Extensive military instructions were an important part of the expanded Rule. Setting up camp and maintaining discipline within the camp were discussed at length. Instructions were given regarding conduct during charges, as well as in battle, and included the proper protocols for handling the Order's piebald standard. The hierarchy of discipline in the field was clearly delineated and options in defeat carefully enunciated.

The reception of a brother into the Order is described in detail in the expanded Rule. First the Chapter Master determined that no one present opposed the candidate, who was then told of the harshness of the Templar life. A highly personal interrogation of the candidate's character and life history next took place. He was questioned as to his willingness to give up his former life and surrender himself to a life of service to the Order. Each new member heard the secret Rule read for the first time at his ceremony of initiation. He was required to swear an oath of absolute obedience and loyalty to the Master and to the Rule, to take vows of poverty and chastity, and to swear to capture and defend Jerusalem. Finally, he was given instructions regarding the disciplines he was to follow for the rest of his life. The ceremony of reception as described in the Rule has no indication of the behavior charged by the fourteenth-century Inquisition.

An issue that has perplexed scholars, and that later caused serious problems for the Order, was a change in the Rule between the Latin and French versions regarding contact with excommunicated knights.

The Latin Rule forbade contact, although it did allow for acceptance of gifts and alms from the excommunicated. The French translation of the Rule commanded the brothers to go where excommunicated knights were gathered. An excommunicate was even allowed to join the Order. Whether the change between the Latin and French Rules owes its existence to a translator's error, Robert de Craon's insistence on his independence, or an exaggerated form of Christian charity extended even unto the damned is impossible to say. At this time the Rule was secret, so that neither Saint Bernard nor Innocent II would have necessarily been aware of the change.

Punishment for infractions against the Rule ranged from lesser humiliations such as being forced to eat from the floor for as long as a year and a day, or the loss of one's habit and all privileges and responsibilities of knighthood, or expulsion from the Order, to the possibility of perpetual imprisonment. In 1301, the Master of Ireland, William Le Bachelor, was excommunicated and starved to death in a tiny cell overlooking the church. His crime was selling Templar land without permission. From his cell, he could observe the Mass and the brethren taking part in the Communion from which he was excluded.

Weekly chapter meetings were held in Templar houses in which four or more brothers lived. After a sermon, the floor was opened to brothers who wished to confess violations of the Rule. Punishment would be assigned by the chapter acting in concert while the brother left the room so the discussion could be private. Accusations might take the place of confession during these sessions. If the guilt of those accused was proven, offenders were punished more severely than those who voluntarily confessed. Accusations were later made by the Order's enemies that this self-policing practice was intended to be the equivalent of the sacrament of penance which required a priest. While this was not true, some of the simpler-minded brethren were unclear on the issue. A reading of the Rule can help us to understand their confusion.

The Rule states that no brother was supposed to confess to anyone but a chaplain brother, "for they have greater power to absolve them on behalf of the pope than an archbishop."[11] Yet chaplain brothers were not able to absolve certain specific sins: killing a Christian; striking a brother so that blood flows; laying a hand on a man of another order whether clerk or priest; renouncing one's vows to another order upon joining the Templars; or becoming a Templar through simony. These sins could only be absolved by the local patriarch, archbishop, or bishop.

Initially nine offenses merited expulsion from the Order. These were simony; disclosing the secrets of a chapter; killing a Christian man or woman; theft; leaving the house other than by the gate (which implied thievery or other sinister motive); conspiracy between brothers; treason with the Saracens; heresy; and fleeing the raised piebald standard during battle from fear of the enemy. "[T]he filthy stinking sin of sodomy"[12] was later added as an expellable offense, as was entering the Order as a layman and taking ordination without the permission of the house.

## IN PRAISE OF THE NEW KNIGHTHOOD

Bernard made another contribution of such vast importance to the Order's recruiting efforts and subsequent myth that an English translation of the most relevant portion has been included as an appendix (see p. 277). Bernard wrote a long letter to Hughes in which he expounded in detail on his views of the code of chivalry and his concept of the ideal of the holy knight. The treatise was entitled *Liber ad milites Templi: De laude novae militae*, "The Book of the Knights of the Temple: In Praise of the New Knighthood," and is believed to have been written in 1135.

The letter was designed to be a guide for current and future members of the Order; to encourage prospective members to apply for admission; and to provide a rationale for the Order within the context of Christianity. It was also an answer to those critics who believed Christianity had no place for an armed brotherhood of warrior-monks whose dual goals of salvation and soldiering were said to be mutually exclusive.

Bernard harshly criticized the vanity and pompousness of secular knights with their flowing hair, silks and jewels, plumed armor, and painted shields, calling them "the trinkets of a woman." He laid out the Christian equivalent of the Islamic jihad in words that could as easily have been spoken by Hasan-i-Sabah to his *fidais*. The new knighthood is described as one that "ceaselessly wages a twofold war both against flesh and blood and against a spiritual army of evil in the heavens." The knight-monk is a soldier of Christ. "Neither does he bear the sword in vain, for he is God's minister for the punishment of evildoers and for the praise of the good. If he kills an evildoer, he is not a mankiller, but, if I may so put it, a killer of evil." The essential religious justification for the slaying of the enemies of Christ by so respected a theologian as Bernard established the concept above the reach of further criticism.

The primary quality for which the Templars were long to be known, in addition to their discipline, was their courage. The Muslims respected them for this as much as the Europeans did. Despite frequent losses over the next two hundred years, Templar courage was rarely questioned. Roots of this may certainly be traced to Bernard's exhortations in *De laude:* "Truly, he is a fearless knight and completely secure. While his body is properly armed for these circumstances, his soul is also clothed with the armor of faith. On all sides surely he is well armed; he fears neither demons, nor men. . . . When readying for imminent battle, their inner faith is their protection. On the exterior, steel, not gold, is their security — since they are to strike fear in the enemy, not provoke his avariciousness. They need to have horses that are swift and strong, not pompous and decorated. Their purpose is fighting, not parades. They seek victory, not glory. They would rather strike terror than impress. . . . They rush in to attack the adversaries, considering them like sheep. No matter how outnumbered, they do not consider the savage barbarians as formidable multitudes."[13]

## THE STRUCTURE OF THE ORDER

The expanded Rule gave careful attention to the hierarchical structure and military functions of the Order. The Master was the supreme head, but he was also responsible to the Order as a whole. He could dispose of some property and was entrusted as the guardian of the Order's wealth. In all important decisions, such as major property transfers, declarations of war, concluding a peace, planning a campaign, even receiving a new brother, the Master was obligated to consult with a chapter of knights. Though his opinion was respected, he possessed only one vote.

The Seneschal was second in command. He carried the Order's battle standard, the *gonfalon baucent,* the piebald standard, a vertical rectangle composed of a black square above a white square. The Marshal was third in rank, as well as the supreme military commander. The Commander of the Kingdom of Jerusalem was the treasurer of the Order. He shared the responsibility for protecting the Order's wealth with the Grand Master. The Draper was responsible for all clothing needs and bed linen.

Next in rank below these five officials were the Regional Commanders. The Commander of the City of Jerusalem was responsible for the health and well-being of the brothers and also bore the primary responsibility for protecting pilgrims, and transporting of the Order's holiest relic (the fragment believed to be a relic of the True Cross). There were also Commanders for Tripoli and Antioch. Next in rank were the Regional Masters who were in full charge of all activities in their area unless the Master of the Order was visiting. The Commanders of the Houses were charged with overseeing the day-to-day activities in the Order's castles and farms. They answered to the Regional Masters. In the thirteenth century, a new office was created, that of Visitor of the Order, who was in overall charge of the Order in Europe and second in command to the Grand Master.

The knights were, of course, the prime element of the Order. The bulk of the Rule applied to their conduct. There was no actual training program for knights. One was expected to be a fully functional warrior upon joining the Order. Knights were drawn exclusively from the nobility. The actual percentage of knights within the overall membership of the Order of the Temple was always quite small after its earliest beginnings. It is estimated by various historians that ten percent is the most reasonable figure. Henry Lea estimates the size of the Order just prior to its downfall at fifteen thousand members, of whom ten percent were knights.[14] The knights were the only members entitled to wear the celebrated white robe and red cross.

The bulk of the members, quite literally a supporting army, were charged with administering the vast requirements of the elite core of heavily armed and mounted knights. The sergeants were the ranking members of this elaborate logistical system. Their duties included everything from cooking to warfare. Their uniforms were a black tunic with a red cross on the front and back and a black or brown mantle. The sergeants were entrusted with responsibilities often equal in scope to that of the knights, despite their lesser status. They would be in full charge of running the Templar household when the knights were away.

A class of associate membership was established that could include married brothers. If a married Templar associate died before his term of service expired, his wife was entitled to death benefits from the Order. Some associates joined the Order for a stated period of time or for the duration of a single crusade. Another class of associate members were those who contributed yearly fees and hoped thereby to gain some of the spiritual blessing of the Order. Women could participate in this group. Other associate members included those without resources who simply offered themselves in service to the Order, receiving sustenance in return for their labor.

Numerous serving brothers functioned in various capacities as foot soldiers, clergy, recruiters, armorers, blacksmiths, grooms, cooks, brewers, tanners, engineers, masons, carpenters, architects, medical personnel, servants, and laborers. The care of horses was one of the most important activities. Vast resources and energy were required to ship, house, feed, and maintain the equine army. (Each knight was allowed to possess up to three horses.) A large number of Templars administered the finances of the Order as it grew to be one of the wealthiest institutions of medieval Europe. Others were charged with maintenance and administration of the vast tracts of land donated to the Order. Templar farms required experts in agriculture and animal husbandry as well as field hands. A distribution apparatus for produce, wool, meat, and other products developed over time. Donated lands might be let out for rental income, and facilities such as mills, wine presses and mines also served as sources of income. In later years, the Templars became involved in shipping, developing their own fleets to move pilgrims, soldiers, and supplies along the Mediterranean route to the Holy Land, which naturally expanded to include trade. Templar houses were maintained in key port cities.

The purpose of these varied activities was to raise the funds and materials necessary for the campaign in the Holy Land. The vast European support network was one of the most important accomplishments of the Order. Without it, the Templars would have ceased to exist after their first major defeat. The European supply base of money, goods, and manpower kept the Order alive through two centuries of continual warfare.

## TEMPLAR WEALTH AND THE PRACTICE OF INTERNATIONAL BANKING

The Knights Templar established the practice of international banking. Their numerous fortresses along the routes leading eastward naturally suggested themselves as depositories for gold and other valuables to kings, nobles, merchants, crusaders, and pilgrims. It was safer to trust the Templar network for monetary transfers than to carry large sums of cash along dangerous routes. Funds deposited with the Order in Europe could be claimed on arrival in the Holy Land as needed. The paper records between Templars in various locations establishing these deposits and payments ultimately led to the modern practice of drawing checks against an account.

Those about to embark on the years-long and dangerous journey abroad would often draw up wills and leave these safely in the hands of the Templars. Thus the Order might be required to fulfill the fiduciary duties of executor for estates left in their care. The Templars were also frequently the recipients of grants of large amounts of cash. In some cases, the money would be specifically earmarked for a crusading purpose. In other cases, the money would be donated as a gift to the Order. Record keeping had to be precise.

As time went on, the financial skills developed by the Order became even more sophisticated. In France especially, the Templar financial bureaucracy was utilized to perform extensive banking services for the monarchy. These activities included assessing and collecting taxes, transmitting funds, managing debt and credit, and paying pensions. The nobility, encouraged by the confidence shown by royalty, made similar use of the brothers.

The armed security offered by the well-guarded Templar houses was so impressive that they were used to hold deposits of royal treasure in England as early as 1185. The crown jewels were deposited in the London Temple in 1204. Templar depositories were also used to hold funds in escrow accounts for contractual guarantees among parties. In addition to valuables such as gold, jewels, and documents, livestock and even slaves are known to have been entrusted to Templar safekeeping in Aragon.[15] Again, superior record keeping was necessary to the success they enjoyed, as was a proper and trustworthy assaying bureaucracy capable of accurately establishing the value of deposited goods.

The papacy also made use of the Order's financial expertise. The Templars began this aspect of their financial activities by arranging loans for Pope Alexander in 1163. In 1198, Pope Innocent III began to levy taxes on the clergy, and in 1208 he called upon the Templars to help him collect the tax. His successor, Honorius III, turned to the Templars to help collect funds for the Fifth Crusade, arranging for clerical taxes to be paid directly to the Paris Temple and then transferred to the papal legate who commanded the crusading army in Egypt. In 1307 and 1308, after the arrest of Order members in France, Pope Clement V exempted his Templar financial staff from the fate of their brothers.[16]

The overall European Templar network was instrumental in contributing to the development of a cash-based economy for the first time in Europe. For example, Templar farms originated the practice of raising crops for sale. Before this, farming was practiced for the sustenance of those who provided the land and/or labor. The constant demand for funds to pursue the crusading effort forced the Templars to become financial innovators. The Holy Land already functioned primarily on a cash economy. Disposable wealth counted for more than property, which was vulnerable to the constantly changing strategic situation. The Templars were able to adapt to this circumstance. Familiarity with the workings of a cash economy gave the Order the experience that would place it at the vanguard as the European economy gradually shifted itself in this direction.

The medieval prohibition against usury was carefully skirted by sophisticated forms of contracts. Interest payments were concealed as administrative expenses, deducted in advance from the moneys received by the borrower or achieved through careful manipulation of the exchange rates of foreign currencies. Money lending by the Templars dated back to the Order's earliest days under Hughes de Payens, who perceived it as one of the duties of the Order — in spite of the fact that Bernard was virulently opposed to materialism and the money trade in general. Almost all European monarchs had occasion to borrow from the Templars, as did several monasteries.

Although the Templars were wealthy in both land and hard assets, the fabulous wealth often ascribed to the Order is undoubtedly an exaggeration. The enormous costs associated with conducting a two-hundred-year military campaign must be factored into the myth of their extraordinary wealth. Funds were constantly required for the normal expenses associated with equipping, transporting, housing, and feeding the vast number of personnel involved. In addition, castle construction, maintenance, and rebuilding were huge financial drains, as were the large sums paid in ransom, lost in unrepaid loans, and seized by the enemy in battle.

# CHAPTER FOURTEEN

# THE EARLY YEARS

## THE RISE OF THE TEMPLARS IN EUROPE

The support of Bernard, papal recognition in the form of the Rule, and the status conferred by the Council of Troyes all contributed to an increase in membership in the Order.[†] The promise of glory, danger, travel, religious expiation, and the chance to fight to establish God's kingdom on earth fell upon waiting and ready ears. The concept of a military-religious order of knight-monks was an idea whose time had come. Within a short period of time the Templars began to amass stores of wealth and land donated by aristocrats excited by their charisma and seeking remission of sins through acts of generosity to a holy order of the Church. Hughes de Payens was one of the first to donate his own lands. France was naturally the first area of expansion, as the prime participants were native to the country. Hughes soon appointed a National Master of the Temple for France, thus laying the foundation for an international bureaucratic structure.

He next visited England and Scotland, where he also received donations of land, money, and volunteers. He established the London Temple in 1128 or 1129. The English branch of the Order prospered greatly under King Stephen, who ascended to the throne in 1135. Stephen's father had participated in the First Crusade, and his wife was the niece of King Baldwin I of Jerusalem. Exemption from the heavy layers of English taxation proved enormously helpful to the growth of the English Temple.

In 1130, the Order was established on the Spanish peninsula, the scene of the first Templar military campaign against the Moors. The Templars of Aragon were uniquely required to swear an oath of loyalty to the king in addition to their oaths to the Order. Under the patronage of the rulers of Catalonia and Aragon, they received large land

---

[†] Owing to the dating-system problems already referred to, Hughes's recruiting efforts may have begun the year prior to the convening of the council. This would have had the effect of increasing the order's strength, thus recommending it for greater consideration by the council.

grants in recognition of the value of their military support. The Aragonese king, Alfonso I, who died in 1134, bequeathed one-third of his kingdom to the Order. This immediately led to a series of power plays by members of the nobility and Alfonso's family. The Templars wisely demurred and, under Grand Master Robert de Craon, renounced their right to rule, instead receiving six castles and other financial grants and privileges. In neighboring Portugal, Queen Theresa donated a castle and surrounding land.

The growth of the Order was slower in Italy because of the fragmented political organization of the country. Italy, however, did have a number of port cities along its coast from which Crusaders, merchants, and pilgrims embarked to the Holy Land. The Order established a presence in each of these.

Under the masterships of Hughes de Payens and Robert de Craon, the Templars were granted six hundred charters "with half of that number being in Provence and Languedoc, a third in north-east France, and Flanders, and the remainder in England, Spain and Portugal, and elsewhere in France."[1] These grants included land, revenues, market rights, rents, and so on. (The extraordinary popularity of the Order in Provence and Languedoc should be noted here. It is sadly ironic when considered in relation to the participation of the Templars in the unconscionable thirteenth-century Albigensian Crusades.)

GROWTH IN THE HOLY LAND

In 1129, Count Fulk, an early friend of the Order, accompanied Hughes de Payens on his return to Palestine (which came to be known as Outremer, "Beyond the Sea"). Baldwin II, who had no male heir, had offered Fulk the hand of his eldest daughter, Melissande, in order to cement the lineage of the kingdom of Jerusalem. Fulk and Hughes traveled with as many as three hundred new members who had joined the Order to serve in the Holy Land. Other new members from Hughes's successful recruitment campaign remained in Europe. Payen de Montdidier, the Master of the Temple in France, was entrusted with overseeing all European Templar activities. Many of the new volunteers made substantial contributions of material wealth to the Order upon their renunciation of secular life.

Fulk and Melissande were married at the end of May 1129. Baldwin immediately enlisted Fulk and the newly enlarged Templar force in his plan to attack Damascus. The battle took place in October. The Christians were thoroughly beaten. The inexperience of their recently arrived European recruits contributed to the clumsiness of the Templar efforts. The defeat, however, did not lessen their prestige either in the Holy Land or Europe. Reports of Templar bravery traveled home with secular knights and returning pilgrims. A conference took place in Toulouse whose purpose was to confer gifts upon the Order. Forty-five donors contributed money and property. The Order's fame, wealth, and membership continued to grow.

The ongoing success of the Order's recruiting efforts was particularly welcomed in Outremer. The rise of the Muslim warrior Zangi — a former Kurdish slave of the Seljuk sultan Malikshah who went on to found the Atabeg dynasty — was correctly perceived as a particularly threatening development to Christian interests. In 1128 Zangi became governor of Aleppo, and by 1130 he was the master of northern Syria.

When Prince Bohemond of Antioch was killed in battle in 1130, his widow Alice, youngest daughter of Baldwin II, declared herself regent of Antioch and offered her allegiance to Zangi. This was an intolerable situation for Baldwin. He and Fulk immediately intervened and Alice was banished. Baldwin again became regent of Antioch, a position he had gladly relinquished to Bohemond and Alice in 1126.

Baldwin II died in August 1131 and was succeeded by the joint rulership of Fulk and Melissande, crowned together in September. Alice soon returned to Antioch to plague them. Fulk managed to subdue a threatened rebellion. In 1136, he craftily contrived a marriage between Alice's nine-year-old daughter Constance and Raymond of Poitiers. Raymond's presence added strength once again to the region as he and Fulk were able to function as a united Christian front.

There is little record of Templar activity during the 1130s. They were undoubtedly engaged in integrating new members and building the training programs needed to transform European knights into soldiers capable of dealing with the varied tactics and strategies they would encounter in their new environment. The enormous and sudden increase in Templar numbers created other practical and logistical demands that would require full attention to accommodate successfully. The Order was given its first group of castles along the northernmost frontier of the Holy Land, the Amanus Mountains, either by Fulk in 1131 or by Raymond in 1136.

As the European occupation of the Holy Land continued, the Order's original goal of protecting pilgrims gradually assumed less importance. The Knights Templar increasingly evolved into a crusading fighting force. The Muslims followed battle tactics entirely different from those commonly employed by European soldiers, and as a result, several early military actions ended in unmitigated disaster for the Europeans. The firsthand, hard-won experience the Templars were to gain from their military encounters with the Muslims would recommend them as advisors to the kings and nobles who came to fight their season in the Holy Land.

Hughes de Payens died on May 24, 1136. The Order he founded was successfully established and would become an eternal mythic component of Western civilization. The deaths of Hughes and Baldwin II heralded the end of the first generation of Crusaders.

## "Every best gift" and Later Papal Support

Another antipope had arisen in Rome in 1130. The dying Pope Honorius II had recommended to the cardinals that Innocent II succeed him. Innocent had been accepted by four cardinals and secretly elected as pope through an electoral subterfuge. He was forced to struggle with Anacletus II, a wealthy and ambitious Roman who had been accepted by two cardinals. Anacletus took over the Basilica of Saint Peter by force, stole its treasures, and began to buy as much support as he could. Soon after, both men were consecrated as pope in different parts of the city. Innocent, fearing for his life, fled to France.

Louis VI decided to support Innocent and enlisted Bernard of Clairvaux to judge the conflict. Bernard endorsed Innocent. In 1135, Innocent excommunicated Anacletus at the Council of Pisa. Innocent returned Bernard's support by becoming a major advocate for the Templars. He granted the Order an annual papal tribute during the council. Other clerics in attendance enlarged upon this from their own resources. In January 1138, Anacletus died. Innocent was able to safely reenter Rome as the undisputed pope. Here he met with Templar Grand Master Robert de Craon, an intelligent and persuasive diplomat.

De Craon carefully explained the financial and administrative burdens facing the Order as it expanded to fill the ever-increasing needs of the campaigns in the Holy Land. Innocent listened carefully. The struggle with Anacletus had convinced him that the Church must maintain the physical muscle to protect its spiritual mission.

On March 29, 1139, Innocent II issued the fundamental papal bull on the Templars, *Omne datum optimum,* "Every best gift." Bernard was in Rome at the time and must have rejoiced. This landmark edict proclaimed the Templars as the "true Israelites" who followed the precepts of spiritual charity and divine love. The bull created a new category of chaplain brother, or priest, within the Order to minister to the spiritual welfare of knights and serving brothers throughout the widespread houses of the Order, thus freeing the Templars of all local ecclesiastical authority. The Order was responsible to the pope alone. The Templars were his private army; he their sole authority. They were granted the right to construct their own churches to protect themselves from the company of sinners. They were allowed to retain any booty seized in battle. They were exempted from all church tithes and authorized to collect tithes for themselves. They were freed from all authority except that of the pope. This included kings and emperors as well as the entire church hierarchy. The Patriarch of Jerusalem who had presided over their founding was stripped of any authority over their behavior. No one was permitted to require an oath of a Templar. No one who was not already a Templar could be elected as Master of the Order (making it more difficult for a king to "fix" an election). All changes to the Rule were to be made only by the Master and a chapter of knights. Furthermore, the bull not only identified the Templars as protectors of pilgrims en route to Jerusalem, but asserted that God and Saint Peter had authorized them to protect the Catholic Church itself and to defend it against enemies of the Cross.

*Omne datum optimum* was frequently repeated by succeeding popes who further strengthened the Order with later bulls. In 1144, Celestine II issued *Milites Templi,* which awarded indulgences to benefactors of the Templars. It also granted permission to supporters to hold collections for the Order once a year in churches. It allowed for the celebration of Mass in areas under interdiction when Templar collectors were present. Pope Eugenius III, a disciple of Bernard's, issued *Milites Dei* in 1145, which authorized a change in battle-standard design from the rectangular piebald battle standard to an eight-pointed black Maltese cross on a plain white background. *Milites Dei* further gave the Order permission to build chapels independent of diocesan authority and to bury Templar dead in graveyards attached to these independent chapels.[†] *Omne datum optimum*, *Milites Templi*, and *Milites Dei* quelled any moral doubt about the Templar mission in orthodox Catholic thought. The holy warrior, who wielded his weapons of destruction in the establishment and protection of Christ's kingdom on earth, was to be aided and abetted by all, loved and respected, and showered with material gifts.

[†] This particular privilege was to become problematic in later years as corruption tainted the Order. Excommunicated nobles paid to be admitted to membership upon their deathbeds so they could be buried in consecrated Christian ground, effectively circumventing one of the worst consequences of excommunication.

CHAPTER FIFTEEN

# THE SECOND CRUSADE

The decade beginning in 1130 represented a turning point in the history of Outremer. The European occupation would require more sophisticated organizational strategies to remain viable after the loss of the initial emotional fervor that followed in the wake of the victory of the First Crusade, and it was rekindled by the meteoric success of the Templar recruiting efforts. The politics of the Holy Land had become very complex indeed. The European inhabitants, collectively known as the Franks, were divided into four separate Crusader states: the king-dom of Jerusalem, the principality of Antioch, the county of Tripoli, and the short-lived county of Edessa. These states were often in conflict with each other.

The decentralization of the Muslims and their own conflicting centers of power further contributed to the instability and fluidity of the political situation. Various temporary alliances and arrangements were made with one or another ruler or group as seemed useful. Land and castles shifted hands frequently, both through conquest and by treaty. Sometimes enemies, plotting against each other, allied across religious and cultural lines to attack their coreligionists.

The Byzantines, as discussed, had a long-standing relationship with the Muslim states that preceded the Crusades. Their Islamic alliances were of a more permanent and practical nature than those formed by the inflamed passions of the Crusades. In addition, the Greeks understood that if the European power in the Holy Land was encouraged to grow unchecked, it could rival and surpass their own.

The alliance between the Frankish and Byzantine Christians burst apart in 1137. During the First Crusade, an agreement had been made between the Eastern emperor and the crusading armies. The Franks would receive the full support of the emperor if they agreed that any captured Muslim land that had previously belonged to the Byzantines would be returned. Antioch was one such territory, yet it had remained in Frankish hands since 1098. In 1137, Emperor John Comnenus laid siege to Antioch. Christian battled Christian. Worse, King Fulk of Jerusalem refused to assist Prince Raymond of Antioch despite their alliance. Thus Antioch became a Byzantine territory again, and Raymond was forced to pay homage to the emperor.

The interreligious hostilities and continually shifting alliances of Outremer were not limited to the Christians. The Seljuks (representing the Abbasids), Fatimids, and Omayyads were engaged in constant power struggles with one another, and all were severally engaged in hostilities with the Assassins (as described in part 2). Alliances such as that between the Damascene sultan and King Fulk against Zangi in 1139 would have been incomprehensible to the medieval European unfamiliar with the harsh diplomatic realities of the Holy Land. The Templars were faced with a complex web of intrigue that often defied the simple idealism inherent in their founding — and would later return to haunt them with accusations of treason.

In 1144, the county of Edessa was taken after a four-week siege by Zangi. News of this buoyed up the Muslims with enthusiasm and self-confidence, while it left Europe with a sense of despair and anger. It marked the first great Christian defeat since the victory of the First Crusade fifty years before. Pope Eugenius III immediately began to call for a new crusade. He chose the French King Louis VII as the leader of the mission. Bernard of Clairvaux was passionately involved in preaching for the Second Crusade. He began in France in 1146 and traveled widely through Europe, everywhere exhorting the crowds to action. This was to be the largest of the Crusades; it included French, German, English, and Italian troops. Military actions were also fought against the remaining Moors in Spain and the Wends in Germany.

Louis VII, Bernard, and Pope Eugenius, accompanied by some three hundred Knights Templar and four archbishops, gathered at a Templar chapter meeting in Paris in 1147 to inaugurate the Second Crusade. Louis was presented with the *oriflamme*, a scarlet banner emblazoned with a golden flame and mounted upon a golden lance. Eugenius granted the Templars the exclusive right to wear a red cross upon the left breast and shoulder of their mantles, thus adding the red badge of martyrdom to the white robe of purity.[†]

---

[†] Curiously, if Joseph von Hammer-Purgstall is accurate here, these were the same colors worn by the Assassin *fidais*, who, he writes, wore red turbans, boots, or girdles with their white robes. Von Hammer-Purgstall ascribes white to innocence and devotion and red to blood and murder. See *The Assassins*, p. 56.

Everard des Barres, the Templar National Master of France, participated as one of three ambassadors in a successful diplomatic mission to the Byzantine emperor to negotiate a peaceful passage for the French army. He also joined in intimate sessions with Louis, arranging for the necessities of the Crusaders. The Templars fought and behaved admirably and with great dignity during the hazardous journey from Constantinople across Asia Minor to Antioch. During the long march, they reaffirmed their reputation as warriors, and functioned as moral examples of loyalty and courage to the European troops. The French force was a motley crew, composed of assorted groups of soldiers loyal to various nobles who were often rivals of each other. Adding to the confusion was the presence of the German army under King Conrad III. The combined forces lacked overall coordination and cohesion. This contrasted with the iron discipline of the Templars inspired by their Rule. King Louis eventually placed the Templars in military command of all the troops. In 1148, each soldier took an oath that he would obey Templar instructions.

During the Second Crusade, the Templars made a historic loan to Louis. The king had spent much more money than expected on supplies and shipping during the journey to Antioch. By the time the army arrived in March 1148, he was in severe need of funds, which could only be repaid upon his return to France. The Templars were able to come to his assistance. "Thus, during that important crusade, sponsored by the Templars' own spiritual patron, Bernard of Clairvaux, the twin functions of permanent fighting force at the service of the Holy Land and financiers to the royal courts of Europe came simultaneously to the fore."[1] From this point on, the Knights Templar became an essential component of any European plan or campaign undertaken in the Holy Land.

In June 1148, the Templars gathered near Acre with the Hospitallers, King Baldwin, the patriarch Fulcher, Kings Louis and Conrad, the archbishops of Caesarea and Nazareth, and other leading nobles and church officials. It was decided to attack Damascus. A force of fifty thousand Christians laid siege to the city but failed to attain victory. A series of bad decisions caused the great army to disintegrate within five days. Rumors and accusations of treason, bribery, and treachery were made against various leaders. Blame was laid at the feet of the European kings, who were accused of ambition and stupidity for choosing to attack the friendly Damascenes. The Palestinian barons were accused of committing treason out of jealousy for the initial successes of the visiting kings or in return for a bribe paid by the Damascenes. The Templars were accused of accepting enemy bribes to set up the army for failure.

The Second Crusade was a blistering defeat for Europe. A great deal of resentment was directed toward the Byzantines. Their treacherous alliances with the Turks had caused much loss of life for the European forces as they marched overland to Antioch. Louis left Palestine after his defeat at Damascus calling for a crusade to be launched against the Byzantines. Bernard, bitterly disappointed by the failure of the Second Crusade, lent his support to a Byzantine Crusade. Everard des Barres, who succeeded Robert de Craon as Grand Master, accompanied Louis to France to help plan the new crusade. Christian was preparing to go to war against Christian.

The brothers in Outremer, however, faced a perilous new situation. Zangi had died in 1146 while his army laid siege to Damascus. His son and successor, Nur al-Din, defeated a Frankish army and killed Prince Raymond in a battle near Antioch. The Templars attempted to help Baldwin III, who rushed to fight Nur al-Din, but most of the Templar force was killed by the Islamic army. André de Montbard, Seneschal of the Order, wrote Everard imploring him to return after alerting Europe to the seriousness of the new developments. Everard did return in 1152, but shortly thereafter resigned as Grand Master to become a monk under Bernard at Clairvaux.

The Templars succeeded in securing a military base at Gaza, ten miles south of Ascalon. The Fatimid stronghold at Ascalon had been a continuous menace to the kingdom of Jerusalem since the First Crusade. From Gaza, the Templars launched repeated swift attacks against Ascalon in imitation of Muslim tactics. Their success with this strategy greatly altered the balance of power in the southern region of the Holy Land.

Ascalon, however, was to be the scene of one of the worst accusations of cupidity made against the Templars. A long siege against the city was undertaken in January 1153 by the army of the kingdom of Jerusalem. On August 15, a breach was opened in a wall near a Templar camp. The new Grand Master, Bernard de Tremelay, reportedly refused to allow any other troops to enter the breach so that the Order alone could reap the first spoils. This act of apparent greed resulted in the

Master's own death along with that of thirty-nine of his knights. The Muslims soon sealed the breach, and the forty Templar corpses were hung from the castle the next morning, while their heads were sent as trophies to the caliph in Cairo. Ascalon fell a week later, but the Templars were denied any credit for the victory or any share in the copious booty that befell the conquerors.

Bernard died on August 20, 1153. Pope Eugenius died the same year, and André de Montbard became the fifth Master of the Temple. In 1154, Nur al-Din fulfilled his father's dream by taking Damascus. The idea of a Byzantine crusade lay dormant.

CHAPTER SIXTEEN

# SALADIN AND THE BATTLE OF HATTIN

The mid–twelfth century witnessed the development of an important new trend among the Franks. Secular lords began to donate castles to the military orders and to rely on the orders to defend the territories included in these grants. The baronage realized that the cost of maintaining sufficient troops and supplies was simply too high; it was cheaper to contribute excess property to the military orders than to be forced to defend it. It has been estimated that by the time of the Battle of Hattin in 1187, the Templars and Hospitallers held about thirty-five percent of the lordships in Outremer.[1] The military orders were thus tending to become independent factors in the political equation of the region — sometimes at odds with each other, sometimes at odds with the barons. Political fragmentation and rivalry among the Christians thereby increased.

In 1162, the throne of Jerusalem passed to Amalric, younger brother of the recently deceased King Baldwin III. Amalric was a powerful leader who, like his rival Nur al-Din, recognized the strategic importance of Egypt. If Egypt were in Islamic hands, the Europeans would be totally surrounded. If it were in Frankish hands, the Muslims would remain permanently splintered. Amalric attacked Egypt in 1164 and again in 1167. Nur al-Din sent his Kurdish general, Shirkuh, against Egypt in 1164 and 1167. Although Amalric was repulsed both times, his second campaign resulted in a mutually favorable treaty with the Fatimids, who sought his aid against Shirkuh. When Amalric proposed a third assault on Egypt in 1168, in violation of his treaty, the Templars refused to support him. They claimed it would be dishonorable for the king to break his word. Amalric proceeded without the Templars and was defeated.

Enemies of the Order claimed they had violated their mission to defend the kingdom of Jerusalem. Yet even William of Tyre, one of their harshest critics of the day, believed they acted honorably in this instance. A practical consideration influencing their decision may have been the incredible financial drain of the disastrous Second Crusade. Templar resources were also strained by their efforts to protect their northern fortresses from Nur al-Din. The Hospitallers were in the midst of a major financial crisis from which they hoped the Egyptian campaign might provide relief. Instead, it worsened their situation to such a degree that the Master of the Hospital resigned in disgrace. Another Templar motivation may have been lingering resentment against Amalric for his actions against a small garrison that had surrendered to Shirkuh in 1166. Amalric had rushed to reinforce them but arrived too late. In his fury, he decided the Templars had not put up sufficient resistance and executed twelve men by hanging.

Shirkuh was the uncle of the legendary Muslim leader Saladin, "Righteousness of the Faith," who would one day be responsible for the singular accomplishment of uniting the numerous Islamic factions. Saladin was born in 1138 in Syria, east of Beirut, and died in Damascus in 1193. Saladin's father, Ayyub, was the governor of Baalbek under Zangi, and then of Damascus under Nur al-Din. Saladin grew up following the pursuits of a young nobleman. He studied the Koran, Arabic poetry, and philosophy. He became expert in hunting, riding, chess, and polo. Saladin's martial prowess was developed as he fought in Shirkuh's campaigns. During the battles against Amalric in 1167, Saladin was given his first command. He managed to withstand a seventy-five-day siege by the Christian army. In 1171, he launched an attack against Amalric from Egypt.

Shirkuh took the office of vizier, or sultan, under the Fatimid caliph al-Adid in Cairo in 1169. Upon the death of Shirkuh, Saladin assumed his uncle's position. Within two years, he overthrew the caliph and became the ruler of Egypt. After two and a half centuries, Ismailism ceased to be the state religion, as Saladin returned Egypt to the Sunni fold. The fourteenth Fatimid caliph al-Adid died of illness soon after at the age of twenty-three. Upon the death of Nur al-Din in 1174, Saladin had himself crowned as the first king of the Ayyubid dynasty. He believed he was destined to be the leader of the jihad against the European infidel. A man of simple tastes, he died with barely enough money to pay for his funeral. Yet he routed the infidel, and his tomb in Damascus is to this day a pilgrimage site. Saladin was considered by friend and foe alike to possess the universally respected virtues of justice, courage, fairness, faithfulness, and piety. He never broke a treaty.

Nevertheless, the Muslims were far from unanimous in supporting Saladin's growing power. For example, in 1172, the Assassins under Sinan made a diplomatic overture to King Amalric. They were alarmed at the success of Saladin's political ambitions and the fervor of his support for Sunni orthodoxy. They proposed an alliance with Amalric against Saladin. Their sole condition was that Amalric lift an annual tribute of some two thousand gold pieces they had been paying to the Templars for two decades to guarantee Templar nonaggression.

Amalric promised the Templars he would make up for any financial loss they might suffer and sent the Assassin ambassador back to Sinan with his message. During his return journey, the ambassador was murdered by a Templar knight named Walter de Mesnil. The recently elevated Templar Grand Master was the fiery-tempered Odo de Saint-Amand. It is not known if Odo ordered the slaying, but he did support Walter. Amalric demanded Walter be turned over to him and tried. Odo refused, invoking the privileges extended to the Order by *Omne datum optimum*. Amalric, enraged, burst into the house where Walter was staying, arrested him, and threw him into prison. Walter henceforth disappeared from the historical record. The possibility of an alliance with the Assassins was lost.

The Templars came under an increasing barrage of criticism during this period as Saladin's victories mounted. In 1160, Pope Alexander III, a strong supporter of the Order, issued a bull forbidding people to pull Templars from their horses, obviously in response to anti-Templar sentiments. King Amalric intended to express his concerns about the growing power and arrogance of the Order to other Christian leaders; however, he died of an illness in 1174. In 1175, Pope Alexander III criticized the Order for the burial of excommunicated persons in Templar cemeteries. In 1179, the Third Lateran Council condemned the Templar abuse of the privileges granted by earlier popes. The ecclesiastic leaders demanded the return of all recently acquired churches and tithes, later defined to mean within ten years of the council. While these demands were never satisfied, they indicate a turn of emotion against the Order.

Saladin laid siege to Damascus in 1174, but the city was rescued with the assistance of the Franks. Yet nothing could prevent him from assuming the leadership of Islam. In 1177, he seized Ascalon with an army of twenty-six thousand men. Here, he received his most humiliating defeat from the combined forces of the Templars and Baldwin IV at Mont Gisard. His opportunity for revenge came shortly thereafter, however, when he took the castle of Le Chastellet near Jacob's Ford in 1180. The castle had just been completed the previous year. It was built to block one of Saladin's major military routes. His first attack against the castle failed, but he defeated the Christian army assembled against him at Marj Ayun. Odo de Saint-Amand was taken prisoner and died in a Damascene dungeon in 1181. Saladin sent sappers to dig underneath the outer walls of Le Chastellet in order to weaken the castle's foundation. When the walls collapsed, the Muslim army attacked. The Templars lost eighty knights and seven hundred fifty sergeants in the battle. Saladin captured seven hundred prisoners and dismantled the castle down to the last stone.

The death of the young Syrian king in 1182 finally allowed Saladin to assume the throne of Damascus. He had thus overcome the last element of fragmented Sunni power and was able to take the title "Sultan of Islam and the Muslims." The Crusaders now faced a united enemy, commanded by a single leader whose sole purpose was their eradication in the name of Allah.

Disunity among the Crusaders fed directly into Saladin's ambitions. For example, when he invaded Tripoli, the Templars possessed one castle in the area and the Hospitallers another. The orders had recently settled a dispute between themselves over territory. Each was so concerned about protecting its own property that the knights remained inside their castles as Saladin's army passed by. Count Raymond of Tripoli was unwilling to engage in a major battle alone against Saladin. Thus, while three separate Christian armies were in immediate proximity, Saladin's force was able to move unmolested through the area, setting fire to harvests, stealing cattle, and killing civilians.

One small, if pathetic, display of unified Frankish behavior occurred in 1184, when the Grand Masters of the Templars and Hospitallers accompanied the Patriarch of Jerusalem on a mission to Italy, France, and England to warn Europe of the dangers of Saladin and to plead for economic and military assistance.

A new crisis over succession to the throne of Jerusalem, however, was about to plunge Outremer into even worse conditions of factionalism, approaching civil war. King Baldwin IV suffered from what was believed to be leprosy. As he became weaker, he appointed his brother-in-law Guy de Lusignan to rule the kingdom and lead the army. Guy's authority was supported by the Templars and their new Grand Master, Gérard de Ridefort, as well as by other Crusaders. An opposing camp supported Baldwin's cousin, Count Raymond III of Tripoli. When Baldwin died in 1185 at the age of twenty-four, Raymond was chosen as regent for Baldwin's nephew and successor, Baldwin V. The boy king died at the age of ten, however, and Guy de Lusignan immediately seized the throne and proclaimed himself king of Jerusalem.

Saladin was able to take diplomatic and military advantage of the intractable inter-Christian hostilities. For example, the Byzantine emperor made a treaty with Saladin in 1185 in which he promised not to come to the assistance of the Europeans. Count Raymond was also driven into Muslim arms. Gérard de Ridefort had a long-standing personal hatred of Raymond. De Ridefort attempted to convince King Guy to attack Raymond and force him to accept Guy's claim to the throne. In response, Raymond made a treaty with Saladin in 1187 in which he promised to make Raymond "King of all the Franks."[2] While this could reasonably be perceived as treason, at least by King Guy, Raymond made no attempt to conceal his actions.

Guy sent a mission to Raymond to attempt to enlist him in a combined effort against Saladin's forthcoming attack. De Ridefort, one of Guy's ambassadors, originally intended the mission to be a military assault on Raymond. But Guy was dissuaded from this course by the other members of the group. As the men were traveling to meet Raymond, a scene was occurring that would soon lead to tragedy. Raymond, following the terms of his treaty with Saladin, had granted safe passage across his lands to a Muslim reconnaissance force of seven thousand soldiers led by Saladin's son, al-Afdal. The permission extended for twenty-four hours. Surrounding villages were alerted and the inhabitants told to remain safely within their dwellings.

When Guy's representatives arrived at Tripoli, de Ridefort learned of the Muslim reconnaissance mission and was determined to attack al-Afdal's army. He made this decision despite the fact that the combined Christian force numbered only some 140 knights, including 90 Templars. The objections of the other leaders to this foolhardy and ill-planned effort served only to fuel Gérard's determination. He prevailed, and on May 1, 1187, the Templars lost 87 knights, including the third-ranking Marshal of the Temple. Gérard himself escaped but was badly wounded, and the Master of the Hospitallers was killed.[†]

---

[†] Gérard's hotheadedness was not incompatible with Bernard's rhapsodizing on Templar courage in De laude: "They rush in to attack the adversaries, considering them like sheep. No matter how outnumbered they do not consider the savage barbarians as formidable multitudes. Not that they are secure in their own abilities, but they trust in the virtue of the Lord Sabaoth to bring them to victory. . . . We have seen one man in hot pursuit put a thousand to flight and two drive away ten thousand." This was pointed out by Malcolm Barber in The New Knighthood, p. 181. For a translation of De laude, see appendix 2.

This catastrophe further exacerbated the hatred between Gérard and Raymond. On the other hand, Raymond voluntarily submitted himself to Guy in guilty acknowledgment of the disastrous consequences of his treaty with Saladin. The Muslims were encouraged by their bloody victory and prepared for a full-scale attack on the kingdom of Jerusalem.

The decisive Battle of Hattin occurred just over a month later. (The plain of Hattin is located approximately sixty-five miles north of Jerusalem and twenty miles east of Acre.) Saladin had amassed an army of twelve thousand knights against King Guy's force of twelve hundred knights and about fifteen thousand foot soldiers and light cavalry. The animosity between Raymond and Gérard was again to result in disaster for the Christians.

Gérard prevailed on Guy to attack Saladin despite Raymond's objection. Raymond insisted the army should remain where it was, despite the fact that his wife was trapped at Tiberias, where she had been defending their castle. Raymond knew the summer heat could be used to Frankish advantage if they would simply outwait Saladin and allow his troops to be weakened by the oppressive weather. Most of the men present agreed that Raymond was right. Gérard, however, railed impetuously against this view. He called Raymond a traitor because of his unwillingness to break the treaty with Saladin weeks earlier. He mocked Raymond's attitude toward his wife's predicament and called him a coward. He claimed the Templars would be forced to put aside their white mantles and pawn their possessions in shame if they failed to avenge their recent defeat at Saladin's hands. Guy sided with Gérard.

The Christian army therefore left its campsite, a well-watered meadow, to march through a fierce desert. Saladin's army had made camp in another meadow near the Horns of Hattin. On July 4, 1187, the Christian army was decimated. Although the Templars fought valiantly, Saladin took full advantage of the weakness of the strategic position of the Franks. Thousands were killed. Thousands more were captured. The Muslims took the royal tent and the True Cross. Some two hundred surviving Templar and Hospitaller knights were beheaded. (While it was the medieval practice to ransom captives, Saladin made exceptions of the military orders because of their warlike nature and threat to Islam.) Two hundred thirty Templars died at Hattin, either in battle or by execution. Gérard de Ridefort lived but was imprisoned along with King Guy and a group of barons to be ransomed.

The entire Palestinian region had been left unguarded by the general Christian mobilization in preparation for the Battle of Hattin; few troops remained in place to defend their positions. Within two months, Saladin took Acre, Nablus, Jaffa, Toron, Sidon, Beirut, and Ascalon. He laid a twelve-day siege against Jerusalem, which fell to the Muslim army on October 2, 1187. Saladin immediately ordered the city cleansed of the hated Christian presence. He had the great cross removed from the Dome of the Rock. The cross was paraded through the streets for two days while it was beaten with sticks. This was the prelude to purifying the mosques with rosewater and restoring them to their pristine condition. Yet Saladin also demonstrated his legendary chivalry by freeing the twenty thousand Christian civilians who had survived the siege. Seven thousand were ransomed with money taken from the treasuries of the military orders; the balance were simply set free. Native Christians were allowed to remain in the city. Ten Hospitaller brothers were permitted to stay in the Order's house, where they could treat the sick for one year.

During the next year Saladin continued his victorious war against the Christian armies. In a two-year campaign, he had reclaimed the Holy Land for Islam. The military orders had been crushed. The remaining Christian territory was reduced to areas along the Mediterranean coast, including the cities of Tyre and Tripoli, a castle at Beaufort, and a few other scattered castles. Saladin allowed Bohemond, former ruler of the principality of Antioch, to retain the city of Antioch and one castle.

# CHAPTER SEVENTEEN

# THE THIRD CRUSADE

The defeat at Hattin and the subsequent territorial losses were a defining experience for the Frankish community as they entered the last decade of the twelfth century. The Palestinian Templars were broken men. Their Grand Master remained in Saladin's prison; their numbers were severely reduced; they had lost the respect of others; their pride was shattered.

In Europe, Pope Gregory VIII sent emissaries to all European kings to enlist support for a Third Crusade. His call was enthusiastically received. First to respond was the Holy Roman Emperor Frederick Barbarossa, who left Europe with an army of one hundred thousand men in 1189. After a series of difficulties on the journey, he died by drowning in Armenia, and his army disintegrated. Meanwhile, Kings Philip Augustus of France and Richard I of England prepared for their departures.

A number of European nobles arrived in the Holy Land during the summer of 1189. Many were crammed together within the walls of Tyre where they quarreled among themselves. They were divided between those loyal to King Guy, which included the Templars, and those who supported his rival, the newly arrived Conrad of Montferrat. Guy's power base had been weakened by his imprisonment and bad judgment in listening to Gérard de Ridefort. He had been ransomed from Saladin's prison in July 1188. Conrad, a powerful German marquis, had arrived in Outremer to fulfill his crusading vow in 1188. The fortuitous timing of his arrival, combined with his military prowess, saved Tyre from Muslim conquest. The majority of barons in the city supported him as their natural leader. He established a legitimate claim to the throne of Jerusalem by marrying Isabel, daughter of Amalric.

The conflict with Conrad led Guy and his Templar supporters to a decision to attack the Muslim-controlled city of Acre so that Guy might have a territory in which to exert his full authority. They began the siege in August 1189. Saladin came to the defense of Acre and the Franks attacked him. Saladin defeated the attack. Among the thousands of casualties was Gérard de Ridefort. He had recently managed to ransom himself by ordering the Templars to surrender their castle at

Gaza. The strategic loss of this "doorway" from Egypt to Palestine must have seemed to many a high price to pay for Gérard's life.

The main force of the Christian army was able to continue the siege of Acre despite the lost battle. They would remain there for two years. In the meantime, King Richard had set out from England, and King Philip sailed from France. They traveled by separate routes. Richard attacked Cyprus on the way and took possession of the island. He continued his journey, reaching Acre on June 8, 1191. Philip Augustus had just arrived. The two monarchs assisted the wearied army in taking the city on July 12, 1191. Richard ordered the slaughter of his Muslim prisoners during the final battle. In sight of Saladin, his men slew twenty-seven hundred prisoners. Richard's reasons for this uncharacteristic brutality are unclear.

Philip Augustus, largely uninterested in crusading, left for Europe within three weeks of the victory at Acre. King Richard remained. His subsequent activities in the Holy Land gradually helped rebuild the Templar reputation and self-image. Richard decided to sell Cyprus and offered favorable terms to his friend Robert de Sablé, the new Templar Grand Master. Templar ownership of the island would prove an unfortunate experience. They were forced to put down an armed rebellion engendered by their mistreatment of the population and disposed of the island within the year.

In September 1191, with Templar tactical advice to guide him, Richard defeated Saladin at Arsuf in a brilliantly executed battle strategy. He thereby demonstrated to Christian and Muslim alike that Saladin was not invincible. Shortly after this battle, Richard offered his daughter in marriage to al-Adil, Saladin's brother, in an attempt to create a treaty with Saladin. Richard proposed they co-rule Jerusalem and that Saladin return some properties taken from the military orders. Saladin refused the offer. Richard spent a year battling fiercely against him. Richard's army arrived within sight of Jerusalem, but they sadly turned back without reclaiming it for Christendom. Richard was persuaded by the wisdom of the Templars, Hospitallers, and native barons of the futility of conquering the isolated city. He understood that Jerusalem would be impossible to defend once he and his army returned to Europe. Instead the Franks decided to rebuild Ascalon as a barrier against the free passage of Saladin's armies from Egypt, which helped to compensate for the loss of Gaza.

Richard, meanwhile, was receiving regular reports from England of the treachery of his brother John, who was attempting to take advantage of his absence to seize the throne. Richard was forced to prepare for his return. He therefore inserted himself deeply into the politics of the region. Some historians suggest he may have contracted with the Assassins to slay Conrad of Montferrat.[1] (Other possibilities were discussed in part 2.) Whether Richard was a party to Conrad's death or not, he arranged for his nephew Henry, count of Champagne, to marry Conrad's widow Isabel within days of Conrad's death, and thus to supplant Guy de Lusignan as king of Jerusalem. Henry was also the nephew of Philip of France, so he was an ideal choice to encourage continued European allegiance to the needs of Outremer.

In September 1192, after several more battles, Richard succeeded in signing a five-year peace treaty with Saladin. The treaty returned cities south of Jaffa to Christian control and opened a safe passage to pilgrims visiting Jerusalem. The Templars sold Cyprus to Guy de Lusignan, which conveniently removed him from the region and that troublesome piece of real estate from their concerns. After a two-year crusade, Richard set off for England in October 1192 disguised as a Templar. Thus began an arduous and adventure-filled two-year journey during which he was captured, imprisoned, and ransomed by the German emperor Henry VI before returning to England.

Saladin died in 1193, a particularly welcome event for Crusaders. Islam fragmented once again, Saladin's hopes for the leadership of his own Ayyubid dynasty notwithstanding. Outremer had managed to survive to enter the new century. The Franks were able quietly to rebuild while the attention of both Islam and Europe was focused elsewhere. The Templars had experienced a renewal through their contact with the legendary King Richard the Lionhearted.

# CHAPTER EIGHTEEN

# The Fourth Crusade

The accession of Pope Innocent III in 1198 was another source of good fortune for the Templars. He was a powerful and influential leader who would reign for eighteen years. He maintained an iron will toward establishing the Church as the supreme ruler of a theocratic feudal hierarchy, in which all Christian kings would willingly submit themselves to the authority of the pope. Innocent lavished his protection on the Templars, pointedly reminding the clergy of exemptions and special privileges in matters of financial and religious independence awarded the Order in the past. Yet, he ruled the Templars with an equally firm hand, upbraiding them in a letter in 1207 for their pride and greed and for abusing the grants with which they had been endowed. He criticized the practice of granting membership and burial privileges to excommunicated nobles in return for money. He bade them reform themselves. The Knights Templar became Innocent's personal army, the militia of Christ, by which the pope would enforce his will and attain his goals. Among these goals was the liberation of Jerusalem and the elimination of Catharism in Europe.

In 1202, Innocent preached a Fourth Crusade whose glory would equal that of the first. Egypt would be the initial target. Innocent hoped to avoid what he perceived to be the mistakes of the Second Crusade, when the multinational forces experienced crippling language barriers and the rivalry between proud kings doomed the efforts of Christendom. The army of the Fourth Crusade was led by various nobles deemed loyal to Innocent, of whom Boniface of Montferrat, brother of Conrad, was the overall leader. The Templars helped fund the European armies as they assembled and began to travel east. Upon the Crusaders' arrival in Egypt, the plan called for the Palestinian Templars to meet and reinforce them, forming a united and powerful Christian force. However, this was not to be.

Merchants of the city of Venice had been enlisted to provide the required ships and passage arrangements for the army as well as a year's supply of food. The Crusaders were not aware that the Venetians had made a simultaneous trade agreement with the sultan of Egypt, promising him that no European army would land in Egyptian territory. The Venetians demanded of the Crusaders a price for their services that exceeded the available resources of the leaders of the nearly thirty thousand assembled troops. Then the Venetians proposed a deal. If the Crusaders would capture the Dalmatian port of Zara for Venice, the Venetians would extend credit to them for the balance owed. Although Zara was a Christian city, the Crusaders agreed, and within five days delivered the city to the Venetians. Innocent was mortified at the shedding of Christian blood and excommunicated both the entire city of Venice and the crusading army. Soon after, realizing the army had been manipulated, he lifted their excommunication.

Next, the Venetian leader Enrico Dandelo — who maintained a long-standing grudge against Constantinople — suggested the conquest of that city as a detour of opportunity for the Crusaders. They could stamp out the Byzantine heresy and unite all Christendom under the pope; they could avenge the Byzantine treachery of the Second Crusade; and they could avail themselves of the legendary wealth of Constantinople to pay their Venetian debt. The Crusader leaders agreed and attacked Constantinople in 1204. Wholesale looting and pillage followed, inevitably accompanied by drunkenness, sacrilege, murder, and rape. Thousands were killed. Innocent's dream of a united Christianity was destroyed. The Fourth Crusade extinguished itself without ever reaching the infidel. The Latin kingdom the Fourth Crusade established in Constantinople fell back into Greek hands within sixty years.

The opening of new campaign fronts in the Byzantine Empire and Cyprus was welcomed by many as a new arena for European knights. Now, one who sought the glory and opportunities for wealth and expiation afforded by battle — but who shunned the difficulties of travel to the distant and alien culture of Palestine — had his burden considerably reduced. As a result, since the beginning of the thirteenth century, the military orders composed the virtually exclusive European military presence in the Holy Land.

# CHAPTER NINETEEN

# The Cathars and the Albigensian Crusade

I nnocent's disappointment and horror at the sack of Constantinople may have contributed to the fervor with which he pursued his next major military objective, the Albigensian Crusade. Beginning in 1209, this bloody war against heresy lasted for twenty years, ultimately evolving into the Inquisition. Its victims were the peaceful Cathars of the Languedoc region of France, whose primary center of activity was near the city of Albi. The Cathars were dualist Christians whose antipapist reformist teachings enraged the Church hierarchy. Throughout the Dark Ages, Europe had remained relatively unconcerned with heresy. The Donatist, Arian, and other doctrinal variants mentioned earlier had largely been defeated. By the sixth century, material conditions would become too harsh to allow for much focus on philosophy during the next four or five centuries. In the eleventh century, however, Manichaean dualism rose again to challenge the exclusive religious hegemony of the Church.

Augustine, the fourth-century theologian who founded the first Christian monastic order in 388, had been a member of a Manichaean sect for nine years prior to his conversion. He is responsible for introducing the accusation that licentious sexual practices took place among the Manichaean elect, who, he said, consumed a eucharist of which human sperm was an ingredient. In the early years of the eleventh century, the soon-to-be common tale emerged of a heretical group who chanted demonic names until the evil spirit entered the room. The heretics then extinguished the lights and engaged in an indiscriminate orgy. The ashes of a baby conceived during such an orgy were mixed with excrement and consumed as a eucharist of Hell by the demoniacs. According to historian Malcolm Lambert, the name *Cathar* (often attributed to Greek or Latin roots meaning "cleansing" or "pure") probably comes from the word *cat*.[1] Twelfth-century enemies of the Cathars believed their rites included ritually kissing the anus of a cat, in which form Lucifer was said to appear. Toward the end of the twelfth-century, the Cathars were also slandered by the term *bougre*, from "Bulgaria," known to be the source of their heresy. Later the word came to mean "sodomite" and is the root of the British slang *bugger* and *buggery*.

As late as 1233, the Roman Catholic Church offered its decisive definition of the Cathar heresy when Pope Gregory IX issued his bull *Vox in Rama*. Here he denounced Cathar worship of Satan and purported to describe their beliefs and practices. He stated that Cathars believed God had erred in casting out Lucifer from Heaven and that Lucifer would return in triumph to reward his faithful. He described the course of an initiation ceremony into the sect: First, a monstrous toad appeared to the Cathar novice. This was followed by the appearance of an ice-cold pale man. When the novice kissed the pale man, all traces of the Christian faith would depart from his heart. After a banquet celebrating the reception of the new member, a black cat appeared. All those attending the initiation festivities offered it the anal kiss. Finally the lights were extinguished, signaling the beginning of an orgy that included homosexual congress. The intensity of Gregory's accusations was matched only by the apparent sincerity of his belief in the charges — and the suffering that awaited those against whom his charges were leveled.

Medieval European dualists were certainly not Manichaeans in the sense of an unbroken tradition dating back to the third-century Persian Mani. In reality, the eleventh-century heresies were isolated and independent of each other. While they shared certain features in common — most notably dualism, anticlericalism, asceticism, antimaterialism, idealism, iconoclasm, and revulsion at ecclesiastic corruption — there was no united ideology such as would later emerge among the Cathars. The first record of the Cathars comes from Germany in the mid–twelfth century. "[T]he heresy was an ideology, with a body of belief and practice, potentially supra-national, impersonal, exceeding in durability the individual, idiosyncratic teachings of this or that charismatic personality, which had hitherto formed the stuff of the heretical episodes recorded by Western chroniclers."[2]

The Cathars were mystical Christians who believed in the direct, personal experience of God as the basis of all spiritual progress. Their origins trace back to the tenth-century Bulgarian dualist Bogomils, who disputed with the Byzantine Church. Both groups had much in common with the Christian Manichaeans of the fourth century. Most Cathars were moderate dualists — in other words, they believed that God was stronger than Satan, that God had allowed Satan to create the world, and in the end would crush all works of evil. On the other hand, it is easy to see how a radical dualist — one who perceived evil as an exactly co-equal force — could tend toward the type of Satanic worship of which many moderate dualists were falsely accused.

Cathars taught that Satan or Lucifer created mankind from clay, and that the God of the Old Testament was in fact Satan. They therefore rejected the Old Testament. They believed the human soul was a fallen angel trapped in a material body, while the true spiritual body remained in Heaven. Through gnosis, or knowledge, the soul could be united with spirit. Without gnosis, the soul would be condemned to migrate to another body in an endless succession of agonizing rounds of material imprisonment.

Cathars believed that matter was intrinsically evil and incapable of redemption. The first woman was tempted to commit the sexual act and thereby the soul was lost; sexual intercourse was the greatest sin because it perpetuated material evil. They rejected all belief in Hell or Purgatory; imprisonment within a physical body was punishment enough. They viewed Jesus as an emanation, or an angel, sent by God out of pity for fallen humanity to teach man the means of escape. Jesus was a part of God — neither God Himself nor man. His body was a projected illusion; pure spirit would have no contact with impure matter. Christ neither suffered nor died on the cross. The cross was an evil symbol of materiality to be despised, not venerated. The concept of Christ's physical resurrection was rejected. The Roman Church was built on the false worship of the creator God, in fact, of Satan. The Mass was rejected as a ritualized worship of matter.

The Cathar elect, the "Perfect," followed the true message of Christ — to reduce one's contact with the material world. They rejected the Church with all its hierarchy. Cathar initiates wandered throughout southern France as simple ascetics. They embraced a strict vegetarian diet, intensive fasting, and a life of poverty. Women had full clerical equality, although the diocesan hierarchy was all male. The oath of the Perfect, known as the consolamentum — the baptism of fire or of the spirit, the superior baptism promised in the New Testament — was ritually administered. A copy of the New Testament was placed on the candidate's head so that its message could infuse the psyche, while the initiator recited invocations and adorations of the Holy Spirit, directly transmitted to the candidate through the laying on of hands. The "kiss of peace" was exchanged among the Perfect administering the ritual and any simple Cathar believers present.[3]

The Catholic baptism of water mimicked the lower baptism of John the Baptist, who himself stated it was inferior to the baptism of fire: "I indeed baptize you with water unto repentance: but he that cometh after me is mightier than I, whose shoes I am not worthy to bear: he shall baptize you with the Holy Ghost, and with fire."[4] The fact that Catholic baptism was performed on an infant without free choice rendered it meaningless. Worse, it was a link to Satan through the corrupt church. Cathar teachings were based solely on their interpretation of the New Testament. They traced their lineage to the Eastern churches mentioned in the Acts of the Apostles and in the Apocalypse.

The Perfect participated in a monthly rite of collective confession, known as the *apparellamentum*, before Cathar deacons or bishops who traveled throughout Cathar territories to administer this sacrament. The spiritual renewal and purification offered to the Perfect by the ceremony also provided the opportunity for the Cathar hierarchy to collect information on the state of various territories. The Cathar episcopate was responsible for the formal training of the Perfect in missionary and liturgical work.

The Perfect, or "Good Men," were materially sustained by the rank-and-file Cathar believers, those who hesitated to embrace the rigorous lifestyle to which the Perfect were bound. The Perfect were held in the highest esteem by Cathar believers, much as are Catholic saints. The *medioramentum* was an act of ritual adoration of the Perfect made by believers. Under the Cathar doctrine, those unwilling to undertake the oath of the Perfect were in the thrall of Satan. Prayers were therefore ineffective unless rendered by the Perfect.

Many Cathars took the *consolamentum* on their deathbeds, thus avoiding the danger of breaking their vows. In the final years of the fourteenth century when Catharism was all but wiped out, the practice of *endura* became increasingly common. This involved suicide by starvation by one who had just taken the *consolamentum* and who was determined not to prolong the possibility of failure to live up to its rigorous demands nor to be captured and forced to renounce by the authorities.

Prior to the persecutions, the sect spread easily through Germany, southern France, and northern Italy. The Muslim presence in the Languedoc in the first half of the eighth century may have had something to do with the region's traditional religious tolerance and relaxed sexual mores. The simple and pious Cathars were perceived by their neighbors as motivated by spiritual concerns alone — no tithing, demands for material possessions, or political power accompanied their gentle faith. No churches were required. The apparent ethical superiority of the Cathar movement presented a very real threat to the

Church. Cathar support has been estimated at ten to twelve percent of the population of Albi.[5] A number of noble families of the Languedoc were Cathar supporters, further encouraging the growth of the sect among their dependents, either by active support of Cathar preaching efforts or passive acquiescence in the spread of the heresy.

Certain aspects of Cathar belief worked against the growth of the sect. They rejected marriage as perpetuating the reign of Satan. So violent were their feelings that they sometimes mocked pregnant women as carrying demons in their bellies and declared women who died pregnant incapable of salvation. They rejected the eating of food produced by sexual means, although they ate fish, which they believed reproduced asexually. The Perfect were enjoined to strict celibacy. The antisexual, antifamily teachings of the Cathars eventually contributed to their decline, as they were unable to replenish their membership by the most natural means available. Another article of faith that worked against their growth was their uncompromising rejection of materialism. Cathar belief offered scant comfort to the poor, who were not attracted to a movement that remained unconcerned with bettering either their poverty or social status. Finally, a tinge of hypocrisy colored Cathar behavior during the persecutions. The strict oaths against the shedding of blood by the Perfect forced them to rely on the theoretically less pure Cathar faithful for defense against the military assaults of their enemies.

The efforts of the Church to counter the heretics had grown increasingly well organized since the preaching campaign in the Languedoc by Bernard in 1145 (he also suspected Cathars of libertinage) and the sporadic burnings by local bishops, priests, and even vigilante townsfolk terrorized by the threat of demonic alliance. In 1206, two Castilian clergymen, Bishop Diego of Osma and his subprior, the canon Dominic de Guzman, volunteered to undertake a preaching campaign modeled on vows of poverty and simplicity like the campaigns of the first- and second-century apostles. They argued and debated with the heretics and traveled widely throughout the land. In 1207, Diego returned to Spain, while Dominic continued with his efforts. He later became the founder of the Dominican Order.

In 1208, the murder of a papal legate by an officer of the pro-Cathar nobleman Count Raymond VI of Toulouse so angered Innocent that he demanded a crusade against the Cathars, offering indulgences to those who committed to at least forty days of military service. This crusade was an attractive proposition when compared to the rigors demanded by military service in the Holy Land. Travel was effortless. Forty days was an extremely modest commitment for the remission of sins. Killing defenseless heretics seemed far less dangerous than fighting Arab warriors. Finally, the pope suggested that the property of landowners who supported and protected the heretics might be seized, and the Languedoc was known to be filled with appreciable wealth.

Southern France was particularly susceptible to the political tensions caused by the declining power of feudal nobles and the corresponding increase in the power of the Capetian king, complicated by the ambitions of the indigenous clergy and the pope. The northern invasion of the Languedoc broke the power of the local southern nobility and paved the way for the extension of Capetian rule over this heretofore independent region.

Following the culmination of two decades of active military aggression, the Inquisition was officially born in the year 1233. "It cannot be repeated too often that the Albigensian Crusades did not wipe out heresy. They killed some of the 'perfect'; they ruined many of the protectors of the Cathars and so they prepared the way for the really effective attack on heresy — the Inquisition."[6] Gregory IX assigned the task of pursuing heresy to the Dominicans, granting them full power to make judgments, assigning them to work in specific dioceses of southern France, and appointing a special papal legate responsible for heresy to assist in their efforts.

Death was considered the proper remedy for heretics in order to root out the powers of the devil and his demonic spawn, and thereby protect the larger Christian community from the spiritual treason of the minority. An increasingly sophisticated alliance between church and state imitated the earlier Roman persecutions. Accusations of heresy rapidly became a convenient and effective smear against enemies. The flames of the Inquisition and the sword of intolerance would rage through southern France against the Cathars for over one hundred years. The last Cathar community of Perfect at the mountain stronghold of Montségur fell to renewed military campaigns in 1244. By 1325, Catharism seems to have been completely stamped out as a recognizable religious form.[†]

---

[†] A highly recommended study of European Christian heretical sects from the eleventh through sixteenth centuries is Norman Cohn, *The Pursuit of the Millenium* 3rd ed. (New York: Oxford University Press, 1970).

Participation in the Albigensian Crusades was one of the most shameful activities of the Templars. It proved to be a dress rehearsal for their own destruction. Though rationalization may make nearly anything palatable, the Templars lent their efforts to the wholesale extermination of Christians. Although they acted at the behest of Innocent III, their actions thoroughly violated the very principles upon which their Order was founded. This medieval anticult pogrom was the occasion for the legendary reply of the papal legate, Arnaud Amaury, to soldiers concerned about distinguishing between Cathars and Catholics, "Kill them all, God will know his own." Although the literal occurrence of this statement has been disputed by numerous historians, the learned Amaury may actually have been quoting from two biblical verses: the first a letter from Paul to Timothy, "The Lord knoweth them that are his," in which Paul makes reference to a statement by Moses on the eve of battle, "Even tomorrow the Lord will shew who are his, and who is holy; and will cause him to come nearer unto him; even him whom he hath chosen will he cause to come near unto him."[7]

CHAPTER TWENTY

# THE FIFTH CRUSADE

I nnocent was followed by Pope Honorius III, who continued to show-
er the Templars with his support for the next eleven years. Events in
the Holy Land left numerous opportunities for diplomatic maneuvers by
the Order to consolidate its power and forge alliances to help rebuild
itself. Templars looked after their own interests and developed their
remaining holdings into self-sufficient feudal communities. Castles were
reinforced in keeping with the lessons of siege. The skill with which
Saladin's sappers had been able to undermine castle walls was not forgotten. Castle Pilgrim at Atlit, between Jaffa and Haifa, marked the
ultimate in medieval castle design. Construction began under the
Templar Grand Master William of Chartres in 1217. Built on a promon-
tory, the castle was surrounded on three sides by the sea and could hold
out indefinitely against land-bound armies. It was never taken by an
enemy.[†]

The Fifth Crusade began in 1217. It was a chaotic multinational
task force composed of volunteers from Cyprus, Hungary, Italy, France,
England, Holland, and Austria. The Crusaders attempted to take the
Egyptian city of Damietta, hoping that a strategic victory against the
Ayyubid sultan al-Kamil would allow them to successfully continue on
to Jerusalem. The overall commander of this crusade was a papal legate,
a Spanish cardinal named Pelagius. His inept handling of tactical matters allowed the Christians to virtually snatch defeat from the jaws of
victory. The underlying assumption defining the strategy pursued by
Pelagius and Pope Honorius was the late Pope Innocent's interpretation of Muhammad as the Great Beast prophesied in Revelation, whose
evil empire would fall of its own accord. Thus the counsel of the Templars, the Hospitallers, and any other qualified military leaders could be
ignored in favor of religious prejudice.

Francis of Assisi visited al-Kamil at Cairo during the siege of Damietta. Through Francis, the sultan offered the Christians a truce. If they
would leave Egypt, he would return the True Cross (taken by Saladin at
Hattin) and give them the area around Galilee and the whole of cen-

---

[†]Although most of Castle Pilgrim was dismantled by the Mamelukes, Atlit today
serves as an Israeli naval base.

tral Palestine, including Jerusalem. Pelagius refused, believing it was sinful to negotiate with the infidel. The more sophisticated military leaders knew that Jerusalem would be in a strategically indefensible position because the sultan insisted on keeping two castles that could be used for future Islamic attacks. They also reasoned that the sultan must be weaker than they had estimated if he was willing to offer such favorable terms. They attacked Damietta with renewed enthusiasm and the city fell in November 1219, upon which they learned that it had been ravaged by plague.

Templar Grand Master William of Chartres had died that summer of complications from wounds. He was succeeded by Pedro de Montaigu, whose leadership inspired morale and confidence among the Templars. Pelagius, meanwhile, held the army within a twenty-mile radius of Damietta for the next two years, to the increasing disgust of the military leaders. Since the Templars were bound by their strict allegiance to the pope, they were forbidden to disobey his direct representative no matter how incompetent he might have been.

Finally, motivated perhaps by the anger and impatience of his allied forces, Pelagius ordered the assault force of over six hundred ships and nearly fifty thousand troops on toward Cairo in July 1221. He could not have chosen a worse moment, as the annual inundation of the Nile was due. After a twelve-day march, the Frankish armies came to a plain from which vantage point they were able to see the Muslim army that had surrounded them undetected throughout their march. The Crusaders attempted to retreat only to have the Muslims open the Nile flood gates, nearly wiping them out. The Fifth Crusade ended in complete disaster. While al-Kamil generously offered to return the True Cross as part of the truce ending the Crusade, it was apparently of so little value to Islam that it had been misplaced over the decades. The Sultan ordered a careful search but it was never recovered.[†]

---

[†] Malcolm Barber, on the other hand, says it was returned. See *The New Knighthood*, p. 130.

# CHAPTER TWENTY-ONE

# The Sixth Crusade
## and the Battle of La Forbie

The Sixth Crusade was led by Frederick II in 1228. Frederick was an intriguing and exotic personality who spoke six languages fluently, including Arabic. He was liked and respected by the Muslims. He enjoyed long-standing friendships with various members of Islamic royalty, kept a harem in Sicily, and was schooled in Arabic philosophy and mathematics. He had little interest in Christianity, although as a child he had been the pupil of Pope Honorius III, who maintained a lifelong affection for Frederick despite their differences. Frederick was known to his contemporaries as Stupor Mundi, the "Marvel of the World." Crowned king of Germany by Innocent in 1215, he immediately announced his intention to go on a crusade. This commitment seems to have been part of a strategy to retain papal favor while consolidating his rule in the Lombard region. In 1220, he was crowned Holy Roman Emperor by Pope Honorius without yet having troubled himself with crusading. In 1225, he was married to the daughter and heiress of John of Brienne, king of Jerusalem. John apparently assumed the marriage would encourage Frederick finally to begin his crusade. Still he delayed.

In 1227, Honorius died. He was succeeded by Gregory IX, who immediately ordered Frederick to fulfill his promise to begin the crusade. When Frederick quickly returned, claiming illness, Gregory did not believe him. He excommunicated Frederick both for his premature return and his military efforts against the Templars and other loyal Catholics in the short time he was away.

Frederick set off again in June 1228, this time presenting the slightly absurd picture of an excommunicated king leading a crusade while the pope sent an army against him in Sicily. Frederick's resolve to fight a crusade for two years was initially received with enthusiasm by the Templars and Hospitallers. Yet soon after his arrival in Acre, a letter from the pope ordered the Templars to play no part in Frederick's effort because of his excommunication. The pope soon sent another letter to the Templars announcing that he had just excommunicated Frederick a second time. It was forbidden for an excommunicate to take part in a crusade.

Although the Templars were bound by their vows of obedience to follow the pope's orders, they understood that any changes Frederick might effect in the balance of power with the Muslims would carry great consequences. Therefore they felt they needed full knowledge of his moves, and in the event of any military or territorial gains, they wanted to be included. Thus they decided on a compromise: they rode one day's journey *behind* Frederick so they could not be accused of marching *with* him. Later they marched alongside him. The terms of this arrangement were that Frederick would stipulate that his orders were being given in the name of God, rather than in his own name, that of an excommunicated emperor!

In February 1229, Frederick negotiated a ten-year treaty with al-Kamil for the return of Jerusalem and a corridor of land leading to the Mediterranean. In addition, the sultan agreed to the return of Nazareth, western Galilee, and the lands around Sidon and Bethlehem. In March 1229, Frederick crowned himself king of Jerusalem. The very next day, the archbishop of Caesarea excommunicated the entire city of Jerusalem for harboring the excommunicate emperor.

Although Frederick negotiated his treaty in the name of all Franks, he never received their permission to do so. The Templars were angry that the site of their original Temple would remain in Muslim hands. The treaty also forbade the military orders from making improvements on a number of their most important castles. The holy war against the infidel was the raison d'être of the military orders, and Frederick had just undermined it. Feelings were so strained between him and the Templars that he feared for his life and left Jerusalem after only a two-day stay.

Jerusalem had been placed in a strategically unsound position by Frederick's treaty, particularly for those less able than he to exercise diplomatic finesse with the Muslims. The Templars joined in a plan with the Patriarch of Jerusalem to take back Jerusalem in the name of the pope. Although they quickly reconsidered and withdrew from the plan, Frederick learned of their activities. He called them traitors, expelled them from Acre, and disarmed them to the extent that he was able. He helped strengthen the strategic position of the newly arrived Teutonic Knights, a German military order founded in 1198, and patterned after the Templars.

The pope, meanwhile, had undertaken a crusade against Frederick in Italy. The Templars attempted to persuade Sultan al-Kamil to turn against Frederick. Furious, Frederick attacked Acre and attempted to take Castle Pilgrim at Atlit, which survived his assault because of the superiority of its design. Finally, on May 1, 1229, the pressures to protect his kingdom from the pope forced Frederick to return to Europe. He continued his campaign against the military orders in Sicily, confiscated property belonging to the Templars and Hospitallers, and managed to regain the territory that had been lost in his absence.

The situation of the Templars improved in Outremer during the decade that Frederick's truce was in effect. The Order received further grants of castles and lands. The success of their European wealth-building and recruitment efforts allowed them to undertake the defense and management of Latin interests in Syria. They began to involve themselves again in the shipping and protection of pilgrims and merchandise traveling from Europe. Skirmishes with the Muslims replaced major campaigns. The truce ended in 1239, and the Muslims retook Jerusalem, exactly as the Templars had predicted.

While the various treaties of the post-Hattin period had been of considerable help in rebuilding European strength, internal divisiveness among the Franks seemed to be working equally hard to undermine it. Widespread charges of abuse of power were made against the Templars. They were accused of contributing to the loss of cities and castles and weakening commerce because of their feuding with other military orders and the Italian merchant corporations. Violent confrontations between the military orders sparked by rivalry and jealously frequently erupted in bloodshed.

In 1240, the Templars successfully negotiated with the Ayyubid sultan of Damascus for possession of the castle of Safed in Galilee in return for an alliance with him against his rival, the Ayyubid sultan of Cairo. Safed was a powerful strategic prize, and the Hospitallers were jealous of the Templar gain. Allied with Richard of Cornwall, brother-in-law of Frederick II, the Hospitallers negotiated a treaty with the sultan of Cairo that, although it included the return of Jerusalem, was otherwise hostile to Templar interests. Later that year in Acre, fighting broke out between the Templars and Teutonic Knights and grew so violent that the Templars burned a church belonging to the Teutonic Knights. In 1242, a virtual civil war between Templars and Hospitallers led to battles in the streets between rival order members throughout Outremer. The Templars laid formal siege to the Hospitaller compound at Acre.

Juxtaposed with conflicts between the military orders were conflicts between the various political powers. The interests of the pope and the allied Capetian dynasty were often in overt conflict with those of the Hohenstaufen dynasty under Frederick. The Palestinian baronage represented another source of disharmony. The barons had been established for a century and a half, and from their point of view, their political priorities were mature. Finally, the merchants of Venice, Genoa, Pisa, and Barcelona were engaged in corporate rivalry with each other, and they frequently aligned themselves severally with rival political or military interests.

The Ayyubid dynasty itself was in a virtual civil war between Egypt and Syria, with smaller sultanates variously allied with the larger combatants. Alliances were frequently proposed to the Franks by the conflicting Muslim powers. This had the net result of further exacerbating conflicts among the already disunited Christians. Gregory IX was attempting to launch a new crusade in Europe. A few nobles, such as Count Theobald of Champagne, responded to his call and made exploratory journeys to the Holy Land. These potential Crusaders walked into a situation so complex that it eliminated any preconceptions they may have entertained about a simple conflict between Christian and infidel.

Then the Khwarazmian Turks made their appearance. The great Mongol leader Genghis Khan had been extending his empire westward by the fearsome power of the Mongol sword. The Khan's armies had succeeded in driving the Khwarazmian Turks into exile, turning them into a roving mercenary band. They were hired by the sultan of Cairo to storm Jerusalem, which they conquered in July 1244. Only three hundred residents escaped the slaughter and pillage. So terrible was the Khwarazmian threat that the Templars and Hospitallers laid aside their differences. They cooperated with the baronage to raise a united Frankish force, which was joined by the army of the sultan of Damascus.

On October 17, 1244, the Khwarazmian Turks and the armies of the sultan of Cairo faced the assembled Templars, Hospitallers, Palestinian baronage, and the armies of the sultan of Damascus at La Forbie near Gaza. The Christian-Damascene army suffered terrible losses. Grand Master Armand de Peragors was blinded and taken prisoner. The post-Hattin Christian gains of the last half century were virtually wiped out. Back in Europe, Frederick II blamed the Templars for not supporting his alliance with the Egyptians. He accused them of treason for their support of the Damascenes, angrily stating (apparently quite disingenuously in view of his own extensive Muslim friendships) that the Templars entertained Muslim princes with great pomp and allowed Muslim visitors to perform their unholy invocations of Muhammad within the gates of the Temple.

# CHAPTER TWENTY-TWO

# THE SEVENTH CRUSADE
## AND THE RISE OF BAYBARS

The last great crusading effort began under the French king Louis IX after the defeat at La Forbie. Louis, born in 1214 in southern France, was an intensely spiritual man who was canonized twenty-seven years after his death. He brought a holy passion for the Crusades that seemed to hearken back to the victorious First Crusade, well before the cynicism and disappointment engendered by defeat, diplomatic maneuvering, and the enormous financial drain had taken their toll. Louis's enthusiasm, sincerity, and piety allowed him to overcome the contemporary attitude and gain support for a new effort. The Templars were instrumental in helping him finance the crusade and organize its logistics. Renaud de Vichiers, the Templar Preceptor of France, was a personal friend of the king. Louis set sail in August 1248, accompanied by de Vichiers, and arrived in Cyprus in September.

There they were joined by Grand Master Guillaume de Sonnac and a group of knights who had sailed from Acre. An emir representing the Egyptian sultan contacted Guillaume in an attempt to negotiate a peace treaty. When Louis learned of this, he forbade the Templars from continuing the discussion. Like Pelagius before him, Louis felt it was beneath Christian dignity to negotiate with the infidel. The plan of the Seventh Crusade mirrored that of the Fifth. It called for a landing at Damietta, with the intention of taking Cairo, then proceeding to Palestine. Strong winds separated the attacking Christian fleet so that some galleys landed as far away as Acre. Louis, along with seven hundred knights, landed at Damietta on June 5, 1249. Fortunately for Louis, the illness of the sultan in Cairo, and the fierceness of the Crusaders' approach, frightened the Damiettians into abandoning their city to the small Christian force.

Also like Pelagius, Louis insisted on waiting in Damietta. He planned to let the Nile floods recede before proceeding to Cairo. Guillaume de Sonnac recommended instead that they attack Alexandria and then proceed to Cairo. The king overruled him. After months of waiting, the Christian army began the slow march to Cairo in late November. They were continually attacked by Muslim raiding parties along the way. Louis forbade any retaliation. Exasperated during one raid, Guillaume disobeyed the king and charged the Muslims. Six hundred enemy troops were killed, which heartened the Christians, and the march picked up tempo.

In December, the army reached the canal separating them from Mansourah, scene of the final defeat of the Fifth Crusade. On the other side of the canal were the armies of two leading Islamic generals, Fakhr ad-Din, a friend of Frederick II from twenty years earlier, and the Mameluke general Baybars, whom we encountered in part 2. The Muslims held the Crusaders in place until February 1250, when part of the Christian force was able to ford the canal and attack the Muslim camp at dawn. Fakhr ad-Din was killed as he leapt naked from his bath. The Crusaders continued to Mansourah, where Baybars tricked them. His soldiers hid themselves within the walls of the town. The Christians unknowingly stormed through the gates, where they were ambushed, cut down nearly to the man. Of 290 Templar knights, only 5 survived. Count Robert of Artois, the fiery-tempered brother of the king, died along with 300 secular knights. Meanwhile, the balance of the army crossed the river and were attacked by the Egyptian force. They suffered great casualties, including the loss of Guillaume de Sonnac, who was blinded and mortally wounded.

Louis hoped that the death of the Ayyubid sultan might plunge Egypt into revolt, but the succession was peaceful. In April, Louis was forced to request negotiations for his army's survival. His offer was refused, and the Christians began their retreat. They were pursued by the Muslim army and lost thousands of men. Louis was captured and imprisoned. His courage and uprightness so impressed the Ayyubids that they agreed to release him on his promise that he would pay his ransom as soon as he was able.

But on May 2, 1250, the newly installed Ayyubid sultan was murdered by his Mameluke bodyguards. The Mamelukes had figured prominently in the Egyptian army since the twelfth century, participating in all of Saladin's campaigns. Now they were responsible for terminating Saladin's dynastic bloodline. The Mamelukes rushed to fortify their rulership of Egypt against a potential Christian rescue attempt of King Louis. The new Mameluke sultan, Aybeg, agreed to abide by the treaty to release Louis. The Franks surrendered Damietta, and Louis was released on May 6. One of his brothers was held for security while the king arranged his ransom payment.

Unable to raise the full amount required, Louis's representatives approached the Templar Commander for a loan. He refused, saying that funds left in deposit with the Templars could only be returned to their rightful owners. However, Louis's friend Renaud de Vichiers, recently promoted to Marshal of the Temple, suggested that, under the circumstances, the French might take the money by force, leaving the Templars no choice in the matter. Louis's representative was rowed to the Order's flagship. He climbed aboard and threatened to smash open the Templar vault with an ax. De Vichiers immediately handed him the key to a strongbox in which were found the funds necessary for the ransom.

De Vichiers became the new Grand Master. Louis made his headquarters at Atlit. The good relationship between the king and the military orders worked to Frankish advantage when an Assassin delegation arrived at Acre to demand a protection tribute from Louis. Three Ismailis holding daggers walked in front of a fourth bearing a shroud in a display calculated to frighten the king. The Assassins explained that other European heads of state who had dealings in the region, including the emperor of Germany and the king of Hungary, paid them tribute, as did the sultan at Cairo. They added that if Louis preferred not to pay, they would accept cancellation of their tributes to the Templars and Hospitallers.

Louis scheduled a second meeting to give himself time to consider the offer. At the second meeting, he was accompanied by the Grand Masters of the Temple and the Hospital, de Vichiers and William of Chateauneuf. Both Grand Masters were unrelenting with the Assassins and demanded a third meeting alone with them. The next day they warned the Assassin envoys that the king's honor had been insulted and that the Assassins were lucky not to have been tossed into the sea. The ambassadors returned to their leader. The Old Man replied by sending several gifts to Louis, the most important of which was the chief's own shirt. Since it was worn close to his body, it symbolized his intimacy with his new ally. He also sent a gold ring with his name engraved upon it. One gift, a set of beautiful crystal, was so heavily decorated with amber that it perfumed the room. Louis sent gifts in return, along with an Arabic-speaking Christian missionary who had deep conversations on biblical doctrine with the Syrian chief. Thus did the Assassins enter into a nonaggression pact with King Louis.

Louis's wife gave birth to a son at Atlit in 1251. Renaud de Vichiers became the boy's godfather despite the prohibition against this in the Rule. In 1252, however, a conflict arose between Louis and the Templars that led Louis to publicly humiliate his friends. The warring Muslim sultanates of Cairo and Damascus had both sent delegations to enlist Frankish help against the other. Renaud presented Louis with a signed treaty the Templars had negotiated with their traditional Damascene allies that simply awaited the king's approval. Louis was furious at this perceived usurpation of his authority. While he was now sufficiently acclimatized to the realities of Outremer to accept treaties with the infidel, he leaned toward an alliance with Cairo. He hoped that he could thereby help to free the remaining members of his invading force still languishing in Muslim prisons. In anger, he forced the Templars to publicly assemble. He demanded they stand barefooted while de Vichiers loudly proclaimed to the Damascene ambassadors that he had made a treaty without the king's permission and therefore it was void. The Master and the Templars then knelt before the king, begged his forgiveness, and surrendered the Order's possessions to him. The Marshal of the Temple, who had done the actual negotiating, was banished from Outremer.

King Louis left the Holy Land in 1254. A disastrous civil war between Venetian and Genoese merchants erupted in the port city of Acre shortly thereafter. Acre had replaced Jerusalem as the headquarters of the military orders since the loss of that city to Saladin at the end of the twelfth century. During the course of the conflict, the Templars joined with the Teutonic Knights and the corporate powers of Venice and Pisa against the Hospitallers and the corporate powers of Genoa and Barcelona. This vicious internecine conflict, known as the Saint Sabas War, may have been responsible for the deaths of as many as twenty thousand Christians between 1256 and 1260.[1]

This period was also fraught with danger from the Mongols under the leadership of Huelgu, as discussed in part 2, chapter 8. The Mongols had issued threats to the Templars and Hospitallers in 1255. In 1258, Huelgu took Baghdad. In 1260, Aleppo fell, as did Damascus shortly thereafter. The Templars, Hospitallers, and Teutonic Knights sent representatives to Europe to raise troops and funds. The Mongol ferocity caused anxiety throughout Europe. As events would later prove, however, the more dangerous threat was closer to home. In September 1260, the great Mameluke general Baybars defeated the Mongols at Ain Jalut, just south of Nazareth.

General Baybars murdered his sultan in October 1260 and seized the Mameluke throne. He reigned until 1277. He was a brave, ruthless, unscrupulous, and immensely talented military leader, responsible for some of the most important victories in the history of Islam. These included defeats of the Mongols, the Christians, and the Syrian Assassins. The Mameluke empire eventually included Egypt, Palestine, Syria, and adjoining territories. In 1265, Baybars launched his offensive against Outremer. He took Caesarea, Haifa, and Arsuf. In 1266, he took Safed, which had grown during the last twenty-five years to a fiefdom that included 160 villages and ten thousand peasants.[2] "As soon as Baibars had taken control of the castle and the Templars, he gave them that night to decide whether they would choose conversion to the Islamic faith, or death. . . . [T]he Templars to a man chose death rather than give up the cross."[3] In 1268, Baybars took Beaufort, Antioch, Jaffa, Banyas, and Baghras, the first Templar castle in Palestine. In 1271, Chastel Blanc fell.

# CHAPTER TWENTY-THREE

# THE EIGHTH CRUSADE AND FINAL DEFEAT

Pope Clement IV pleaded in despair for help from all the European crowned heads. King Louis, now fifty-four years old and the father of eleven children, again answered the call of Christian duty. His family included his young grandson Philip, nicknamed le Bel, "the Fair," who had inherited his grandfather's good looks, if not his saintly character. Louis left France for his second crusade on July 1, 1270. He arrived at Carthage in Tunisia on July 17, where he contracted dysentery accompanied by fever and convulsions. On August 27 he died, whispering with his last breath, "Jerusalem, Jerusalem!"[1]

Prince Edward of England led a crusading force that arrived in Acre on May 9, 1271. Baybars had just taken the Hospitaller fortress of Krak des Chevaliers and the Templar castle of Safita. When Louis and his army had arrived in North Africa the previous summer, Baybars was forced to turn his attention from his Palestinian campaign. Therefore the timing of Edward's entrance in the northern region seems to have contributed to Baybars's willingness to offer the Franks a ten-year truce. When the Templar Grand Master Guillaume de Beaujeu signed a non-aggression pact with Baybars, he effectively nullified the Templar role in Palestine.

Edward's truce with Baybars allowed Outremer to survive long enough for the last major player to enter the political stage. Charles of Anjou was the brother of Louis IX and a close ally of Pope Gregory X, who had declared Charles the Capetian king of Sicily in 1266. Charles sought to expand his realm throughout the Mediterranean and to rule in Palestine. In 1268, he executed the last of the Hohenstaufen claimants to the throne of Jerusalem. The Franks elected King Hugh III of Cyprus as their next king. Hugh traced his bloodline to Queen Isabel I, daughter of John of Brienne and wife of Frederick II. Isabel's granddaughter, Maria of Antioch, however, opposed her cousin Hugh's claim. She argued that she was more closely related to Isabel and therefore entitled to the succession.

Charles of Anjou supported Maria. She traveled to Europe to present her case to Pope Gregory, who also accepted her claim. Charles spent several years negotiating with Maria for her rights to the crown. The pope helped persuade her to accept the generous offer of Charles, which she did in 1277. Charles thus supplanted Hugh as the king of Jerusalem. Hugh had returned to Cyprus in 1276, angered by Templar support for Charles and their open refusal to acknowledge his authority. He retaliated by seizing and destroying Order property in Cyprus.

Charles, in contrast, had long enjoyed a comfortable relationship with the Templars. Guillaume de Beaujeu, who rose to become Grand Master in 1273, was one of his relatives. De Beaujeu had represented the Order at the Council of Lyons, convened in 1274 by Gregory X to consider a new crusade and related matters. During the council, the Templars rebuffed a major offer of manpower and supplies from King James of Aragon. Malcolm Barber suggests the reason for their uncharacteristic lack of enthusiasm for this offer may have been their support for Charles of Anjou. If a fight with the Mamelukes erupted during the sensitive negotiations between Charles and Maria, the likelihood of Charles successfully achieving his goal would have been diminished.[2]

Upon the death of Baybars in 1277, the Knights Templar were in a perilously weakened condition. The joint menace of Baybars and Huelgu had reduced the Franks to their lowest level of military power in nearly two hundred years. Yet, perversely, the Order involved itself in a civil war in the county of Tripoli between 1277 and 1282. This unnecessary and wasteful abuse of power turned many in the Christian community irrevocably against Guillaume de Beaujeu and the Templars. Their distrust would have tragic consequences over the next decade, as we shall soon see.

In 1281, the Mongols launched a new attack against the Mamelukes. Baybars's successor, Sultan Qalawun al-Malik al-Mansur, offered the Franks a new ten-year truce in 1282 in an effort to avoid an alliance between the Franks and the Mongols. When Charles of Anjou died in 1285, the throne of Jerusalem reverted to the two sons of King Hugh of Cyprus, who ruled in succession after Charles.

In violation of the truce, Qalawun began to attack Frankish territories in 1285. By this time, the Christians of Outremer were reduced to a pathetic state in which all moral force had long since been spent. In place of the zeal to reclaim Palestine through Holy War in the name of Christ remained the desire for commerce with the Muslim infidel. In 1289, the residents of Tripoli invited Qalawun to intervene in their internal civil affairs. He humored them and made use of the opportunity to seize Tripoli. Guillaume de Beaujeu had been alerted to the sultan's intentions by his network of spies. He attempted to warn the

Christians but had so discredited himself in their eyes that they refused to believe him. Qalawun destroyed the city and slew its inhabitants. Cynically, he declared that the truce was still in effect despite his own behavior. The weak and frightened Christians accepted this absurd statement.

In 1290, a riot broke out in Acre and several Muslims were killed. De Beaujeu was informed by his spy network that Qalawun was amassing an army to move against Acre. De Beaujeu proposed that Christian prisoners held by the military orders and the merchant powers be turned over to the sultan and blamed for the riots in order to placate the Mamelukes. (Since the prisoners were already facing the death penalty, he reasoned this was an intelligent ruse to save the greater population.) His plan, however, was rejected. De Beaujeu next privately negotiated with Qalawun to spare Acre for the price of one gold coin for each resident. When he announced this arrangement to the people, they pronounced him a traitor.

Qalawun died in November 1290 and was succeeded by his son, al-Ashraf, who swore to continue in his father's footsteps. On April 5, 1291, al-Ashraf laid siege to Acre. On April 15, Guillaume de Beaujeu led a night attack against the encamped Muslim army. The knights initially had the element of surprise in their favor, but in the darkness they became entangled in the Muslim tent ropes and were beaten back. On May 18, the Muslims broke through the city's defenses and entered the walls of Acre. The Templars fought valiantly, and in the battle de Beaujeu was mortally wounded.

Only the Templar castle at the southwest of the city remained in Christian hands. Surviving Templars assembled there along with some citizens of Acre who had joined them. The Marshal of the Temple, Peter de Sevrey, was in command. On May 25, al-Ashraf offered him and all occupants of the castle safe passage to Cyprus if they surrendered. De Sevrey agreed and opened the castle gates. The Mameluke soldiers went wild when inside, attacking men, women, and children indiscriminately. The Christians managed to fight them off. De Sevrey sent the Commander of the Temple, Theobald Gaudin, to Sidon with the remaining treasure and holy relics of the Order. Al-Ashraf renewed his offer of safety. This time de Sevrey left the castle to discuss terms, only to be beheaded in sight of the remaining garrison. The sultan's troops stormed the castle, and on May 28, 1291, Acre fell. All present were killed.

CHAPTER TWENTY-FOUR

# The Last Years of the Knights Templar

Theobald Gaudin was elected Master of the Order in Sidon. After a large Mameluke army appeared, he left for Cyprus carrying the Order's remaining assets with him. Sidon was abandoned on July 14. Tortosa was evacuated on August 3. By August 14, 1291, Castle Pilgrim was abandoned. The Holy Land was empty of Christian power for the first time in two hundred years.

Upon the death of Gaudin in April 1293, Jacques de Molay was elected the twenty-third and last Grand Master of the Knights Templar. Born in France in 1244, de Molay joined the Order in 1265 and was soon sent to the Holy Land. He was outspoken and critical of what he found there. He felt the business of the Templars was fighting the infidel and viewed any treaties with the Muslims as weakness at best, and treason at worst. He was openly disdainful of Guillaume de Beaujeu and his efforts at diplomacy. De Molay rigidly maintained his opinionated demeanor through the twenty-seven years of his service in the Order. He made a convincing appeal to the brethren of his own fitness to lead.

In 1294, de Molay left Cyprus for a three-year journey through Europe to meet with the heads of state of England, France, Naples, and Aragon, as well as the pope. He was working to gain support for the Order so that it could rebuild in preparation for a new crusade. He was successful in gaining some tax exemptions and import and export allowances from the various kings. Pope Boniface VIII mediated a dispute between the Templars and King Henry of Cyprus, who claimed authority over the Order because it was situated in his domain. The pope granted the Templars the same privileges on Cyprus they had held in Syria. He urged King Henry to treat them well in consideration of their great suffering in defense of the Holy Land.

The Templars did their best to pursue their goals. A small garrison had been left at Ruad, an island two miles off the coast of Tortosa, in 1291. The Order worked to increase its naval capacity and took part in raids against the Muslims. The garrison at Ruad was gradually reinforced until 1302, when it was attacked and destroyed by a Mameluke naval force. As late as 1306, the Templars participated in a major political intrigue in Cyprus, aiding Amaury de Lusignan in deposing his brother, King Henry. The Hospitallers joined them on Amaury's behalf. The intention behind the participation of the military orders was to strengthen Cyprus as a crusading base against the Mamelukes. The Templars also supported efforts to build an alliance with the Mongols against the Mamelukes.

Long-held resentments against the Knights Templar were, however, now able to rise unchallenged to the surface. In defeat they became a convenient target. They had long been viewed with suspicion and distaste because of their unique papal privileges. In addition to isolating the Templars from the communities in which they lived, the Order's papal privileges tended to reduce the independence of local parishes. The papacy had extended its long tendrils directly into the lives of remote countryside towns and villages. Henry Lea also reminds us that these privileges extended to all Templars, the noble-born knights as well as the lower-class serving brothers, some ninety percent of the Order's membership. The churlish behavior, of which many must have been guilty, would be another ready source of hostility from their neighbors.[1] Finally, the apparent extent of Templar wealth and power contrasted poorly with their overall record in battle.

The Templars were thoroughly identified with the Crusades. The obvious question of God's support for the Christian cause pressed more and more heavily on the pious heart as defeat was added to defeat. Disillusionment replaced enthusiasm and praise gave way to blame. As the success of the Crusades had been the cause of the incredible rise of the Templars, so defeat would herald their tragic demise. They had suffered catastrophic losses in the past and recovered each time. But the loss of their assigned protectorate was a blow from which they never recovered. Bravery could not absolve defeat.

Malcolm Barber estimates the membership of the Order to have included some seven thousand knights, sergeants, serving brothers, and priests at this time. Associate members and allied individuals brought the number much higher. The Order possessed at least 870 castles, preceptories and houses.[2] Their independent, armed presence in Europe could not fail to produce tension. The Templars retained the power to declare war and make peace on their own terms. They could not be ordered to fight for kings and were exempt from royal taxes and tolls. They stood apart as a feudal anachronism from the ever-growing central power of the monarchy.

## Proposals for Unification of the Military Orders

The loss of Palestine acted as crisis often had before, becoming a cata-
lyst for the drive for a new crusading effort. This time, however, it
would carry sinister consequences for the Knights Templar. Europe had
changed greatly during the two hundred years of the Crusades. Feudalism was evolving into nationalism, while Christianity was losing its
iron grip on medieval culture. The considerable financial burden of the
Crusades was finally encouraging monarchs and church leaders to seek
relief. The leading powers came to the conclusion that a unification of
the wealth and assets of the Templars, Hospitallers, and Teutonic
Knights — including personnel and leadership — might combine to
make a whole greater than the sum of its parts. King Louis IX had first
advanced a proposal for unification of the military orders as early as
1248.

At the Council of Lyons in 1274, one of the issues under consideration was a general overview of attitudes toward the Crusades. The
guiding light of the council was the Spanish mystic Raymond Lull, a
former knight who had became a preacher. Lull was also a Muslim
scholar and linguist. He believed that Islam could be converted to
Christianity, for the most part peaceably, by well-prepared preachers;
however, he accepted that the process must involve a certain amount
of force. He was a strong advocate of consolidating the military orders.
Pope Gregory was apparently convinced by Lull's arguments, but Gregory died in 1276. Six short-lived popes followed over the next twelve
years, so no further progress was made toward uniting the orders. In
1287, Lull first presented his ideas to the newly crowned French king,
Philip IV.

In 1288, Nicholas IV assumed the papacy. His thoughts turned
immediately to the Holy Land. He was a strong advocate of uniting the
orders and caused the first important work to be published on the subject in 1291. The fall of Acre created additional impetus for the idea.
In 1292 the Council of Salzburg officially approved union of the military orders. The death of Nicholas in April 1292, however, once again
delayed implementation.

Pope Boniface VIII reigned from 1294 to 1304. He exhibited little
concern for either the issue of unification or the continuation of the
Crusades. As a lawyer, his primary focus was the codification of the
body of Church law and the consolidation of papal power against the
reigning secular monarchs of Europe. When Jacques de Molay traveled

to Europe in 1294 to visit Boniface, he was unaware of, or chose to ignore, the growing sentiment for unification of the orders that merely awaited papal interest.

## PHILIP IV AND CLEMENT V

The grandson of King Louis IX, Philip the Fair, who was crowned in 1285 at the age of seventeen, had become the most powerful king in Europe. He was a man who understood power. He was manipulative, cunning, cold, intelligent, and determined, with an instinctive grasp of psychology and an almost modern appreciation for the power of the "Big Lie." At the same time that he embodied the psychological quali-ties of a ruthless politician, Philip was viewed as a semidivine being. The Church taught that the monarchy was appointed by God to rule the faithful; Philip had been anointed at his coronation with the leg-endary holy oil of the Capetian dynasty; he was known throughout Europe as "the most Christian King of France." These cultural beliefs appear to have been internalized within his own psyche.

Philip faced a very difficult financial situation. The ambitious growth of France as a world power had cost dearly. War debts from his father's crusade against Aragon in 1284–85 remained unpaid. Philip's own war against England and Flanders during the 1290s added a further burden of debt. The lack of a predictable source of royal income was characteristic of the feudal economy. Philip exhausted himself with plans to overcome his chronic shortage of funds. His currency manip-ulations alone devalued the coin of the realm by two-thirds during the decade beginning in 1290. He inaugurated a plethora of new taxes including a national sales tax. Philip levied special taxes on the Lom-bards and Jews, two wealthy minority groups from whom he was accus-tomed to borrowing heavily.

Philip's financial woes caused him to take the unprecedented step of levying taxes against the Church. This placed him in direct opposi-tion to the equally ambitious Pope Boniface VIII, who issued the bull *Unam sanctam*, which proclaimed the sovereignty of the pope over all secular rulers. The power of the kings was born from original sin, while that of the popes came from God. As may be imagined, Boniface and Philip remained locked in a furious power struggle throughout Boni-face's papacy. In 1296, Boniface issued a bull forbidding clerical taxa-tion. Philip responded by prohibiting the export of bullion from France, thus effectively severing the flow of tithes to Rome. The battle between these two mighty contestants escalated incrementally until Boniface excommunicated Philip in 1303. The pope next intended to place the entire nation of France under papal interdict. At this Philip balked. He brought legal proceedings against Boniface in France and sanctioned an armed arrest of the pope while Boniface vacationed at his summer residence in Anagni outside Rome. The raid, conducted with a force of sixteen hundred soldiers, occurred the day before the pope was to issue his bull against France. The frail eighty-six-year-old Boniface was imprisoned for three days before he was liberated by the populace of Anagni, but he died within a month of the attack.[†]

Guillaume de Nogaret had led the raid against Boniface. He had once been the legal counselor to the king of Majorca and, later, a professor of law at Montpellier University in France. He joined King Philip in the early 1290s. He was made "first lawyer of the realm" in 1302. De Nogaret was a fanatic who was expert in smearing his victims with accusations of magic, heresy, and sexual perversion — the appropriate contemporary shibboleths that could be used to incite the irrationality of the population. De Nogaret had made these accusations against the bishop of Pamiers in 1301, and he repeated them against Boniface in 1303.

Boniface was succeeded by Pope Benedict XI. In audience before Benedict, de Nogaret accepted full responsibility for the raid against Boniface. This allowed Benedict to lift Philip's excommunication but forced him to excommunicate de Nogaret. This presumably had little effect on the French lawyer because of the depth of his hatred for the papacy. Contemporary accounts stated that his parents were Cathars who had been burnt alive as heretics during the Albigensian Crusades.

---

[†] In order to place Philip's treatment of Boniface in context, it should be pointed out that in 878, Pope John VIII had been imprisoned and starved by a nobleman who sought papal sanction for a candidate he proposed as Holy Roman Emperor. In 897, Pope Stephen VI had the corpse of his predecessor exhumed, robed, and tried before an ecclesiastic council, where it was found guilty, stripped, mutilated, and flung into the Tiber. A revolt in Rome the same year resulted in Stephen being imprisoned and strangled in his cell. A century later, after a virtually continuous line of corrupt popes, Otto I, king of Germany and Holy Roman Emperor, deposed Pope John XVI, gouged out his eyes, cut off his tongue, and paraded him through the streets of Rome turned backward on an ass. In 1052, Pope Leo IX was imprisoned for nine months. As late as 1075, Pope Gregory VII was physically attacked while celebrating Christmas Mass and carried off by agents of a Roman nobleman.

Philip's extraordinary actions against the pope were dramatically illustrative of the struggle for power between secular kings and the papacy during the early fourteenth century. This conflict had persisted throughout the Templar story. From the theocratic dreams of Gregory VII in 1073 to the horror and impotence of Boniface in 1303, the battle had gradually been turning in favor of the monarchs. One reason for the decrease in papal power was the cynicism engendered by the political successes of the thirteenth-century popes. They had exterminated the Cathars, battled the Hohenstaufens, and built the Inquisition. Yet, in the words of Malcolm Barber, "this had been achieved at a high cost to papal prestige. To many people, the papacy had degenerated into just another political power, devoid of any moral purpose or lofty spiritual aims."[3] The attack by King Philip against the Templars must also be viewed in the wider context as an attack against the papacy by an ambitious secular power.

Pierre Dubois, a Norman lawyer and publicist who had been a propagandist for Philip, wrote three separate pamphlets beginning in 1300 in which he promoted the value of uniting the Templars with the Hospitallers and combining their assets to finance a new crusade. Dubois further suggested the Church organize a common treasury for the forthcoming crusading effort, bypassing the traditional Templar role of financier. In his last pamphlet, released in the summer of 1307, Dubois added a note proposing that the Templars be totally abolished and their assets seized to finance a crusade. This seems to have been added with foreknowledge of Philip's intentions to conduct the arrests.

Raymond Lull had modified his original emphasis on peaceful conversion of the infidel after the loss of Acre. In 1292, he advanced the idea of a new crusade to be fought by a unified military order commanded by Philip or one of his sons. The position of master of the new order was to be hereditary or appointive. The master would reign as king of Jerusalem. He would be known as Bellator Rex, the "Warrior King." Lull spent some years at Philip's court attempting to acquire support for his plan. Philip obviously would have found the idea attractive, as such a position held by the Capetian dynasty could only strengthen its power over other European monarchs and the Church. Malcolm Barber shows the extent of influence Lull may have had on Philip. Barber writes that a report, issued in 1308, stated that after the death of Philip's wife he asked the pope to unite the military orders and offered to step down as king of France to become the king of Jerusalem and master of the new Order of the Knighthood of Jerusalem.[4] Although it strains credibility to imagine Philip willing to abdicate the throne of France for leadership of a military order and kingship of Jerusalem, the report adds evidence of a continued momentum for radical change.

Pope Benedict XI died after only eight months in office. Philip succeeded in having the archbishop of Bordeaux, Bertrand de Got, a Frenchman, elected as Pope Clement V in November 1305. Clement's background included training in Roman and canon law. He had served as a papal diplomat prior to his elevation. He was, however, sickly, psychologically weak, indecisive, and greedy, a man who would become little more than a tool in Philip's ruthless hands. For example, of the twenty-four cardinals whom Clement would appoint during his papacy, twenty-three were French. By 1308, some three years after his accession, Clement had not yet even visited Rome because of the incessant demands upon his time and energy made by the French king. The height of absurdity was reached that year when Clement, under pressure from Philip, moved his headquarters officially from Rome to Avignon in southern France, some fifty miles northeast of Marseilles. Avignon was owned by some of the pope's vassals. In 1348 it would become papal property. It served as the seat of the papacy through seven popes until 1377, a period known as the "Babylonian captivity."

Philip's financial problems continued to mount. In June 1306, he announced that France would return to a full-valued currency, instantly tripling prices. Violent riots took place throughout Paris with angry mobs in deadly skirmishes with royal troops. Philip took refuge in the Paris Temple for three days, during which he was reminded firsthand of the military and financial strength of this kingdom within his own kingdom of France. (The previous year, Philip had sought membership in the Temple after the death of his wife. His application was refused, fueling his resentment against the Order.) His intractable financial problems drove him to another radical act that was to be a grim preview of coming attractions — Philip arrested every French Jew on July 21, 1306. This statewide operation, supervised by Guillaume de Nogaret, was successful in adding a great store of seized assets and wealth to the needy royal coffers, as well as canceling many debts the French king had owed to Jewish moneylenders.

Pope Clement V sent out letters on June 6, 1306, summoning the Grand Masters of the Templars and Hospitallers to an audience at Poitiers to discuss a new crusade. The Hospitaller Master Fulk de Villaret was unable to travel since his Order was engaged in setting up headquarters on the newly acquired island of Rhodes. De Molay signaled his intention to meet with the pope toward the end of the year. Clement instructed him to travel as inconspicuously as possible. Instead de Molay brought sixty knights and stores of gold and jewels in an ostentatious display of Templar wealth and power. He journeyed first to Paris, where he deposited his valuables at the Temple and met with the French king. Philip apparently flattered and deceived the old warrior, who left assured of the continued good relations between the Order and the French crown. It should be remembered that even at this late date, the Templars continued to be entrusted with the financial management of Philip's kingdom.

Jacques de Molay traveled on to Poitiers to meet the new pope. In the nineteen months of his reign, Clement had bowed before King Philip on numerous issues left over from the king's battle with Boniface. Clement, however, was now facing the most troubling problem of all. Philip had recently presented him with a series of terrible allegations of heresy and immorality against the Templars. He assured the pope that these charges had been made by a reliable witness, and he demanded that Clement hold a full papal inquiry into the matter.

Clement informed de Molay of the situation. The Master was furious and incredulous, vehemently denying any wrongdoing. The pope was satisfied with his answers and perhaps felt he could simply wait out Philip's fury. De Molay returned to Paris for a secret chapter meeting in July 1307. A circular was sent throughout all Templar houses in France reminding the brethren of the Rule's prohibition against discussing any of the secrets of the Order.

De Molay returned to Poitiers, where he presented two documents to the pope, one being a discussion of, and an argument for, a new crusade. The other was an essay on the issue of uniting the orders. De Molay placed himself squarely against this idea for a number of reasons, none particularly compelling. He argued that the Hospitallers and Templars each had their own identity and that merging them would weaken the good works of which they were each capable — the Hospitallers focused on charity, the Templars on militarism. He stated that recruits were attracted to each order for different reasons and it would be unfair to deny them the opportunity to choose. He added that competition was a valuable means of ensuring self-improvement. Copies of the papers were sent to Philip. "The Grand Master rejected the idea of union, and may have accelerated the process of suppression in doing so. . . . [O]nce Philip the Fair had espoused the cause there could have been little doubt concerning the outcome."[5]

The Hospitallers were quicker to recognize the precarious situation in which the loss of the Holy Land had placed the military orders. After securing their base on Rhodes, they reorganized themselves to become an effective maritime force fighting against Muslim pirates in the Mediterranean, helping to make European commerce and travel safer. The Templars were less flexible. De Molay seemed to remain completely unaware of the gravity of the situation that faced him. In fairness, it should be stated that while his blind eye may certainly have contributed to the destruction of the Order, it is doubtful whether he or anyone else might have averted the outcome by more intelligent behavior.

On August 2, 1307, Clement sent a bull to Edward I at the request of the English Temple, exempting the Order from the king's tithe. Clement referred to the Templars in the same language of loving papal superlatives that had been used in the Order's favor for nearly two hundred years. Clement's strategy of passive resistance to Philip had thus far been successful. Later in the month, however, de Molay again visited the pope and may have fatally aggravated the situation by demanding a full papal inquiry to clear the Order's name of the slander and suspicion under which he had been chafing.

# CHAPTER TWENTY-FIVE

# THE END OF THE ORDER

The primary original witness against the Templars was one Esquin de Floyran, a disaffected French Templar who had first attempted to convince James II of Aragon that the Templars were criminals. He was unsuccessful, since James enjoyed a good relationship with the Order. Esquin returned to France to lay his charges before Guillaume de Nogaret. De Floyran appears to have later received some Templar land from Philip in return for his testimony and to have sought payment from other monarchs when his accusations resulted in convictions. Three other witnesses were found who supported his account, two ex-Templars and a cleric. Philip authorized twelve new brothers to join the Order in France during the summer of 1307. Guillaume de Plaisians, a member of Philip's inner circle of lawyers, stated that the spies reported back that the accusations against the Templars were true. A trickle of other witnesses came forward as well, each held in some form of disrepute by the Order.

After the pope informed Philip of his intention to conduct an inquiry, Philip issued a sealed mandate on September 14, 1307, to his police officers throughout France. It called for discrete preparations to be made for the arrest of every French Templar at dawn on October 13, 1307. The warrant accused the Order of unspeakable crimes against God, Christ, the Church, Europe, and common decency through heresy, witchcraft, treason, and sexual perversion. The charges bore the characteristic hand of de Nogaret, whom Philip had promoted to chancellor of France and guardian of the king's seal. The intention of such a strongly worded document was to convince Philip's police to overcome their own scruples and act against these highly regarded men — their neighbors and friends.

In order to attach an air of legality to his actions, Philip claimed the arrest order had been prepared at the request of the Inquisitor-General of France, the Dominican friar Guillaume de Paris. While no direct evidence exists for this specific claim, Guillaume was an active participant in the affair. Philip had attempted to control the Inquisition in France for a decade, and Guillaume was his private confessor. Guillaume would have been within his legal rights as head of the Inquisition to seek the aid of the secular monarch to assist the Church in the matter of heresy. On September 22, Guillaume wrote the inquisitors of Toulouse and Carcassone, listing the crimes of the Templars, advising them of the forthcoming arrests, and preparing them for the difficult task ahead of collecting and recording depositions.

On October 12, 1307, de Molay was honored as one of the pall-bearers for the funeral of King Philip's sister-in-law. The next day, Friday the thirteenth, he and every Templar in France were in jail. Of approximately five thousand French Templars, fewer than twenty escaped. Philip's precipitous arrests had the effect of avoiding a prolonged inquiry while the brethren were still at liberty and able to defend themselves by legal means. Philip next employed a sophisticated medieval version of "spin control." On the day after the arrest, Saturday, October 14, the masters of the university and cathedral canons were assembled in Notre Dame, where de Nogaret and others addressed them regarding the crimes for which the Templars had just been arrested. On Sunday the fifteenth, an invitation was extended to the French people to come to the garden of the royal palace, where they were addressed by spokesmen of the king and Dominican inquisitors. Similar town meetings were held throughout France to mold public opinion. On Monday, October 16, Philip sent letters to all kings and princes of Christendom to explain his actions and enlist their support against Templars in their own lands.

"Due process" for an imprisoned medieval Frenchman opened wide the gateway of judicial abuse to authorities. Torture was the legal and accepted method of conducting interrogations. The Inquisition exerted its brutality convinced of its divine mission. The Templars were doomed. The French secular officials conducting the arrests were instructed to begin interrogation and torture at once. Within days, these tasks were transferred to the authority of the Inquisition. The monarchy participated to varying degrees depending on the regional personnel needs of the Inquisition.

The excruciating reality of torture demands a descriptive paragraph. The technology of torture during this period included the rack, to which the ankles and wrists of the victim were tied with ropes attached to a windlass. As the crank was turned, the arms and legs would be progressively stretched until they dislocated from their sockets. Another infamous method of torture was the strappado. This involved tying the hands with a rope behind the back and throwing the other end of the rope over a ceiling beam. The victim would be hoisted upward and precipitously dropped — then yanked to a halt inches from the floor, cracking and dislocating arms, shoulders, wrists, and ribs. Weights might be attached to feet or testicles to increase the agony. Torture by fire was conducted by smearing fat on the soles of the feet and holding them to the flames. One unforgettable account of this came from a Templar priest whose bones dropped out of his feet several days after the torture. He brought the bones to his hearing before the papal commission. Other forms of torture involved such time-proven techniques as beating, starvation, diets of bread and water, sleep deprivation, restriction in irons or chains, unspeakable sanitary conditions, and verbal and psychological abuse. Many Templars died in prison — some took their own lives in desperation.

By October 25, two weeks of imprisonment had succeeded in preparing these fallen warriors for the first scene of the terrible tragedy that would crush them utterly over the next seven years. On that day, Grand Master Jacques de Molay admitted the Order's crimes to a prestigious assembly of legal scholars held at the University of Paris. (While many believe de Molay confessed from fear of torture alone, in a letter dated January 1308, he wrote that the brutality he had suffered included having the skin torn off his back, belly, and thighs.[1])

The next day, thirty more leaders and other handpicked Templars added their confessions to buttress de Molay's accounts. They testified that their ritual of reception included the denial of Christ, spitting on the cross, obscene kisses, and the worship of a hideous idol in the form of a human head. De Molay thanked the "Most Christian King Philip" for exposing these sins and wrote an open letter to the brethren, ordering them to confess.

On November 9, Hugh de Pairaud, Visitor of the Order, second-in-command to de Molay, also confessed and thereby further demoralized any who may have tried to defend the honor of the Order. De Pairaud held a long-standing grudge against de Molay because he believed de Molay had usurped his own rightful claim to the succession as Grand Master. This may help to explain his particularly damaging testimony regarding the famous "Templar head" or idol, which he claimed to have carried about from chapter to chapter in his journeys through France. He described it as having four feet, two in front and two in back. Others later claimed it was too terrifying to describe: that it had a beard; or a demon's face; or two faces with two beards; or three faces; that it was made of silver with carbuncles in the eye sockets and a texture of old skin; that it was completely smooth to the touch; that it was a painting or a small brass or gold statuette of the figure of a woman. The Templar head, described so differently by the very few who even mentioned it, invariably calls to mind descriptions and illustrations of the nightmare creatures depicted in medieval grimories — stylized by Eliphas Lévi as the Devil Card of his Tarot, Baphomet, the androgyne Lord of Initiation, a conscious reference on Lévi's part to the Templar legend.

Despite the thoroughness of the king's search, only one head was turned up in the Paris Temple. This was a large, hollow, silver female bust, in which was found a skull, wrapped in a red linen shroud, with a label identifying it as "Caput LXVIII" or "head no. 58." Testimony explained that it was the skull of one of the eleven thousand martyred virgins. This referred to the martyrdom of Saint Ursula, patron saint of virgins, and eleven of her companions during the early centuries of the Christian era. Due to a mistranslation of the text, eleven virgins became the eleven thousand of legend.[2]

Geoffroi de Gonneville, born of a wealthy and powerful French noble family, was the Preceptor of Aquitaine and Poitou, the fourth-ranking dignitary of the Order. He stated in his confession of November 15, 1307, that he was told by the Grand Master of England, who received him in 1279, that the practice of denying Christ and defiling the cross was enjoined on the Order by the pledge of an evil Grand Master imprisoned by a Muslim sultan. In order to secure his release, the Grand Master swore to introduce the denial of Christ into the Order's reception ceremony henceforth.[3] Later in the deposition, he opined that the custom may have been in imitation of Saint Peter's threefold denial of Christ. Gérard de Ridefort might seem a candidate for this dubious distinction after his capture by Saladin. Thomas Béraut, nineteenth Grand Master (1256–73), has also been suggested as the originator of this custom, because he had been captured by the Muslims and abjured the Christian faith in order to gain his freedom. Roncelin de Forz, the Master of Provence in the late thirteenth century, was also mentioned by de Gonneville as a possible source for the heresy. "Master Roncelin" is credited as the source of the spurious nineteenth-century "secret Rule" published by Merzdorf.

One hundred thirty-eight depositions survive from the examinations held in Paris between October 18 and November 24, 1307. Of that number, only four Templars proclaimed their innocence: Jean de Chateauvillars, Henri de Hercigny, Jean de Paris, and Lambert de Toysi. One hundred twenty-three Templars confessed to spitting on or near the cross.[4] The records of the examinations seem to indicate that many Templars confessed to denying Christ with relief, as if the tortures of their own conscience were as harsh as the tortures of the Inquisitors. Yet Malcolm Barber provides an important reminder for anyone too eager to accept the confessions as true: "Few people, surveying the events of the twentieth century, can have any illusions about the capability of the state to oppress organizations, groups or individuals, indeed, even to effect a complete change in mental outlook in those in its power."[5] The vast majority of French Templars were middle-aged members of the European support network, with no combat experience, who quickly confessed under torture or the threat of it and the demoralizing example of their leaders. At least twenty-five Parisian Templars died from torture during the fall of 1307.[6]

Philip's appeal of October 16 to the other European monarchs to arrest the Templars was rebuffed. They did not believe him, being well aware of his character. James II of Aragon and Edward II of England refused to arrest the Templars in their kingdoms and wrote letters to other monarchs and to the pope in the Order's defense. Yet the effeminate Edward II was a weak-willed opponent who had only recently ascended the throne after the death of his father in July 1307. He was betrothed to Philip's daughter Isabella. Edward I had been a powerful ruler and a staunch defender of the Order. The Templars had most recently assisted him against the Scottish rebellion led by William Wallace. Philip may well not have dared to attack the Templars had Edward I still lived.[7]

Pope Clement's power was necessary to legitimize Philip's actions. The Church's imprimatur would allow Philip to rob the Templars not only with impunity, but with sanctification. Clement appeared to take control of the proceedings. On October 27, he wrote an uncharacteristically courageous and angry rebuke to Philip for interfering with papal authority in Church affairs. The king was a secular ruler who had arrested members of a religious order, responsible to the pope, for crimes of heresy. The proper authority for crimes committed against Christ was the Church, acting through its judicial arm the Inquisition. (In this complaint, Clement overlooked the alleged request for Philip's help from Guillaume de Paris.) For their part, the Templars looked to the pope for protection from the persecution of the king and rescue from their predicament, or at least some guarantee of justice and a fair hearing. De Molay clung to this misplaced hope for years.

Following the declaration of his independence, Clement immediately capitulated by issuing the bull *Pastoralis praeeminentiae* on

November 22, 1307. The bull required the kings of England, Ireland, Castile, Aragon, Portugal, Italy, Germany, and Cyprus to arrest the Templars within their borders and sequester their property, *but* to do so in the name of the pope. Clement announced that he would investigate the charges against the Order, and that he would be especially pleased if they were proven baseless. The pope had placed himself in the center of the hurricane that Philip had unleashed. Philip undoubtedly hoped the matter might be over within a couple of weeks after the arrests. Clement's intervention stalled the proceedings for seven years.

The first papal investigations in France began with two cardinals sent by Clement in December 1307. They dutifully queried the inquisitors and the king's counselors and reported back to Clement that everything was being handled properly. Clement impatiently sent them back to question the prisoners. The cardinals soon reported the shocking news that Jacques de Molay, Hugh de Pairaud, and sixty other brothers were retracting their earlier confessions made under torture.

By the terms of the Inquisition, the accused *were* guilty. There was little chance or interest in determining innocence. The accusation was the crime. There were no provisions for mounting a defense; no legal counsel was allowed. Witnesses were reluctant to testify on behalf of the accused lest they be branded as accomplices. Witnesses for the prosecution could remain anonymous. The accused was allowed to make a list of known enemies. If those names coincided with the names of his accusers, some doubt might be cast on the accusations. Confession was the only practical avenue — if no confession was received, torture would certainly follow. In rare cases where a confession was not obtained by torture, excommunication as a demonically inspired heretic would be followed by burning at the stake. If a confession obtained by torture was retracted, the same punishment awaited the unfortunate soul, for he was perceived as a relapsed heretic and the revenge of Christ would follow. Confession and repentance allowed for a reconciliation with the Church prior to the imposition of punishment, which could range over varying degrees of severity, from monetary fines for small infractions to lifelong imprisonment for major crimes.

Clement suspended the French Inquisition in February 1308 to collect together the evidence and court records to date. (On December 21, 1307, obviously responding to the anxiety of the Hospitallers, Clement issued a bull confirming their status and ordering their protection.) Clement insisted that the proceedings against the Templars would be fairly conducted by an independent papal commission. By now, King Philip had placed his reputation, personal safety, and leadership of France on the line. There was no retreat. He insisted the Order was guilty. He may have even begun to believe his accusations. He and de Nogaret initiated a campaign of vilification and slander against the pope through anonymous pamphlets, accusing Clement of protecting heretics because of his own corruption. Philip returned to the legal scholars at the University of Paris to get a favorable ruling on his legal rights in the matter. After a month of deliberation, however, they informed him on March 25 that he had no authority either to judge the Templars or to dispose of their property. Therefore Philip convened the Estates General in May 1308. After a week of listening to de Nogaret's accusations, the two thousand representatives of the nobles, clergy, and commoners voted their support for Philip's actions and the destruction of the Order.

Later in the month, Philip traveled to Poitiers with a small armed force to discuss the matter with Clement. A public consistory had been called by the pope beginning May 29. Those present included cardinals and royal counselors, as well as lesser ecclesiastics and laymen. Guillaume de Plaisians addressed the group, badgering and even threatening the pope. But Clement responded that he would hold firm to his decision to handle the matter in a legal and proper fashion. He declared his hatred of heresy but spoke of his duty to fairness. De Plaisians responded in an even more threatening manner on June 14. Clement held fast.

Philip next tried conciliation. He would, of course, submit to Clement's authority, but since the pope had no jails, Philip would help him by keeping the Templars in France's prisons. On June 27, he arranged for seventy-two handpicked Templars to come before the pope and confess their crimes directly. This finally left Clement some latitude. He said that the confessions were convincing. He negotiated certain concessions from Philip regarding property. Next, he split the inquiry into two separate categories.

Category one was a papal commission of inquiry to judge the Order as a whole. Clement announced that it would report to the Council of Vienne, scheduled two years from then in October 1310. (The council was delayed until October 1311.) Category two involved reinstituting the Inquisition, suspended since February, to judge the guilt or innocence of individual Templars. This investigation would be conducted at the diocesan level by provincial councils presided over by the local bishop. But as noted above in the controversy over lay investiture, local bishops were appointed with the concurrence, and upon the recommendation, of the secular king. Thus Philip had virtual control of the inquisitorial activities of the provincial inquests.

Despite Clement's various stratagems to save face and maintain the appearance of papal independence, he had little if any genuine concern for the members of the Order. The Minstrel of Hell was playing the tune to which both Philip and Clement danced. On August 12, 1308, Clement released the articles of accusation against the Templars, *Faciens misericordiam*. The list included 127 offenses, many of which repeated others. The most serious charges were the following:

- That at the ceremony of reception (or sometime after the ceremony) the Order demanded its new members deny Christ, or Christ crucified, sometimes Jesus, God, the Virgin, or the Saints.
- That the Order taught that Jesus was not the true God, that he was a false prophet, that he had not suffered on the cross, that he had died not for the redemption of humanity but for his own sins, that neither the receptor nor the candidate could expect salvation through Jesus.
- That at the ceremony of reception, the candidate was told to spit on the cross, or an image of the cross or of Jesus. That they sometimes trampled the cross underfoot, or urinated upon it, both at the reception ceremony and at other times.
- That they adored a "certain cat" in contempt of Christ and the orthodox faith.
- That they did not believe in the sacraments of the Church.
- That Order priests did not properly consecrate the host nor speak the correct words during the Mass.
- That the Grand Master, or the Visitor, or even the Preceptors, claimed they could absolve members of sin.
- That there were a series of kisses during the ceremony of reception, by the candidate or by the receptor, either on the other's mouth, navel, bare stomach, buttocks, base of the spine, or penis.
- That homosexual relations were enjoined upon them as licit and that members were instructed that it was proper to submit to advances from brothers.
- That they worshiped and adored an idol as their God and savior. It was variously described as a human head, or heads, sometimes with three faces, or a human skull. It was believed the idol protected the Order, gave it riches, and caused the trees to flower and the land to germinate.

- That in their receptions, they surrounded the idol with a small cord that they then wore at all times around their waists, next to the shirt or on the flesh, in veneration of the idol.
- That the leaders of the Order punished anyone who refused to engage in improper behavior or who complained about the Order's sinful nature.
- That the form of confession that the Order practiced kept these sins within the confines of the group.
- That the Order financially profited by improper and immoral means and refused to give requisite alms and hospitality.
- That they conducted all their business in secret meetings and at night and that the above errors could only flourish because of this secrecy.[†]

In late August 1308, the French investigation took another strange turn. Clement sent three cardinals to question further the five senior Templar leaders. They reversed themselves again, returning to their confessions of nearly a year before. The renewed confessions took place under the watchful eyes of three of Philip's officials — Jean de Jamville, their brutal jailer; Guillaume de Nogaret, whom they knew to be responsible for their travails; and Guillaume de Plaisians, who pleaded with them as a friend to confess their crimes for the salvation of their immortal souls. We must view the actions of these pathetic creatures against the backdrop of the soul-crushing sophistication with which they were brutalized during their long imprisonment.

While the provincial councils pursued their nefarious efforts against individual Templars from the summer of 1308 until the convocation of the Council of Vienne in October 1311, the papal commission on the Order opened its first session in Paris on November 12, 1309, to consider the fate of the Order as a whole. The eight church dignitaries appointed as commissioners by Clement had all received Philip's approval. No one came forward to defend the Order, despite the

[†] G. Legman has pointed out that one thing that makes these charges so interesting is their encyclopedic nature. If Philip and de Nogaret wished solely to destroy the Order, the charges of denying Christ and defiling the cross (the most heinous of Christian crimes) would have been more than sufficient to condemn them to death. He also questions why, if the charges against the Templars were wholly manufactured, some of the contemporary boilerplate accusations, such as bewitching cattle, murdering children, planning to assassinate the king, not to mention the most obvious accusations of usury or financial fraud, were missing. See *The Guilt of the Templars*, p. 42.

invitation to do so that had been issued in August. Philip's jailers, under whom all French Templars were imprisoned, were none too anxious to arrange transport and accommodations for the witnesses.

The strategy of reserving the leaders for separate judgment by the pope appears to have accomplished its purpose — to separate the heads of the Order from the membership, and perhaps to encourage them selfishly to believe they stood a better chance than the brethren. Hugh de Pairaud pleaded for a private audience with the pope. Jacques de Molay, weakened and confused from the effects of his two-year imprisonment, testified twice. Like de Pairaud, he sought an audience with the pope. To add to his confusion, de Molay was cautioned that whatever defense he intended must be weighed against his confessions already made, lest he be judged a relapsed heretic. His halting and weak attempts to speak well of the Order resulted in nearly irrational and incoherent ramblings. On November 28, 1309, Guillaume de Nogaret confronted de Molay with the claim that Saladin had publicly attributed the defeat of the Templars in battle to their practice of sodomy and the betrayal of both their faith and the Rule to which they were sworn. De Molay stated that he had never heard this and despite the accusations against him, he was innocent of any homosexual behavior.[†]

The first session of the papal commission ended on November 28, leaving Philip little cause for anxiety that the commission would be an effective forum for the Order to defend itself.

The second session began on February 3, 1310. Philip, apparently less concerned about any danger the commission might pose to his efforts against the Temple, now ordered his jailers to be more cooperative in bringing forth those prisoners who wished to be witnesses. A group of fifteen Templars came forward to declare the Order's innocence. Suddenly a stampede followed, eventually growing to 597 brothers who offered to present testimony in the Order's defense. On March 28, four brothers were chosen as spokesmen for the group, two of whom, Pierre de Bologna and Renaud de Provins, were able, educated, and articulate Templar priests.

---

[†] Legman suggests that Jacques de Molay was known to be homosexual and that he made a deal in which he admitted to denying Christ and defiling the cross in exchange for not pursuing the more personally embarrassing charge. At least two Templars accused him of a relationship with his valet, who confirmed at least one such incident in his own testimony. The valet also admitted to worshipping the idol. See *The Guilt of the Templars*, pp. 107–8.

On March 31 and April 7, Pierre de Bologna made lengthy statements in which he vehemently denied all the charges. He explained that any confessions made by the brethren had been extracted under torture. He reminded the council that in countries where torture was illegal, virtually nothing was said against the Order. He accused the king and his henchmen of attacking the Order in a shameful vendetta of foul lies. He explained the pernicious effects of torture on the human psyche, stating that torture left its victims devoid of freedom of mind. Keeping the brethren jailed under royal custody, facing the continual threat of murder and torture, made a mockery of any semblance of justice. He objected to the presence of de Nogaret and de Plaisians at the ecclesiastical proceedings, as laymen were specifically prohibited from attending. He reminded the commissioners of the two centuries of service the Order had rendered to Christianity.

Pierre de Bologna stated in his eloquent defense on April 7, 1310, that the kiss of peace was part of the holy affirmation of Christ that each Templar took on his initiation. He stated that anyone who said otherwise was guilty of mortal sin. (In November 1307, he had admitted to denying Christ, spitting on the Crucifix, being enjoined toward homosexual congress with other Templars, and receiving the obscene threefold kiss. He swore at that time the standard formula that he was not acting under pressure but for the good of his soul.[8])

By May 1310, the situation had shifted in the Templars' favor for the first time in almost three years. The clarity, persuasiveness, and intelligence with which the Order's case was being presented threatened the king's campaign of lies, hysteria, and vilification. Philip was forced to take another approach as this sickening saga continued. Philip reopened a provincial ecclesiastical council near Paris on May 11, despite Pierre de Bologna's urgent plea to the papal commission on May 10 to prevent it. This Inquisitional body was convened under the authority of another of Philip's henchmen, the newly appointed archbishop of Sens, Phillipe de Marigny, brother of the powerful royal chamberlain Enguerrand de Marigny. The very next day, May 12, Archbishop de Marigny declared fifty-four Templar brothers — who had just testified in defense of the Order before the papal commission — guilty as relapsed heretics because they had revoked earlier confessions made under torture. The men were immediately taken to a field and burned alive, heroically proclaiming their innocence and that of the Order as they died.

The impact of this atrocity on the witnesses prepared to testify

before the papal commission was as Philip predicted. They were demoralized. The demonstration of the king's ruthless determination to crush
the Order succeeded in silencing the remaining Templar defenders.
Meanwhile, Archbishop de Marigny's burnings continued. Within
days, 120 men perished by fire. The archbishops of Reims and Rouen,
both Philip's appointees, began their own provincial councils. An
uncounted number of Templars went to their deaths, many of whom
were chosen from the dwindling ranks of those willing to testify in support of the Order. Archbishop de Marigny had Order spokesman
Renaud de Provins brought before his provincial council to answer for
his crimes. The papal commission sent representatives to the archbishop to protest that this would make their inquiry a farce. De Marigny
was initially undaunted. He eventually capitulated and arranged for de
Provins to be returned to the papal commission. Then it was discovered
that Pierre de Bologna had mysteriously disappeared from jail; most
probably he was murdered. The second session of the papal commission
adjourned on May 30.

When the papal commission reconvened for its third and final session on November 3, 1310, only a handful of witnesses were found willing to testify in favor of the Order. The remainder of this tragic charade
consisted of confessions made by nearly 200 men, many broken and
trembling, weeping on their knees. On June 5, 1311, the papal commission rendered its findings to King Philip. A complete record of the
hearings was prepared for the pope. The commission concluded that
the case against the Order was unproved. Evidence had been found,
however, that unorthodox practices were taking place that should not
go unpunished. This was enough for Philip.

In the other countries of Europe to which *Pastoralis praeeminentiae* had
been directed in 1307, various actions were taken. Despite the affection
any European authority may have had for the Templars, all Christian
rulers were obligated to comply with the pope's instructions to arrest.
The edict was initially only cursorily complied with in England. Forewarned by news of the French arrests in October, and with the three-
week delay between the receipt of *Pastoralis praeeminentiae* by Edward
on December 15 and his arrest order of January 7, 1308, a number of
English Templars were able to escape. Those who chose to remain were
treated benignly. Templars were confined to their preceptories and were
allowed to keep their possessions, even their weapons.

English common law stipulated trial by a jury of free men, in remarkable contrast to the practices of the Inquisition. Almost nothing happened until October 1309, when two visiting Inquisition officials began conducting interrogations in London without the use of torture. Not one of the 43 brothers admitted to even a single charge. After their dismal failure, the inquisitors begged the king for more latitude in interrogation. Edward condoned the use of mild torture on December 15. Even with this, the interrogations failed to extract any confessions during the spring of 1310. In June, the inquisitors complained that they could find no competent English torturers and begged the king to move the Templars to French jails where they could be "properly" interrogated. This was refused. Edward allowed a second round of torture in the fall of 1310, resulting again in no confessions. In all, 144 English Templars were questioned.

Finally, in May 1311, three Templars made the standard confessions to the charges and were absolved and reconciled with the Church. In order to appease the pope, a compromise was achieved in 1311. The English Templars declared that the Order was so defamed by the charges against it that members were unable to purge themselves. Therefore they requested to be absolved by the prelates of England and reconciled with the Church. The English Master of the Temple proudly refused even this compromise and was imprisoned in the Tower of London where he died in 1313. In Scotland, Robert Bruce had more on his mind than the ambitions of Philip and Clement and welcomed the assistance of skilled warriors in his battles with the English crown. In Ireland, the results were also virtually nil.

James II of Aragon had a change of heart after his spirited defense of the Order. In late November 1307, even before receiving Clement's bull, he ordered the Templars to be arrested and their goods seized. He may have realized that in view of the support of Philip IV, who virtually controlled the pope, his most practical posture would be to appear to cooperate with the tide of events. Also, since his kingdom was an active military front fighting the Moors, the Iberian Templars were well trained and well armed. James may have felt that swift and decisive early action would avoid a larger confrontation in the future. He sent his troops against a Templar castle in December. The garrison, which included the Aragonese Master of the Temple, surrendered peaceably. Other castles resisted, however, hardened in their resolve by the king's unwillingness to negotiate. The popularity of the Templars was demonstrated by the fact that local noble youths joined the knights in their castles to aid in their defense. The last Templar castle surrendered in July 1309.

The papal inquiry in Aragon did not even begin until January 1310. Even though the Order had been engaged in military action against the king for two and a half years, the imprisoned Templars were well treated. While torture was sparingly applied in 1311 on direct orders from the pope, still no confessions were obtained. In Aragon as well as in other countries of the Iberian peninsula, including Portugal, Majorca, and Castile, the Templars were found innocent. After their acquittal, many surviving Castilian Templars went off to live as anchorites in the mountains. It is said that after death their bodies remained incorruptible in eloquent testimony to their innocence and martyrdom.[9]

In Germany, the authorities pursued the pope's orders with varying degrees of commitment and efficiency depending on the local political situation. On May 11, 1310, a group of twenty armed Templars burst into the proceedings of the Council of Mainz, loudly proclaiming their innocence of all charges. They stated that the crosses on the mantles of those Templars already burned had been remarkably untouched by the flames in dramatic witness to the innocence of the Order. When the council reassembled, all thirty-seven Templars who testified were unanimous in declaring themselves innocent. The Order was declared innocent. But Clement was angered and overturned the German verdict.

In Italy the Templars were a small presence. It seems that many were able to flee because very few witnesses were found. Local rulers responded differently to the pope's commands. In Lombardy, despite the orders of the pope, the authorities refused to use torture and the Templars were found innocent. In Ravenna, the Templars were also favorably regarded. Only seven Templars were brought before the council. Torture was not used and all were found innocent. In Naples, the Angevin allies of Philip complied immediately, and some forty-eight Templars were arrested and killed. In the papal states, only eight Templars were found, of whom seven were convicted. In other areas of Italy where torture was legal, such as Navarre and Tuscany, the Templars were found guilty at the first trials.

In Cyprus, headquarters of the Order since the loss of the Holy Land, Amaury de Lusignan had overthrown his brother in 1306 and become governor of the island with the help of the Templars. Upon receiving the pope's directive, Amaury negotiated with the Templars over the terms by which he could comply with the papal directive and make the necessary arrests. In May 1308 the Cypriot Master of the Order and two other leaders presented themselves before the governor, proclaiming their innocence and that of the 118 Templars on the island. On June 1, 1308, Amaury laid siege to the Templar castle at Limassol. The Templars surrendered and were placed under limited arrest. Hearings were not held until May 1310. All those questioned proclaimed their innocence. Amaury de Lusignan, however, was assassinated on June 5, which allowed Clement to institute new trials and make extensive use of torture to reach a more satisfactory verdict.

On October 16, 1311, the general council of the Church, which had been delayed by a year, opened in Vienne, France. Its threefold purpose was to examine the Templar situation, to study the viability of another crusade, and to make plans for reforming the Church. The ambitious council turned out to be very unpopular. One-third of the invited clergy failed to attend and none of the invited European royalty showed up. Clement's concern was clearly limited to the disposal of the Templar property. Among other pressures being exerted on him, Philip and de Nogaret had revived their threat of a posthumous trial of Pope Boniface on charges quite similar to those leveled against the Templars, only worse. His body was to be exhumed and burned, any gains in papal power he had been able to win were to be reversed, and the excommunication of de Nogaret was to be lifted.

As the council drew nearer, Clement realized he earnestly needed more damaging evidence then had so far been collected. With the exception of France, home to Philip's gruesome machinery of state, there had been little confirming evidence of Order-wide guilt. Clement's bull of November 22, 1307, and his activities since then, had irrevocably committed him on the question of the guilt of the Order with which his own fate was inextricably bound. Thus he stepped up his demands for torture. Men throughout Europe who had languished in prison for years since their initial confrontations with the Inquisition were dragged before their interrogators once again. Numerous new confessions and reversals of hitherto retracted confessions resulted from Clement's feverish and bizarre activities to legitimize his papacy.

As if by rote, Clement formally invited the Templars to come and defend themselves. Nine Templars appeared at the council to plead for

the Order, stating that fifteen hundred to two thousand brothers awaited the chance to testify on the Order's behalf. Church members in
attendance, with the exception of the French clergy, wished to allow
the Templar defenders to testify before the council. Clement, however,
ordered the immediate arrest of the small advance group in order to dis-
suade the others from coming forth and rekindling interest and sympathy for the brothers.

Clement was unable to gain ascendancy over the council because
of the transparency of his case. Philip, grew impatient. In February
1312, he sent a delegation composed of de Nogaret, de Plaisians,
Enguerrand de Marigny, and other French nobles and cardinals to plead
his concerns to Clement. This group angered many council members by
spending twelve days in private meetings with the pope. In March,
Philip issued an ultimatum stating that the Order must be suppressed
because evidence of heresy and other crimes had been found in June by
the papal commission. He added that Templar wealth should be reas-
signed to a new crusading order.

Clement's dilemma was finally solved on March 20, 1312, when
Philip arrived with a military force to ensure the action of the council.
The matter was to be forever closed. On March 22, a secret consistory
of the Council of Vienne was convened. Clement presented his bull
Vox in excelso to the assembled cardinals and prelates. In it he stated
that while the evidence against the Order did not justify its definitive
condemnation, the proceedings had so scandalized the Order that no
honorable man would consider membership. This state of affairs would
so weaken the efforts of Christendom in the Holy Land that he was
bound to abolish the Order. The consistory voted by a four-fifths majority to suppress the Order. On April 3, Clement publicly read Vox in
excelso, and the dissolution of the Knights Templar was complete.
Three thrones were erected on the podium for the reading. Clement
was seated in the center with Philip to one side and his son, the king of
Navarre, on the other. "It was done. It was so simple, Clement discovered, after all. In a few sentences and a few minutes he had succeeded
where all the armies of Islam had failed."[10]

While Philip still hoped for the formation of a new order with
himself or one of his sons at its head, he realized this was not to be. His
character had been forever blackened, his dream of ruling a Christian
empire as the Warrior King was over. Clement announced on May 2, in
the bull entitled Ad providam, that all Templar property was to be
assigned to the Hospitallers, and Philip was to be reimbursed for his

expenses since 1307. In Castile, Aragon, Majorca, and Portugal local military orders were to be the recipients of Templar goods and property and were to provide refuge for dispossessed Templars.

As might be expected, the Order's wealth had been systematically looted during the years since the first arrests. With conviction a foregone conclusion, charters granting property had been revoked. Stores of food, clothing, horses, livestock, movable property, and even timber had been confiscated by governments and the Church. Rents due the Order had been collected for years by the authorities. Debts payable to convicted heretics were absolved. This was particularly fortuitous for Philip, who had borrowed vast sums from the Order. Monastic orders maintained scrupulous historical records and documentation of their activities, and undoubtedly the Templars were no exception; however, their archives were forever lost. The Hospitallers, not surprisingly, were able to reap little from Clement's grant. Plunder had been the prime object of suppression and few Templar assets remained for the benefit of the Hospital. It was ten years after Clement issued *Ad providam* before the Hospitallers were able to collect any remaining Templar property.

On May 6, 1312, Clement decreed in the bull *Considerantes dudum* that the fate of leaders of the Order would be dealt with by papal authority, while the brothers would submit to the provincial councils for judgment. Most surviving brothers were treated fairly gently. Those who were found innocent or submitted willingly to the Church were allowed to remain in former Templar houses and were even granted pensions from remaining Order property. Only those who refused to confess, or who revoked their confessions, were punished as heretics and burnt. Many brave knights chose this path.

In 1317, German Templars were allowed to join the Hospitallers. In Aragon, James II founded the Order of Montesa in 1317, which welcomed former Templars. In Portugal, Templars were allowed to join the new military Order of Christ, founded by King Diniz. In 1318, Clement's successor, Pope John XXII, commanded religious orders to support surviving Templars in Naples. He also stated that their vows remained in force. Therefore, for example, they were forbidden to marry. With these statements, he tacitly acknowledged their orthodoxy, completely contradicting his predecessor's actions against them.

The four ranking Templar leaders — Grand Master Jacques de Molay, Visitor of France Hugh de Pairaud, Preceptor of Normandy Geoffroi de Charney, and Preceptor of Aquitaine Geoffroi de Gonneville — were brought before a special papal commission of three cardinals convened in Paris on March 18, 1314. The hearing was to be a mere formality since the leaders had repeatedly confessed; all four were to be imprisoned for life. But de Molay and de Charney revoked their confessions and proclaimed the innocence of the Order. Thus guilty of a relapse into heresy, the two were turned over to the civil authorities for burning that very evening. With great courage, loudly proclaiming their innocence and orthodoxy, Jacques de Molay and Geoffroi de Charney were burned at the stake on Ile de Javiaux, a small island in the Seine. Their behavior was widely admired by the assembled onlookers, who reverently collected their ashes as relics.

Legends were immediately born that seemed to vindicate these once-great warriors against the injustices that had been perpetrated against them. It was said that a group of Templars who had proclaimed their innocence and were being taken to their executions passed by Guillaume de Nogaret. One screamed out a curse against the villainous lawyer: In eight days de Nogaret would appear before the tribunal of the Lord to face his judgment. Eight days later, de Nogaret died. Jacques de Molay is said to have uttered a curse as the flames engulfed him, demanding that if the Order were innocent, the pope be summoned to God's tribunal within forty days and the king within the year to answer for their crimes. Clement died in thirty-three days, Philip eight months later. Three of Philip's sons succeeded him to the throne. All were dead within fourteen years of Philip's demise, thus ending the three-hundred-year reign of the direct line of the Capetian royal family.

# CHAPTER TWENTY-SIX

# REFLECTIONS ON THE TEMPLAR ORDER

The inevitable and immediate question regarding the Knights Templar is, of course, were they guilty? I believe the question should be rephrased: Of what might the Templars have been guilty, and who among them were?

Common sense must accompany any speculation on the question. The story of the Templars contains the entire spectrum of human experience: heroism and cowardice, generosity and greed, intelligence and stupidity, humility and pride, self-denial and self-indulgence, spiritual aspirations and failings, adherence to and betrayal of oaths. To help place these men in context, let us keep in mind that throughout the two hundred years of the Order's existence, the vast majority of its members were little removed from peasants, while most of its knights were far from the spiritual luminaries of myth. On the other hand, I believe that some Templars did live up to the elements of their myth.

The absolute truth of the matter is this: It is impossible for anyone to state with certainty whether the Order was guilty or innocent of the charges leveled against it. The question will forever remain one of the vexing problems of history. Was there a policy of heresy — either passed along in a secret oral tradition widely available to the numerous preceptories throughout the world, or clutched tightly to the breast of each Grand Master and his chosen elite? This is exactly the type of conspiracy the French king and pope accused them of perpetrating. Many Templars died, facing torture and imprisonment, and the Order was ruined as a result of these accusations. Yet, the only conspiracy of which we have unmistakable evidence is that between King Philip, Pope Clement, and Counselor de Nogaret.

For centuries historians, occultists, conspiracy theorists, and others have speculated on the guilt or innocence of the Templars. The question has become a virtual litmus test, an article of faith, among opposing camps. Some believe that the Templars were the mystical harbingers of light and the secret initiators of the Renaissance and all later esoteric movements. Others believe the Order had degenerated into an evil and idolatrous sect, whose spiritual descendants still function as the cynical, atheistic, and nameless forces behind the international statist movement embodied by the United Nations and other prototypical world-government organizations.

A third interpretation is the so-called "rationalist" position, the brightly polished intellectual suit of armor worn by the skeptical historian who essentially states that the Templars were indeed a part of the historical record and were exterminated in the Middle Ages. Those Templars who survived may have joined other religious orders or entered civilian life, but they eventually died out and were forgotten — except for periodic outbreaks of a kind of St. Vitus's dance of mythological passion, fueled alternately by romantics and charlatans. People of this mind-set can point to the lack of tangible documentary evidence of either doctrinal heresy within the Order or the visibility of a "hidden tradition." They satisfy themselves that the cause of historical accuracy has been served by their refusal to see the larger thematic picture.

The scholarly creativity and sense of humor that historian and erotologist G. Legman brings to the discussion is unique. He writes that the Templars were exquisitely guilty as charged — they were a homosexual orgy cult based on Luciferian-dualist principles in which the mysterious idol, Baphomet, is the key. Legman appends the long section on the Templars from scholar-antiquarian Thomas Wright's 1866 essay "The Worship of the Generative Powers" in support of his conclusions. Both Legman and Wright trace the initiation ritual of which the Templars were accused through the Gnostic phallic worship of pre-Christian and anti-Christian cults. Wright ascribes the obscene rites described by early Christian heresiologists to "a mixture of the license of the vulgar Paganism of antiquity with the wild doctrines of the latter Eastern philosophers."[1] He believed that Persian Manichaeans fled persecutions in the east by migrating west and establishing sects of the nature of the Cathars. He further identifies the medieval Satan with Priapus.

The Gnostic model of the bisexual and androgynous nature of divinity has long been taken by various sects as an endorsement of both heterosexual and homosexual contact between adherents. The idea that the Templars were infused with an earlier broad-based sexual magical paganism — whose universality extends through Sufism, Buddhism, Hinduism, Kabbalistic Judaism, Taoism, the sixteenth-century witch cults, and the twentieth-century activities of Gerald Gardner and Aleister Crowley — may seem fanciful. Yet something like this is exactly what we are contemplating when acknowledging a heretical doctrine among the Templars that was not solely the creation of Philip and de Nogaret. To dispute this possibility entirely seems as perilous as embracing it wholeheartedly.

I believe the evidence points to an interpretation that neither exaggerates the realities of history and common sense nor sacrifices the mystery and romance that have accompanied the Templars since the day of their founding. Three critical influences are indisputable in this history, and their effects must be accounted for in any discussion that seeks to accept the facts of human behavior as we know it.

The first factor was the doctrinal creativity employed by Saint Bernard in establishing the Rule of the Order, and the propaganda designed to attract members and financial backers. Bernard made use of a sophisticated interpretive methodology that tended to explore, examine, and create religious dogma. A military-religious order of knight-monks — a warrior clergy — was a new idea for Christianity. Its shadowy origins might easily be traced to the story of King David in the Old Testament, in which David's slaying of Goliath identifies him as a holy killer in the service of the Lord. Jesus often spoke as a warrior, using military analogies to express the unequivocal nature of the commitment required to progress along the spiritual path. When he said, "Think not that I have come to send peace on earth; I come not to send peace, but a sword,"[2] he eloquently expressed the necessity for battle against the forces of darkness.

But the fact is that Bernard invented a new concept. It was elegant and alive. It fit the requirements of the social, political, and spiritual circumstances of the day so well that it was enormously successful. Yet it came at the tail end of a long period of cultural stagnation. That the full weight of the Church proved so receptive to Bernard's spiritual child may have opened a gateway in an otherwise dormant European psyche. Kings and nobles joined their energies to this new idea. It was not science. It was theology. A magnificent change was introduced to European Christianity, and its originator was canonized for his efforts. On the other hand, the saint's spiritual children were to be anathematized and exterminated. What so clearly distinguished the Templars from the Hospitallers and the Teutonic Knights was the exquisite Templar spiritual myth. Their founding was a creative psychic act that briefly illumined medieval Europe; their destruction was a dark event of equal but opposite magnitude.

The second critical factor was the influence of contact with the Holy Land upon Europeans in general, and members of the military orders in particular. Arab culture was infinitely more refined than that of Europe in the Dark Ages. The region was also replete with many other faiths. The mystics, fakirs, Zoroastrians, Gnostics, Sufis, and Buddhists whom they encountered would have presented a kaleidoscopic panorama to the newly arrived Crusaders. It was inevitable that the more intelligent and spiritually inclined knights would compare the superstitions and dogmas of Catholicism with the richness and sophistication of the Oriental theologies to which they were exposed. Increasing doubt concerning the exclusive possession of divine favor by Christianity would gradually undermine orthodoxy. The initial contact between Crusaders and the Assassins occurred during the Qiyama. As the systematic overturning of Muslim Shariah took place among the Syrian Nizaris, some sense of the subtlety of their beliefs may have been communicated to their new acquaintances. The rejection of Islamic orthodoxy by the Ismaili initiate is profoundly reminiscent of the rejection of Christian orthodoxy ascribed to the Templars by the Order's accusers.

The military orders were the most stable European presence among the varied Crusading entities. We have seen the local baronage, financially exhausted by the requirements of self-defense, donate land and fortresses to the orders. European kings and nobles came for a time of crusading and left to return home — undoubtedly enriched by their experience — so that during the two centuries in question European society was certainly influenced by its contact with Outremer. But the military orders were a continuous presence. Members would learn the language, bargain and conduct business, enter personal friendships and political alliances, read literature, discourse on philosophy, and even quietly take lovers. In time, the ranks of the orders would contain people who had spent more of their lives in the East than in Europe, people more at home with oriental culture than with that of their birthplace.

The third factor that must be weighed into the Templar question is the influence of the Cathars. We repeatedly encounter the popularity and primacy of Languedoc in the history of the Templars. From the enthusiastic reception to their earliest promotional activities to their despicable conduct during the Albigensian Crusades, Templar history is inextricably entwined with that of Languedoc. The very heresy they were enlisted to stamp out included elements with which they were accused during their own trials. If heresy did enter the Order, this was a likely area of ingress. For example, the sacred kiss of which the Templars were accused echoes the Cathar kiss of peace among the Perfect. The charge of spitting on the cross seems to be very much in line with the Cathar hatred of the image of the crucified Jesus. The term *bougre*, or *bugger*, used against the Cathars anticipates the charge of homosexuality against the Templars. The collective confession of the *apparella-mentum* among the Perfect seems to be echoed in the Templar chapter proceedings. The rejection of family is common to both, as is their overtly antisexual attitude.

Antinomian Christianity would immediately choose the cross as a primary symbol to disparage in its quest for truth. The loathsome ideal of vicarious atonement, in which an innocent substitute or scapegoat is offered by the coward for his own spiritual redemption, could well be construed as worthy of disdain. Nor is it an impossible journey to imagine the transformation of the Cathar rejection of the physical body and its sexual nature into an embrace of apparent licentiousness. In both responses to the psychobiological needs of the human being, there is an ascetic rejection of one aspect of the psyche — either the physical hunger for sex in the case of the celibate, or the emotional hunger for bonding and personalized affection in the case of the libertine.

We pause here for another word of caution in support of the possible innocence of the Templars. It has been said that no Templar came forward to die for his heretical beliefs as so many of the Cathar martyrs did. Yet Jacques de Molay, for all his wavering, died a martyr proclaiming the innocence of the Order, as did many others who could have easily escaped the flames of the Inquisition if they had simply refused to revoke their confessions made under torture.

For the esoteric student to blandly assume the guilt of the Templars in order to advance a romantic theory of history and initiation may well be to defile the Order's memory with the slanders of the French king. Charles Henry Lea points out that accepting the guilt of the Templars logically implies accepting the Inquisition's later accusations against the witches. He also makes the astute observation that if the Templars really were guilty of founding or promulgating an anti-Christian doctrine, *they would have concealed their heresy* with a carefully graded progressive unveiling of the secret. He dismisses as absurd the idea that any heresy would immediately be revealed to all and sundry at the first occasion of their admission to the Order.[3]

The Templars never had the top-down hierarchical structure we have observed among the Nizaris. There was no Templar Imam. The Grand Master was an *elected* official who might be chosen for his strategic and military prowess or his political connections. Except perhaps in the case of Hughes de Payens, we do not find spirituality to be a prerequisite for acquiring the office. The Grand Master was certainly required by the Rule to be brave, to hold the interests of the Order as primary, to exhibit spiritual humility and generosity, and to bind himself to honor. But, the Grand Master was never conceived of as a channel of Higher Consciousness, as was the Nizari Imam, who was in a position to alter fundamentally the doctrines of the sect. We have seen Hasan II turn Alamut upside down with the Qiyama, while his grandson Hasan III did the same when he forced the Assassins to reject Shiism and embrace Sunnism. Although the Templar Grand Master had the ability to enforce or relax the Rule at his discretion, there is no convincing evidence of a clandestine Rule that enjoined upon the Order as a whole the behavior of which it was accused.

The Assassins under Hasan-i-Sabah were a deeply mystical secret society that did much to alter the political reality of its day in order to spread its religious teaching and establish its own political freedom in a hostile environment. The Knights Templar, as a group, were far less sophisticated. However, the early influence of the mystical teachings of Saint Bernard, the exposure to the rich and varied spiritual traditions encountered in the Near East, and the continual effects of the heretical Cathar current, may have created an inner corps of initiates who developed alternate doctrines of spiritual attainment during their association with the Order. This underground Templar elite, when exposed to the mystical tenets of the Assassins, would have found therein a spiritual richness worthy of their complete attention. The profundity and integrity of the teachings they subsequently developed were utterly defiled by the imaginative and vile slander of King Philip and the Inquisition.

I believe the interpretation of the Order's guilt or innocence that is most consistent with the historical evidence, and with a common-sense understanding of human nature, suggests that an inner corps of Templars quite possibly subscribed to an echo of the behaviors of which the Order at large was accused. And these men, some of whom survived, were the mystical channels by which the Gnostic-Ismaili legacy entered European occultism, where it has continued to influence the Western Mystery Tradition ever since.

PART FOUR

# Afterword

✠

# THE PATH OF THE MYSTERIES

The focus of this book has been intentionally narrowed to explore one of the major nexus points in the development of Western esotericism, the two centuries of the Crusades. This is an era of history that has been carefully researched by scholars and is reasonably well documented. Our thesis has been that the Western Mystery Tradition evolved into its present form largely as a result of the marriage between the mystical teachings of Islam and those of Christianity. Since both Christianity and Islam were founded on Judaism, Western occultism could be described as the fusion of the esoteric currents of our three great monotheistic faiths during the Crusades. When the sons of Isaac and Ishmael celebrated their long-delayed family reunion, they openly embraced the daughters of Sophia, the pagan wisdom of antiquity that had lain concealed within the esoteric doctrines of all three religions. From these unions was born the re-awakened soul of Western culture and its still-unrealized potential.

The following overview of occultism before and after the Crusades is offered in support of my acceptance of this thesis. Although it will be possible only to touch on the highlights of the development of the Western Mysteries, this summary will help illustrate the movement of systems of esoteric truth through different periods and cultures. Beginning with Egypt — home of the first objective historical manifestation of the Mysteries — we will observe a fairly coherent progression of occult knowledge until the Dark Ages fell upon Europe in the sixth century. European pagan philosophers and initiates, forced to leave their homelands, migrated to the more hospitable realms of Persia, carrying with them their Gnostic and Neoplatonic bounty. A number of the most important esoteric components of the Ismaili wisdom teachings will be instantly recognized in the following pages. Next, after the end of the Crusades, the reintroduction of occult teachings to the West will be evident as we observe the flourishing of the esoteric arts and the profusion of mystical secret societies that began during the Renaissance. Finally, broadly tracing these societies and their teachings through to their modern descendents should help establish the personal relevance of much of the complex history we have explored to this point.

## The Origins of the Western Mystery Tradition

**Egypt.** Egypt is known as the mother of civilization and the birthplace of Western esotericism. The Egyptian religion was a magical religion that involved a continuous interaction between the individual and the various deities who constituted its elaborate pantheon. Initiates were required to memorize magical formulas and spells and to demonstrate their proficiency therein; tests of courage and honor were administered by the officers of the Temple. Possession of secret knowledge, along with a highly developed moral character, were necessary to penetrate the deeper levels of the Egyptian psychic road map. Her priests developed a highly evolved system of magic that they represented in written, illustrated, and sculpted form. Egypt's Mysteries were allied with the sacred kingship of the realm. There was thus little need for an esoteric underground of the type we encounter among the Ismailis or in post-Crusade Europe.

Egypt has long been acknowledged as the home of the alchemical arts and sciences. Its moral teaching presented in its wisdom literature and mortuary texts attain to the highest levels of sacred awareness. Egyptian art is awe-inspiring. Its temples, statues, frescoes, carvings, jewelry, painted scrolls, and sarcophagi stand as mute witnesses to a brilliant and lofty spiritual culture that has never been equaled on earth. The silent and stationary images of the Book of the Dead continue to speak and move today, some four millennia after their creation.

**Hebrew Kabbalah.** The Kabbalah is the esoteric Jewish doctrine. The word comes from the Hebrew root *QBL,* meaning "to receive," and refers to the passing down of secret knowledge through oral transmission. The Kabbalah is said to have been taught by God to a select company of angels in Paradise, who conveyed it directly to Adam after the Fall, offering a means by which he could reclaim his former state of spiritual grace. It was passed on to Noah and then to Abraham (early second millennium B.C.E.), who traveled to Egypt, where he shared the doctrines of the Kabbalah with chosen priests. These in turn passed it on to adepts of other nations. Long after, Moses (ca. thirteenth century B.C.E.) was initiated during his desert wanderings, when he too was taught directly by the angels. Moses concealed the kabbalistic doctrine within the first four books of the Pentateuch. Such is the legendary derivation of the Kabbalah, which remained deep within Jewish culture until Rabbi Simeon Ben Jochai's disciples collated his treatises into the central kabbalistic work known as the *Zohar*, which was first published in Spain in the thirteenth century.

The most important graphic symbol of the Kabbalah is the Tree of Life. It is a richly evocative image of the multiplicity inherent in the emanationist cosmos envisioned by the ancient mystics and seers who developed the teaching. The Tree includes within itself the celestial, archangelic, angelic, and planetary realms, as well as the earthly and demonic worlds. Its hierarchical geometric construction begins with an Invisible from which proceeds Unity. All creation flows from that Unity in a series of progressively denser planes of being. The Tree of Life is reflected in the Four Worlds (Archetypal, Creative, Formative, and Material), which correspond to the Four Elements (Fire, Water, Air, and Earth). As a diagram, the Tree is composed of ten spheres, or Sephiroth (representing the numbers one to ten), connected by twenty-two paths (the sacred letters of the Hebrew alphabet). Together they comprise the thirty-two Paths of Wisdom described in the *Sepher Yetzirah*, an early kabbalistic text attributed to Abraham. Within the richness of its symbolism, the Tree of Life provides a structural map of the means of liberation.

A kabbalistic tradition exists among the Arabs and Greeks, both of whose languages are alphanumeric. Thus, like Hebrew, words and phrases can be plumbed for hidden meaning based on their numerical equivalence to other words and phrases. Similarly, numbers can be understood to conceal deeper meaning based on the words they represent. Egyptian sacred art also exhibits a correspondence between the postures of the figures in its vignettes and the shapes of the hieroglyphics.[1] Initiates learned the secret keys that allowed them to decode these symbols and read the concealed messages within the paintings and sculpture.

**Greece.** The Mysteries were carried from Egypt to Greece by the mythic poet and musician Orpheus, credited as the originator of the Greek pantheon. The Eleusinian Mysteries, believed to have been founded about 1400 B.C.E., became the most popular and widespread venue for the communication and preservation of the esoteric truths of Egypt. Many of the principles of the Eleusinian Mysteries have been preserved for the modern world by Plato (ca. 428–348 B.C.E.), particularly in his *Timaeus* and *Critias*, and by the Roman writer and satirist Lucius Apuleius (second century) in his *Transformation of Lucius*, or *The Golden Ass*.

The central drama of the Lesser Mysteries of Eleusis was the abduction of Persephone, daughter of the goddess of nature, Ceres, by the lord of the underworld, Pluto, who made her his bride. The hierophants of Eleusis drew parallels to the imprisonment of spirit in matter, the sepulcher of the soul. Those who persevered through the Lesser Mysteries and indicated their worthiness for advancement were introduced to the Greater Mysteries. Here the path of purification was indicated by the mythic release of Persephone for six months of each year to life on earth. The periodic escape from the material realm of the death of the soul to the Olympian heights of the immortal gods of light was the method by which the soul was initiated. Secret techniques to accomplish this were closely held by the priests and priestesses who administered the Greater Mysteries.

**Gnosticism.** Such themes were a prime component of the next great Mediterranean spiritual current broadly known as Gnosticism. Zoroastrianism (Persian dualism) was spread throughout the Roman Europe by the cult of Mithras and was another major influence on Gnosticism. Gnosticism viewed the world as divided between matter and spirit. Spirit — the spark of the ineffable, eternal, incomprehensible divinity within each individual — was trapped in the material confines of the three-dimensional body under the rule of the Demiurge, or lesser deity. Gnostic emanationist doctrines held that the preexistent irreconcilable antagonists of the Invisible (Spirit and Matter, Darkness and Light) gave birth to a middle ground, or Pleroma, the interstice between them. The Pleroma was the home of the various archangelic and angelic hierarchies from which ultimately proceed human existence in the terrestrial sphere. Reversal of the descent from spirit to matter indicated the path of return. The initiate learned to rise beyond the prison of flesh in a progressive ascent through spiritual realms mapped out in great detail by the various Mediterranean Gnostic communities. Spiritual freedom was promised as the birthright of those bold and persistent enough to claim it.

In the early years of the Christian era, the Essenes in the Holy Land and other pre-Christian Jewish and pagan Gnostics welcomed the Christian revelation. They found in its spirituality a familiar echo of their own. Gnosticism had long continued to expand because of its tendency to inclusive synthesis.

**Hermeticism.** Greek Gnostics went on to create the Hermetic literature in the second and third centuries. Hermeticism was a creative mix of the same themes that formed the background of early Christianity — Gnosticism, Greek philosophy, Jewish and Persian beliefs, and the savior mythos of the divine intercessor. Hermes Trismegistus (Thrice-Great), the Greek conception of Thoth, was said to have taught mankind the arts of writing, music, mathematics, astronomy, medicine, chemistry, magic, and philosophy. Hermes is the initiator, the psychopomp or spiritual guide, through the Invisible. The soul of the Hermetic initiate ascended through the seven planetary spheres, progressively shedding its lower nature, that it might reunite with its spiritual reality, the One who is before the First Beginning.

A considerable number of treatises were ascribed to the authorship of Hermes during the second and third centuries. These covered many topics including astrology, alchemy, magic, and the occult properties of herbs and stones. There were also philosophical and spiritual writings of intense piety with which Hermeticism is most generally identified. The Hermetic school represented the attempt to go beyond the rational and intellectual limitations of traditional Greek philosophy by directly cultivating the mystical faculties.

**Neoplatonism.** During the third to fifth centuries, the Neoplatonic movement arose from the Hermeticists. Plotinus (205–270), Porphyry (234–305), Iamblichus (ca. 250–330), and Proclus (ca. 410–485) were its prime exponents. It was the final development of the Mystery school in the Western world before the crushing silence of the Dark Ages would descend on Europe. It incorporated all the doctrines hitherto discussed and brought them to a new level of refinement. "Neo-Platonism was the supreme effort of decadent pagandom to publish and thus preserve for posterity its secret (or unwritten) doctrine. In its teachings ancient idealism found its most perfect expression."[2] In addition to its embrace of emanationist doctrines, Neoplatonism taught that intellectual knowledge was useless unless accompanied by an elevation of individual consciousness to higher states of perception. Meditation and other spiritual exercises were the means by which the initiate could attain to direct realization of the inner truths of religion and philosophy.

**Islam and the Near East.** As the pagan Mysteries declined under the dual assault of their own bloated corruption and the Christian persecutions, Western Europe plunged into the Dark Ages. The sacred teaching migrated to the Near East as scholars and anchorites forced from Neoplatonic academies and Gnostic communities by Justinian were welcomed by the Sassanian dynasty of Persia. Neoplatonism found fertile soil in the Near East. The ancient Sumerian and Babylonian civilizations had long before developed elaborate mythic pantheons and celebrated their sacred Mysteries. Many centuries after these cultures crumbled, Zoroastrianism appeared sometime between the sixth and seventh centuries B.C.E. Under the combined influence of Islam and Neoplatonism, the remnants of the doctrines of Zarathustra metamorphosed into the indigenous Persian Gnostic movements of the seventh through tenth centuries. While traditional Islam captured the aspirations of many as it spread throughout the Near East, it left a hunger for a richer and more elaborate symbology. The philosophical wealth of Neoplatonism appears to have fit perfectly with this yearning, reaching its Islamic high point in both Ismailism and Sufism.

Islam was the avenue by which the writings of Aristotle (ca. 384–22 B.C.E.) were introduced to medieval Europe. Arabic translations of Aristotle's Greek originals were re-translated into Latin during the twelfth century by Christian, Jewish, and Muslim scholars working in Spain and Sicily. Aristotle's works challenged the medieval superstitions and faith-based exclusivity of Christian spirituality, which tended to be supported by the idealism of his teacher Plato, who excluded physical reality from the concerns of the philosopher. The teachings of Aristotle were the direct antithesis of his master. Aristotle taught a form of rational inquiry and logic, the scientific method of investigation in which the power of the reason is exalted. These disciplines helped to encourage the achievements of Islam in medicine, mathematics, and science. Aristotle's investigations also extended through cosmology, metaphysics, ethics, psychology, and political theory, fields of thought that had been dormant in Europe since the fall of Rome.

**The Crusades and the Occult Underground.** The enforced contact between Christianity and Islam during the Crusades was the occasion for the next migration of the Mysteries. By the time European Christianity came in contact with the Muslim Near East, it was ready for the stimulation that would be offered by Palestine. On the other hand, by the end of the Crusades two hundred years later, the military campaigns of the Crusaders and the Mongols had bled Islam of its vitality. Europe, which entered the Dark Ages as Islam rose to its five centuries of world leadership, experienced a cultural renaissance after the Crusades. Islam was plunged into its own Dark Ages. The Muslim military victory over Europe and Mongolia resulted in social and economic defeat from which Islam is still recovering.

## WESTERN ESOTERICISM AFTER THE CRUSADES

The extensive attention devoted earlier to the Ismaili beliefs and their evolution from the Muslim mainstream makes, I believe, a persuasive case for the influence of Ismaili philosophy on European esotericism. We accept the thesis that the primary source of ingress for the Gnostic-Ismaili teachings into Europe were those individual Templar initiates who managed to escape the destruction of the Order. Templar survivors quietly continued to teach the doctrines and mystic techniques they had learned and developed in the East — the true "secret teaching" of the Order. These gradually gave rise to the flourishing of the occult arts in Europe. The centuries following the Templar dispersion in the fourteenth century have played host to an esoteric revolution that continues to this day.

**Renaissance.** The destruction of the Knights Templar was accompanied by the dying gasps of the Dark Ages. Numerous occult disciplines and secret societies began to surface almost simultaneously, mysteriously infusing the European zeitgeist. This occult flowering was part of the Renaissance, or "rebirth," the period of European history immediately following the Middle Ages, from approximately 1375 to 1575. Characterized by a surge of learning and interest in classical literature and values, it also included the decline of feudalism and growth of commerce; the discovery of America; the substitution of the Copernican heliocentric theory for the Ptolemaic geocentric model; and the invention or use of paper, the printing press, gunpowder, the mariner's compass, and the telescope.

Leonardo da Vinci (1452–1519) has long been heralded as the model of the Renaissance man — a brilliant artist and scientist whose universal interests spanned the entire range of contemporary knowledge. His fellow artists of the Italian school included the sculptor and painter Michelangelo (1475–1564), whose works typify the new spirit animating Europe. Themes of the sacred nature of the individual, which had surfaced in the Grail myths and chivalric romances of the twelfth century, became manifest during the Renaissance. The enforced collectivism characteristic of medieval feudal society and theology was replaced by an acceptance of the individual as one who "could enrich society and illuminate natural order, rather than threaten them."[3] In Renaissance art, man reassumed his rightful place in the cosmos. Michelangelo's God touches the hand of Adam directly, and with love; his David stands naked and unashamed.

Renaissance hopes for a new Golden Age were also identified with the advance of science. Discussing the significance of the discovery of America by Christopher Columbus (1451–1506), the *Encyclopedia Britannica* states, "The first really serious blow to the traditional acceptance of ancient authorities was the discovery of the New World at the end of the fifteenth century."[4] The earth was no longer flat. Soon it would cease to be the center of the solar system. Nicolaus Copernicus (1453–1543), while visiting Italy at the turn of the sixteenth century, was captivated by a Hermetic treatise on the sun written by Marsilio Ficino (1433–99), director of the Florentine Platonic Academy. Copernicus was inspired to spend the next fifty years of his life studying astronomy. His world-shaking book, *On the Revolution of the Celestial Spheres*, was published soon after his death. Copernicus cited Hermes Trismegistus in support of his conclusions that the Earth revolves around the Sun, in contrast to the scientific theories of Ptolemy accepted since the mid–second century. Galileo Galilei (1564–1642) used the newly invented telescope to prove the scientific accuracy of the heliocentric theory. He was brought before the Inquisition for his efforts and forced to recant, spending the last eight years of his life under house arrest. Despite the best efforts of the Inquisition, however, centuries of belief, instruction, and authoritative dogma were crumbling — and with them fell the infallibility of the Church.

**The Protestant Reformation.** In 1517, Martin Luther (1483–1546) publicly attacked clerical corruption and its doctrinal support in the Catholic Church. He thereby inaugurated the Protestant Reformation in Germany. It is staggering to consider how narrow Luther's escape from the flames of heresy must have been. The rise and survival of the Protestant movement demonstrated beyond argument the weakened state of the Church, and the loss of its hitherto unchallenged thousand-year monopoly on the religious life of Europe. Luther embodied religious characteristics similar to those of the Hebrew prophets of the sixth to fifth centuries B.C.E., the canonical acceptance of whose critical rejection of the established powers was unprecedented in the authoritarian climate of the ancient Near East. Luther also reflected the Donatist heresy in which the efficacy of the sacrament was perceived to be dependent on the spiritual purity of the individual who administered it.

## The Disciplines of the Western Tradition

Among the many factors undermining the authority of the Church during the Renaissance was the growth of the esoteric movements. Artists, scientists, scholars, and even politicians embraced mysterious ideas that were as new as they were old, ancient ideals whose acceptance often became a symbol of the most sophisticated modernity. We will now touch on some of the occult disciplines embraced by Renaissance esotericists.

**The Grail Myth.** Among the first subjects to capture the Renaissance imagination were the idealistic yearnings embodied in the Grail Tradition.[†] The Grail warrior faces a series of fearsome dangers and overwhelming enemies, some supernatural, who force him to draw from beyond his own limitations of power and endurance in order to prevail. His only protection is the strength of his faith and his commitment to duty and a higher purpose. The first written literature of the Grail appeared almost simultaneously with the founding of the Knights Templar. The Templars certainly inspired authors like Wolfram von Eschenbach (ca. 1170–1220), whose masterpiece *Parzival* idealized the knights as defenders of the Grail and warriors whose purity enabled them to take their nourishment directly from the sacred stone. Bernard and the Cistercian Order are acknowledged by Pauline Matarasso as the source of the monastic guidance given to Eschenbach's Grail companions. She identifies the white habits of the monks, their consistent isolation as hermits, and the virtues they espouse to the Grail knights as pure Cistercian doctrine.[5]

Chivalric orders based on Grail symbology were instituted among the nobility. The Order of the Garter was founded in England in 1348

---

[†] Thomas Malory's Grail romance, *Le Morte d'Arthur*, was the most popular book in the English language in the late fifteenth century according to Norman Cantor (*The Civilization of the Middle Ages*, p. 538).

by Edward II. The Order of the Golden Fleece was founded in Burgundy by Philip III and was associated over time with the French, Austrian, and Spanish nobility. The elaborate and ornate ceremonial activities of these orders reflected an open embrace by late medieval culture of the higher code of chivalry as an ethical choice suitable for an aristocracy in conditions of peace as well as war.

**Tarot.** The introduction of the Tarot cards to Europe closely corresponded with *Parzival*'s publication in the last quarter of the fifteenth century. The Tarot was said to have been designed by a council of initiates who met in Morocco around the year 1200. Their goal was both to protect the hidden wisdom and to make it accessible across all barriers of language and culture. Their ingenious choice of a vehicle was a common set of playing cards to be carried throughout the known world by wandering gypsy tribes. The Tarot depicts the psychospiritual processes of initiation within its mysterious imagery, believed to encompass all knowledge. Among the rich threads of its symbolic tapestry are a perfect pictorial representation of the Grail myth, along with astrological and alchemical truths. Tarot meditation makes use of magical techniques by employing the cards as energy doorways for the focusing of concentration. In structure, the Tarot is a schematic representation of the Kabbalah. Its twenty-two trumps correspond to the letters of the Hebrew alphabet and paths of the Tree of Life, its four suits to the four Elements and four Worlds, and its ten numbered cards to the ten Sephiroth.

**Renaissance Hermeticism.** The fall of Constantinople to the Ottoman Turks in 1453 forced Eastern scholars to flee to the West with books and manuscripts dating from classical Greece. The influence of the nearly forgotten Hermetic thinkers of the early Christian period blossomed during the Renaissance. In 1460, a Greek manuscript containing the primary writings of the *Corpus Hermeticum* (a collection of fifteen Hermetic treatises) was purchased by the wealthy ruler of Florence, Cosimo de Medici (1389–1464). He had founded the Platonic Academy, dedicated to the study of Greek philosophy, that functioned as a center of Renaissance Neoplatonism. He instructed Marsilio Ficino, director of the academy, to translate his newly acquired manuscript. Frances Yates points out that Renaissance Hermeticists made the primary error of believing these writings dated from remotest antiquity in

Egypt, rather than second- to third-century Greece.[6] The high esteem in which they held this material, however, has been shared by succeeding generations of occultists who are well aware of its provenance.

**Hermetic Kabbalah.** The availability of the Hermetic literature was accompanied by a widespread interest in the Hebrew Kabbalah, promoted by the works of Ficino's disciple Pico della Mirandola (1463–94). The marriage of Greek Hermeticism and Jewish Kabbalah resulted in the Hermetic Kabbalah. Pico's interest, inspired perhaps by his access to unpublished manuscripts of Raymond Lull (1235–1315), later influenced Johannes Reuchlin (1455–1522), Cornelius Agrippa (1486–1535), Robert Fludd (1574–1637), and many others who were deeply versed in the Kabbalah and who, directly or indirectly, influenced the Rosicrucian flowering of the early seventeenth century. In Germany, Knorr von Rosenroth (1636–89) translated a number of texts from the *Zohar* into Latin in his *Kabbala Denudata*. Von Rosenroth helped popularize the notion in Christian culture of the divine origin of the Hebrew language and its ability to open the secret recesses of nature. The open-ended, systematic intellectual model offered by the Hermetic Kabbalah gave occultists of many nations a common structure on which they could build their individual researches, and a common language in which they could share their conclusions.

**Alchemy.** The sixteenth and seventeenth centuries witnessed an outpouring of alchemical literature and activity. While it has become fashionable to describe alchemy as a psychospiritual process, there is no doubt that it was very much a physical experimental science, the precursor of chemistry and physics. Philosophically, alchemy represented an evolution from the extreme Gnostic repulsion toward matter to an acceptance of the material basis of incarnation. Matter was recognized as a potential medium for healing. Subtle and invisible psychic energies could be manipulated and adjusted by contact with various plants, metals, and other natural sources of energy. Alchemy acknowledged the "superiority" of spirit in the sense that matter was capable of transformation. The works of Paracelsus (1493–1541), alchemist, physician, scholar, astrological healer, and those of his teacher Johannes Trithemius, abbot, scholar, and historian, stimulated popular fascination with occult theories of healing, cryptography, Kabbalah, magic, and angelic communication. Paracelsus was so highly regarded by succeeding generations that his writings were said to have been discovered in the tomb of Christian Rosencreutz, about whom more will soon be said.

**Magic.** Magic, like alchemy, celebrates matter as an expression of the divine and as a ladder toward a heavenly return. Magic bases much of its theory and practice on a willing acceptance of the physical world as the basis from which to communicate with the spiritual forces of the invisible planes. The ban on magic by the medieval Church had forced its practitioners to remain concealed. Magic was a socially undesirable pursuit. The translation of the Hermetic writings, however, added an air of respectability and philosophical prestige to the practice of magic for the first time in the post-Christian West. Renaissance adepts such as Cornelius Agrippa in his *De occulta philosophia* (1531) defined magic as the science of the Magi and deemphasized its common connotation with sorcery. Giordano Bruno (1548–1600), a student of the works of Raymond Lull, paid for his interests in cosmology and magic by being burned at the stake by the Inquisition. He supported the heliocentric theory of Copernicus and taught that the universe was infinitely expanding and peopled with extraterrestrial and extra-dimensional life forms. He was an enthusiastic advocate of the magical arts and the deities of the Egyptian pantheon.

## WESTERN SECRET SOCIETIES

Along with astrology, the primary occult teachings, as described above, have been studied, developed, practiced, and taught by numerous mystical secret societies or special interest groups. While the Rosicrucians have traditionally been considered to be the first of these to be formally established in Europe, historian Christopher McIntosh writes that an immediate Rosicrucian predecessor may have been a hidden alchemical society founded in Germany in 1577 as the Order of Inseparables. Its senior members were owners of mines and smelting works. The Order made use of its own alphabet and recorded the results of its alchemical workings in a central secret archive.[7] Soon after, the Rosicrucians burst upon the scene. They have essentially defined the concept of the secret society for the Western world ever since. We now take a brief look at the Fraternity of the Rose Cross and at some of its more illustrious offspring over the next four centuries.

**Rosicrucianism.** The publication of the three Rosicrucian manifestos, the *Fama Fraternitatis* in 1614, the *Confessio Fraternitatis* in 1615, and *The Chemical Wedding of Christian Rosencreutz* in 1616, popularized the concept of a secret order of adepts silently guiding humanity's destiny. The idea fascinated the European mind. The French philosopher and renowned mathematician René Descartes (1596–1650) actively, but unsuccessfully, sought out the Rosicrucian Order in 1619–20 during his travels in Germany. While the manifestos boldly announced the existence and goals of the Rosicrucians, most aspirants found that attempts to contact the brothers went unanswered.

The *Fama* explained that the legendary founder of the Rosicrucians, Christian Rosencreutz, had traveled throughout the Holy Land in search of wisdom in the early to mid–fifteenth century. On his return to Europe, he was scorned by those with whom he attempted to share his knowledge because of their pride and ignorance. Eventually Rosencreutz returned to Germany, where he found three disciples to whom he could impart the sacred wisdom. These four were the initial members of the Fraternity of the Rose Cross. As the Order grew, its purpose was defined as healing. The brothers were sworn to engage themselves in healing without charge, to cultivate anonymity by dressing in the custom of the lands where they traveled, and to meet once a year at their secret headquarters known as the House of the Holy Spirit. Rosencreutz lived for 106 years, after which he was buried in a resplendent vault where he lay incorruptible for 120 years. The discovery of his tomb was the signal for the Order to announce itself to the world and trumpet the dawning of a golden age of spiritual illumination and reformation.

The *Confessio*, in particular, expressed violently antipapist views, identifying the pope as the anti-Christ. Most authorities accept Johann Valentin Andreae (1586–1654), a German Protestant minister, as the anonymous author of at least *The Chemical Wedding*. He appears to have been an active member of a group that labored to transform Europe politically as well as spiritually by establishing a reformist Protestant monarchy in Bohemia in place of the reactionary Catholic Hapsburg dynasty. This effort resulted in the coronation of the Elector Palatine Frederick V (1596–1632) and his English wife, princess Elizabeth Stuart (1596–1662), as the short-lived "Winter King and Queen of Bohemia." Frances A. Yates has described this political effort as " an expression of a religious movement which had been gathering force for many years, fostered by secret influences moving in Europe, a movement towards solving religious problems along mystical lines suggested by Hermetic and Cabalist influences."[8] She credits the end of the six-year burst of Rosicrucian literature in Germany to Frederick's military defeat by the Hapsburgs. This short-lived Rosicrucian flowering has ostensibly had the most far-reaching influence of any occult development in the Western world.

Michael Maier (1568–1622), personal physician to Emperor Rudolf II, was chiefly responsible for associating alchemy with the Rosicrucian mythos. In England, Robert Fludd, the Rosicrucian physician and occultist, wrote a number of influential works on the Hermetic Kabbalah and alchemy. His and Maier's books were illustrated with a series of exquisite drawings, rich in esoteric symbolism, executed by the publisher and engraver Johann De Bry and his talented son-in-law Matthieu Merian (1593–1650). The Enochian magical workings of John Dee (1527–1608) and Edward Kelley (ca. 1555–97) were another nexus point of this current. Dee had been a moving force behind the attempt to establish an anti-Catholic spiritual monarchy in Europe. Frances Yates writes, "[T]here can be no doubt that we should see the movement behind the three Rosicrucian publications as a movement ultimately stemming from John Dee."[9]

Francis Bacon (1561–1626), naturalist, politician, and philosopher, was associated with English Rosicrucianism. His posthumously published utopian tale The New Atlantis (1627) contains unmistakable parallels to the Rosicrucian manifestos. Thomas Vaughan (1622–56), known as Eugenius Philalethes, wrote a number of influential alchemical treatises. He also published the first English translation of the Rosicrucian manifestos in a joint edition as The Fame and Confession of the Fraternity of the Rosie Cross in 1652. The Chymical Wedding was first published in English by Ezechiel Foxcraft in 1690. Elias Ashmole (1617–92), a leading exponent of English Rosicrucianism, was an alchemist, author, and scholar. He founded the Ashmolean Museum in Oxford and was a founding member of the British Royal Society. He was also deeply involved in Masonry, which he joined in 1646, some seventy years before it publicly announced its existence. Isaac Newton (1642–1717), another member of the British Royal Society, is known to have been interested in alchemy and to have possessed copies of the Rosicrucian manifestos as well as an important alchemical work by Ashmole.

In view of the slanders we have seen directed against both the Assassins and the Templars, it is instructive to learn that in 1623, the first of a series of terrible allegations was hurled against the Rosicrucians in an anonymous pamphlet published in France.[10] The now-familiar litany of charges against them included the denial of God, blasphemy, worship of Satan, sorcery, and witchcraft.

**Freemasonry.** The first public link between Freemasonry and Rosicrucianism is cited by Christopher McIntosh as occurring in 1638, the year of Robert Fludd's death.[11] How the Masonic current became infused with the Rosicrucian mythos is impossible to pinpoint but simple to understand. The higher mystical principles of Rosicrucianism would automatically appeal to the sort of mind attracted to the similar principles of speculative Freemasonry. Rosicrucianism has been inexorably entwined with Masonry since the mid–eighteenth century when the Eighteenth Degree of the Ancient and Accepted Scottish Rite was added to honor the Brotherhood.

While there is no universally accepted definitive historical origin for Freemasonry, there are a multitude of theories and speculations that range between fact and fantasy. The most common supposition is that "speculative" Masonry (the modern fraternal secret society open to nontradesmen) evolved from the medieval guilds of builders and stonemasons, or "operative" masonry. John J. Robinson has crafted an excellent argument in *Born in Blood* against this theory, suggesting instead that a Masonic derivation from fleeing Templars makes more sense. English and Scottish Templars had ample warning of the fate that awaited them by observation of the treatment accorded to their French brethren several months before the English arrests. Some were quite likely to have gone underground, perhaps joined by a few of the French Templars who escaped Philip's arrests. The antimonarchical, antipapist basis of Freemasonry would be quite easy to understand in view of the Templar betrayal by Philip and Clement.

The secret signs, grips, and words of Masonry fit the context of a fugitive band of oppressed and excommunicated men facing capital charges from the civil and religious authorities of their day. The Masonic demand for belief in a monotheistic God, along with traditional Masonic respect and tolerance for privacy concerning the specifics of that belief, accord well with the history of the religious warriors of a monastic brotherhood suddenly being pursued as satanic heretics. The Masonic exhortation to exhibit charity to brothers in need also makes sense in the context of a fugitive brotherhood, as does the severity of the penalties invoked by the terrible oaths upon those who betray the secrets of their fellows. The common primacy of Solomon's Temple (built ca. 950 B.C.E.) in both Templar history and Masonic myth is also provocative.

The English Grand Lodge was founded in 1717 in London. Freemasonry spread at a rapid rate. In 1737, Andrew Michael Ramsay (1696–1743), a Scottish Freemason who later became the chancellor of the Grand Lodge of France, introduced the idea of the ancient origins of Masonry and the particular importance of the period of the Crusades. He stated that the Crusades had been inspired by the Masonic desire to restore the Temple of Solomon to Christianity and to allow for the continuation of the practice of sacred architecture. He claimed that Masons allied themselves with the Hospitaller Order. This suggestion soon inspired others to popularize the legend of a Templar-Masonic connection. The Templar mysteries are celebrated in the Masonic York rite in the Order of the Temple Degree, and in the Scottish rite Thirtieth Degree, or Knight Kadosch.

**The Hidden Masters.** The Gold-und Rosenkreuz (the Order of the Golden and Rosy Cross) was founded in Germany in the mid–seventeenth century by Herman Fictuld, about whom little is known. Based on an amalgamation of Masonic and Rosicrucian aspirations, it was deeply involved with alchemy. Its political agenda was conservative, in contrast to the progressive social radicalism and anti-Christian ideals of many other Rosicrucian and Masonic societies then and since. Both Knorr von Rosenroth and the physician, Kabbalist, and alchemist Francis Mercurius von Helmont (1618–99) were members. The Order had nine degrees of initiation. The concept of Secret Chiefs was heavily emphasized by this group and would become an increasingly common component of all subsequent occult secret societies. The similarity between the Secret Chiefs or Hidden Masters of Western occultism and the Ismaili Imam and Mahdhi is striking.

**Eighteenth-Century Secret Societies.** Continental Masonry was far more decentralized and anarchistic than the conservative English craft, tightly controlled by its Grand Lodge. Thus many different lodges with varied influences and practices functioned in Europe under the broad banner of Freemasonry. Baron Karl Gotthelf von Hund founded the Rite of Strict Observance in 1764. French Freemasonry had received an infusion of Catholicism between 1735 and 1740 particularly in the chapter of Clermont. Baron Hund, who had earlier converted to Catholicism, was received into these degrees during a visit to Paris in

1742. On his return to Germany, he established the Strict Observance. A successful organizer and promoter, Hund's efforts prospered. He infused his Order with a Templar mythology — members were known as New Templars. He taught that escaping English Templars fled to Scotland and that Freemasonry was a continuation of the Knights Templar. He established nine organizational provinces and a series of seven grades of initiation, at whose summit were the Unknown Superiors.[12] Alchemy was of great interest to Hund and part of the Order's success was as a clearinghouse for information on alchemical experiments.

Another major influence on German Masonry was an order known as the Clerks of the Temple, founded by Johann August Starck, who was also a Catholic convert, although he later rejected Catholicism and became a Protestant pastor. He sought for the roots of occult wisdom in Assyria, Persia, and Egypt. He claimed the Essenes had passed their secret doctrine on to the Templar clergy, who, he believed, maintained a separate doctrine from the knights. He taught that the chaplain brothers were independent of the hierarchical structure of the Templar Order and in possession of their own initiated wisdom.

On the political front, eighteenth-century Masonic Lodges played a pivotal role in bringing about the French Revolution. The legendary shadow figures of the Comte de St. Germain and Cagliostro were reputed to be organizing rebellion throughout the Masonic network. The reality of St. Germain's possession of the Philosopher's Stone remains an article of faith among occultists. The Bavarian Illuminati, founded by the Jesuit-trained professor Adam Weishaupt in 1776, also made use of the preexisting Masonic network to advance its own claims and carry on recruiting efforts. The Illuminati have been the subject of endless speculations on the nature of political conspiracy. It is still rumored today that the destruction of the monarchy during the French Revolution was organized by Illuminati operating through the Masonic lodges to avenge Templar bloodshed some four hundred years earlier.

Martines de Pasqually (d. 1774) founded the Order of the Elect Cohens in France in 1760. Pasqually's roots are obscure. He may have been a Spanish or Portuguese Jew who converted to Catholicism. His idiosyncratic magical doctrine combined elements of astrology, Gnosticism, and Kabbalah from which he built an elaborate and rigorous series of ritual magical invocations whose purpose was to facilitate the adept's communication with what Pasqually called the "Active and Intelligent Cause."[13]

In 1781, Court de Gebelin (1725–84), in his *Monde Primitif*, first called the Tarot the "Book of Thoth," after the Egyptian god of magic and divination. De Gebelin was also the first to state that the Tarot was derived from Egypt, and that its twenty-two trumps corresponded to the letters of the Hebrew alphabet. Nineteenth-century adept Eliphas Lévi (1810–75) made his famous observation on the Tarot in *Transcendental Magic* (1855–56): "As an erudite Qabalistic book, all combinations of which reveal the harmonies preexisting between signs, letters and numbers, the practical value of the Tarot is truly and above all marvelous. A prisoner devoid of books, had he only a Tarot of which he knew how to make use, could in a few years acquire a universal science, and converse with an unequaled doctrine and inexhaustible eloquence."[14]

**Nineteenth-Century Secret Societies.** Eliphas Lévi, Frederick Hockley, Papus (Dr. Gérard Encausse, 1865–1916), Max Theon (ca. 1848–1927), Marquis Stanislaus de Guaita (1861–97), Franz Hartmann (1838–1912), Theodor Reuss (1855–1923), and others wrote about, practiced, and taught the sacred sciences. P. B. Randolph (1825–75) founded the Brotherhood of Eulis. He claimed Rosicrucian initiation and also initiation by the "Ansaireth or Nusairis of Syria" from whom he received, "the priceless secret of compounding elixir of life, the secret of youth, the mystery of forgetfulness, the stone of the philosophers and the mystery of the magic crystal, which permitted the seer to behold all that transpired on earth and on any of the planets."[15]

Sir Edward Bulwer-Lytton (1803–73) chose the Comte de St. Germain as the prototypical Rosicrucian adept and hero of his unforgettable novel *Zanoni*. Joséphin Péladan (1858–1918) began his Salons de la Rose-Croix in Paris in 1892, which attracted such artists and musicians as Gustave Moreau (1826–98), Félicien Rops (1833–98), George Roualt (1871–1958), and Erik Satie (1866–1925). Madame Blavatsky (1831–91) founded the Theosophical Society in 1875. Her literary accomplishments in *Isis Unveiled* and *The Secret Doctrine* represented the largest and most successful effort to teach and popularize the primary doctrines of occultism since the Christian era began. Blavatsky introduced Oriental religion to Europe and actively promulgated the concept of Secret Chiefs or Hidden Masters invisibly guiding seekers upon the path of wisdom.

The Societas Rosicruciana in Anglia was founded in 1867 by Robert Wentworth Little (1840–78) with the assistance of Kenneth Mackensie (1833–86). Mackensie claimed to have received initiation from German Rosicrucians. Among the SRIA's membership was

William Wynn Westcott (1848–1925), a London coroner and occult scholar who became its head in 1891. Another member and future leader was the learned adept S. L. MacGregor Mathers (1854–1918), who translated von Rosenroth's *Kabbala Denudata*, published in English as *The Kabbalah Unveiled*.

In 1888, Westcott and Mathers, along with Dr. W. R. Woodman, founded the Hermetic Order of the Golden Dawn in London. The Golden Dawn included among its members some of the leading lights of English literary and artistic circles such as William Butler Yeats (1865–1939), Arthur Machen (1863–1947), Algernon Blackwood (1869–1951), George Russell (A. E.; 1867–1935), Florence Farr, and, of course, Aleister Crowley (1875–1947). Mathers systematized the entire Western esoteric tradition to date and built an ingenious synthesis that still forms the dominant intellectual curriculum for English-speaking occultists. He constructed the Enochian system, the singular contribution of the Golden Dawn, which resumes all these threads. The initiatory symbolism of the Golden Dawn is based on the Rosicrucian myth. Its central ritual is a dramatic reenactment of the discovery of the tomb of Christian Rosencreutz.

The influence of the Golden Dawn on modern occultism is ubiquitous. The concept of Secret Chiefs held a position of major importance in the Golden Dawn, which stated that its leaders were in close contact with such beings. According to the Order's own history, its founders had made contact with a female German Rosicrucian adept who authorized them to establish the society. After a time, however, she discontinued correspondence. An associate later wrote that she was no longer available but that the English aspirants had received sufficient instruction to form their own links with the Hidden Masters and therefore had no further need of their German sponsor.

**The Twentieth Century.** The breakup of the Golden Dawn was largely the result of the failure of that communication, at least according to Aleister Crowley, who succeeded Mathers as the direct representative of the Inner Plane Adepts. Crowley was indisputably the greatest occult genius of the twentieth century. He rose rapidly through the ranks of the Golden Dawn. Like Christian Rosencreutz and the Templars before him, he set off on a series of travels that gave him firsthand exposure to the wisdom traditions of the world's many cultures. Crowley always expressed a particular admiration for Islam. In *The Book of the Law*, transmitted in Cairo in 1904, Crowley, like Muhammad, is designated as the Prophet of the New Aeon by Aiwass, "a messenger from the forces ruling this earth at present."[16] Crowley described Aiwass as a "tall dark man . . . with the face of a savage king . . . [whose dress] suggested Assyria or Persia."[17]

Crowley's influence on modern occultism is incalculable, penetrating nearly every Western school. Two allied magical societies continue working in his name today. They are the Ordo Templi Orientis (O.T.O.) and A∴A∴, both composed of men and women who have accepted the principles of The Book of the Law. Crowley's particular genius was first, as a "medium," that he received The Book of the Law, and second, that in designing his unique system of magical training for the A∴A∴, Crowley introduced Eastern techniques of meditation and concentration (yoga) to the Western magical tradition. In this important sense he reaffirmed the spiritual marriage of East and West, consummated during the Crusades, to inaugurate the spiritual renaissance he hailed as the New Aeon. The O.T.O. is based on an interpretation of the Templars. Crowley calls his faithful "knight-monks of Thelema." The Order is structured on strict hierarchical and military lines. Its teaching is said to have sprung from European interaction with Islam during the Crusades.

I accept Crowley as the designated modern expositor of the Western Mysteries. With certain exceptions, Western occultism since his death in 1947 has been built on his work. The exceptions are Rudolf Steiner (1861–1925; himself briefly a member of O.T.O.[18]), who founded Anthroposophy. Although an original and creative school of spiritual development, the structural foundation of Anthroposophy is esoteric Christianity. This fact begins to separate it from the more narrow field of occultism under discussion here. I would also exempt G. I. Gurdjieff (1877–1949) and his equally creative teachings of psychospiritual awareness from this particular category of occultism.

The most notable English-speaking adepts who followed in Crowley's footsteps include artist Austin Osman Spare (1889–1956); Kabbalist Charles Stansfeld Jones, known as Frater Achad (1886–1950); Karl Germer (1885–1962), Crowley's successor as Outer Head of the O.T.O.; Wilfred T. Smith (1885–1957); Jack Parsons (1914–52), a scientist with the Jet Propulsion Laboratory in California whose pioneering work on solid rocket fuel has been honored by a crater on the moon bearing his name; author and healer Dr. Israel Regardie (1907–85); Major Grady L. McMurtry (1918–85), who was identified by Crowley shortly before the latter's death as the future "caliph" of the O.T.O. to succeed Germer, and who reactivated the Order in 1969 and success-fully passed it on to its current leadership; Marcelo Ramos Motta (1931–87); Harry Smith (1923–91) a widely heralded modern genius who made singular contributions in a number of fields including anthropology, art, film, and music, and who played a major role in the magical development of a generation of modern occultists; and Kenneth Grant (b. 1924). One O.T.O. member who has been particularly influential in modern religious movements was Gerald Gardner (1884–1964). A personal friend of Crowley's, Gardner was responsible for the revival of witchcraft (wicca), which has since grown steadily to become an increasingly popular component of the "New Age" spectrum. Another modern adept who has been influenced by Crowley's work is Dr. Michael Aquino. His Temple of Set, founded in 1975, has attracted an intelligent and committed following. Peter Carroll's explorations in Chaos Magick are also worthy of note.

**The Dark Side.** The Templars and Assassins have also attracted the attention of darker souls. The Ku Klux Klan was founded in Pulaski, Tennessee, in 1865 and spread widely in response to the evils of reconstuction after the Civil War. The Klan immediately identified itself as a secret chivalrous military order in defense of Christian virtues and the Constitution of the United States. Klan founder, Confederate general Nathan Bedford Forrest (1821–77), called for the Klan's dissolution four years after its birth. He learned that it was impossible to control the activities of anyone who could hide beneath a sheet and commit criminal acts in the name of the group. Despite Forrest's disbanding of the Klan, irregular activity has continued to this day, with three main periods of waxing and waning growth. The modern robes of the Ku Klux Klan mimic the Templar uniform, with the cross placed as an emblem over the breast. The Klan's cross burnings[†] have been compared to accusations of Templar defilement of that symbol.[19] An allied network of self-appointed assassins committed to the enforcement of their view of Christian Law is known as the Phineas Priesthood. Its mythos focuses on God's approval of the biblical assassination of a couple who

[21] Modern Klan leader Charles Lee describes the burning of the cross as a "lighting." "It represents the light of Jesus Christ in the world, the advancement of the Christian faith." See Howard L. Bushart, John R. Craig, and Myra Barnes, *Soldiers of God: White Supremacists and Their Holy War for America* (New York: Kensington Books, 1998), p. 160.

married outside their faith, as recorded in Numbers: 25:6–13. Author Richard Hoskins compares the modern Phineas priest to the Shiite Assassin, while his polemic on the subject is filled with numerous references to the medieval Templars.[20]

The German *völkisch* ideology of the late nineteenth century, as exemplified by the teachings of Guido von List (1848–1919), was heavily laced with a romantic nostalgia for the chivalric medieval trappings of the Templars and Teutonic Knights. Jörg Lanz von Lebenfels (1874–1954), an influential supporter of List, had been a Cistercian monk prior to developing the racist philosophy and eugenic goals that characterized the later National Socialist program. Lanz founded the Order of New Templars in 1907. He preached a form of Christian racism that is reminiscent of Christian Identity, which teaches that Christian Aryans are the true Israelites and thus the biblical "chosen people." List, on the other hand, embraced Teutonic paganism, totally rejecting Christianity as a false belief.

Building on the work of List and Lanz von Lebenfels, Theodor Fritsch (1852–1914) organized the Germanenorden in 1912. By 1917, Rudolf von Sebottendorff (1875–1945) had become the Bavarian head of the Order that adopted the name Thule Society for concealment. Thule Society members were Hitler's earliest supporters; Von Sebottendorff provided the early Nazi Party in Munich with a newspaper for propaganda purposes. While Adolf Hitler (1889–1945) apparently had little use for the secret mystical brotherhoods of chivalric knighthood, Heinrich Himmler (1900–1945), the founder of the SS, was deeply involved in the myth.

**The Realm of the Imagination.** Modern writers have filled many thousands of pages with carefully constructed scenarios in which the Templars are shown to have possessed the spear that pierced the side of Christ, the physical Holy Grail, or some other priceless physical treasure. Secret attributions and long-hidden mysteries have been uncovered and revealed in an endless number of books. On the political side, otherwise intelligent thinkers concerned with the very real evils of global tyranny have identified the Templars as early proponents of world government because they formed the first multinational corporation. The Assassins have even been accused of financially supporting modern criminal terrorist networks with drug-running operations based in the Middle East.

## Conclusion

The legends of the Templars and the Assassins are indeed very much alive to this day. The long-term survival of the memory of these two rather obscure groups points to various archetypal levels at which they affect the psyche. Meditation on certain concepts may help us better to understand this. Despite the best efforts and tenacity of the modern secular campaign to disparage traditional beliefs and ideals as either outdated or based on erroneous assumptions like God — traditional values somehow survive. The "innate knowledge of the Gods" described by Iamblichus demands of us that we aspire to honor, chivalry, self-sacrifice, redemption, patriotism, courage, and integrity. What better words could be used to describe the ideology shared by the Templars and Assassins of yore?

Other virtues common to both groups included the military standards of esprit de corps and hierarchical obedience. The systematic attempts at the enforced destruction of these qualities in modern America's military notwithstanding, the age-old cross-cultural need intrinsic to members of military bodies for cohesive enthusiasm suggests they too will survive the best efforts of political correctness.

Mystical aspirations and the quest for moral absolutes are another concomitant of "an innate knowledge of the Gods." One might look with jaundiced eye upon the ethical superiority claimed by modern man. Contrast the moral lethargy of today's cynical cult of experts and social planners with the values expressed in Wolfram von Eschenbach's *Parzival*. The inevitable conclusion of that comparison will be of moral devolution rather than evolution.

Modern cognoscenti may still be heard bemoaning "the number of people killed in the name of religion." In fact, during the twentieth century, very few people died in the name of religion. Between 1900 and 1987, however, at least 168 million people were killed by their own governments during times of "peace." During the same period, an estimated 40 million people died because of war.[†] In other words, during

---

[†] R. J. Rummel, *Death by Government* (New Brunswick, N.J.: Transaction Publishers, 1994), pp. 3–4. Professor Rummel conservatively estimates that some 62 million people were killed in Communist Russia, 36 million in Red China, and 21 million under the National Socialists of Germany. See also Stephane Courtois, ed., *The Black Book of Communism: Crimes; Terror, Repression*, trans. Jonathan Murphy and Mark Kramer (Cambridge: Harvard University Press, 1999).

the twentieth century, the average person was four times more likely to have been killed by his or her own government during times of peace than by an enemy during times of war. This chilling statistic implies that in modern life at least, totalitarianism is far more dangerous than religion.

Acceptance of a higher standard by which individual actions and purposes may be weighed is still the most effective means for the encouragement of moral excellence. To both the Templar knight and the Assassin *fidai*, uncompromising valor was a condition of spiritual attainment. To those who continue to seek after that goal today, the same prerequisite still applies.

APPENDIX ONE

✠

THE NINE DEGREES OF WISDOM

This account of the theology and purported nine degrees of the Ismaili system was compiled from several sources. One is Edward G. Browne's *A Literary History of Persia,* vol. I, pp. 410–15. His account is based on that of the Muslim historian an-Nuwayri, who wrote circa 1332 and who cites as his source the tenth-century anti-Fatimid Ismaili Akhu Muhsin. Joseph von Hammer-Purgstall's *The History of the Assassins,* pp. 34–37, is another source, as is Enno Franzius *The History of the Order of the Assassins,* pp. 26–29, and De Lacy O'Leary's *A Short History of the Fatimid Khalifate* (1923; reprint, Delhi: Renaissance Publishing House, 1987), pp. 21–32. Samuel M. Stern's *Studies in Early Ismailism* contains an important discussion of the matter in the chapter entitled "The 'Book of the Highest Initiation' and Other Anti-Ismaili Travesties." My own thoughts have been liberally added to these sources.

I believe the interpretation of the degree structure presented below can be useful as an intimation of the process by which the Ismaili secret doctrine was imparted, as long as the reader keeps in mind that it is speculative and intended at best to be suggestive of a system that has never been publicly disclosed. I do not agree that it presents the Ismailis as sinister proponents of either a cynical agnosticism or an amoral and atheistic doctrine. On the contrary, if this interpretation is reasonably accurate, it describes an elevated and exalted spiritual teaching.

The preliminary conversion-recruiting process began by creating doubt in the mind of the intended convert. Simple but unanswerable questions concerning life and Koranic doctrines would demonstrate to the seeker his own ignorance and the need for an authoritative teacher and guide. "Why did it take God six days to create the world when He could have accomplished it in an instant?" "What do the recording angels mentioned in the Koran look like and why can't we see them?" "Why does man alone of all the animals stand erect?"

Further discussion of the contradictions of religion and the abstruseness of the Koran would fan the doubt to a flame within the mind of the right kind of student. Then he would be told that the answers to his questions were sublime mysteries not to be revealed to the unworthy. Would he be willing to take a solemn oath to the *dai* never to reveal the teachings he might receive; swear to be ever truthful to the *dai*; never join with the enemies of the Ismailis or act in any way against the group; and continue in his normal outward observance of Sunni practice?

**First degree.** Upon the taking of the oath of allegiance and the presentation of an offering to seal the oath, the seeker would be admitted to the first degree of the Ismaili mysteries, in which he accepted that the revelations of the Koran have a superior esoteric meaning, the *batin*, which might be opened to him through contact with a divinely inspired and authorized interpreter. This was the longest degree because the breakdown of past faith would need to be accomplished and its progress carefully observed.

**Second degree.** Next the disciple would be shown, and asked to accept, the error of the Sunni teaching and its inadequacy to answer meaningful spiritual questions. He would also be taught to recognize the need to suspend his own interpretation of the truth in favor of the teaching of the Imam or his direct representative, the *dai*, whose grasp of truth was superior to his own. This degree was the natural stopping place for the majority of converts.

**Third degree.** In this degree, the seeker learned the kabbalistic mysteries of the number seven, which included the seven heavens, seven planets, seven colors, seven metals, and so on. He was taught that this mystery applied to the seven divine Ismaili teachers, the Imams, whose names he would now learn, along with the esoteric words of power by which their aid might be invoked. This level forever separated the student from the more widespread Shiite community that recognized twelve Imams.

**Fourth degree.** The seeker was next taught that God chose to reveal Himself through seven prophets. The line included Adam, Noah, Abraham, Moses, Jesus, Muhammad, and Ismail (or Muhammad ibn Ismail). The acceptance of a Prophet following Muhammad was the highest heresy to the Sunnis, among whose most rigorous articles of faith is the belief that Muhammad is the last prophet. Thus the finality of the Koran as the ultimate revelation of God's Law was denied.

**Fifth degree.** Here the *dai* revealed that the literal interpretation of the Koran was fit only for the uninstructed masses, those who were unprepared to penetrate the *batin* with the guidance of the Imam. The Sunni observances of Shariah were described as steeped in ignorance of the esoteric meaning behind the precepts. A doctrine of twelve apostles extending the true faith was taught, backed up with mathematical and numerological teachings concerning the mysteries of the number twelve, including the twelve signs of the zodiac, twelve months, twelve tribes of Israel, and so on. Practical magical use of kabbalistic knowledge was taught.

**Sixth degree.** Only the most advanced and discreet disciples could proceed to this level, because here they were instructed to abandon Muslim observances altogether, including prayer, fasting, and pilgrimage. These were to be performed only for reasons of social expediency. Their purpose was declared to be meaningless, designed solely for the subjugation of the masses, while there was an allegorical meaning to these practices from which only the wise could profit. The philosophical teachings of Pythagoras, Plato, and Aristotle were introduced, and the use of reason to test religious truth was endorsed. A sixth-degree initiate could become a *dai* himself.

**Seventh degree.** The very few who were admitted to this degree passed from philosophy to mysticism. The dualistic doctrine of first and second causes (the preexistent and the subsequent) was taught, which challenged the belief in divine unity. Initiates of the seventh degree studied Aristotle's theory of the eternity of matter. Creation was explained to be the introduction of movement into matter, which produced time and change.

**Eighth degree.** Here the superfluity of exoteric religious doctrine was further examined. The relativity of morality and consequent indifference of action (or absence of absolute values) were proclaimed. The teachings of this degree further elaborated on the two principles introduced earlier. The nameless first cause is what we know as God. The thought of God is an emanation that becomes the second cause, the Logos, acting as a mediator between God and man. The existence of a formless, nameless, unknowable being anterior to and beyond all previous dualistic conceptions was introduced.

**Ninth degree.** Here the rare initiate studied in depth the Greek Gnostic cosmological teachings of the soul, the heavens, and the celestial intelligences. The ninth-degree Ismaili was a pure philosopher, a law unto himself. The teaching within this degree is the source of the oft-quoted statement attributed to Hasan-i-Sabah: "Nothing is true, everything is permitted." It is reflected in the modern revelation proclaimed through the twentieth-century English magus Aleister Crowley: "Do what thou wilt shall be the whole of the Law." It assumes a level of ego surrender and moral austerity concomitant with a successful search for spiritual truth in which the initiate may at last rely on his own perceptions for an understanding of his mission.

✛

# THE BOOK OF THE KNIGHTS OF THE TEMPLE

## IN PRAISE OF THE NEW KNIGHTHOOD
### *Liber ad milites Templi: De laude novae militae*

To Hughes the Knight of Christ and the Grand Master of the Militia of Christ, from Bernard by the sole title of Abbot of Clairvaux; certain that he fights the good fight.

Unless I am mistaken, my dear Hughes, you have petitioned me not once nor twice but three times to write a sermon of exhortation for you and your fellow knights. Because as you say, if I am not capable to wield a lance, I may at least brandish words against your tyrannical enemies; and that the moral essence of this message, if not just my material support, will be helpful to you. Indeed I have delayed for some time, not because I disregard your petition, but in order that I am not at fault for taking the petition lightly. For I would have preferred that a more distinguished individual complete the task rather than my inexperienced hand, which might leave the task, because of my failed effort, the more necessary and difficult.

Having thus waited for some time to no avail, I indeed have now accomplished this to the best of my ability. Let not my lack of success, however, be wrongfully mistaken as unwillingness. It is for the reader to judge if it is acceptable. Although even if some find my work either minimumly satisfactory or not sufficient, I shall nevertheless be content, for I have not failed in my desire to give my all to you.

## I. A SERMON OF EXHORTATIONS FOR THE KNIGHTS OF THE TEMPLE

1. It seems that a new knightly order has recently been born in that region, which is the Orient, once visited in the flesh from on high. As He then drove out with His mighty hands the principalities of darkness, so now does He attack their disciples, the sons of disobedience, banishing them by the hands of His protectors. Also He brings redemption

to His laity by once more raising the horn of salvation in the noble house of David, His servant.

This new order of knights is one that is unknown by the ages. They fight two wars, one against adversaries of flesh and blood, and another against a spiritual army of wickedness in the heavens. When alone man bravely resists an enemy in the flesh, I do not judge it astonishing, as that it is not rare. And when a virtuous soul battles sin or demons, this also is not extraordinary, although it be praiseworthy, for the world is full of monks. But when a man is mightily armed with swords, and distinction marks his belt, would not anyone present or not consider that it is worthy of all the admirations, since the world is unaccustomed to such things?

Truly, he is a fearless knight and completely secure. While his body is properly armed for these circumstances, his soul is also clothed with the armor of faith. On all sides surely he is well armed; he fears neither demons, nor men. Truly does he not fear death, but instead he longs for death. Why should he have a fear for life or for death, when in Christ is to live, and to die is to gain? He stands faithfully and with confidence in the service of Christ; he greatly desires for release and to be with Christ, the latter certainly a more gracious thing.

Secured, therefore, advance you knights and drive away the enemies of the cross of Christ with an untroubled soul. Be certain that neither death nor life has the power to separate you from the grace of God, in whom is Christ Jesus. Indeed at every kind of danger reply, "Whether we are to live or whether we are to die, we are the Lord's." How glorious to return from the victories of such a battle! How blessed to die a martyr in battle! Rejoice, courageous champion, if you live and conquer in the Lord, indeed there is great rejoicing and glory. If you die, you are joined with your Lord. Life is certainly fruitful and victory is glorious, but a sacred death is truly more important. To be sure, if "they who die *in* the Lord are blessed," how much more blessed are they who die *for* the Lord?

2. Certainly, whether they die in bed or in war, the death of His sacred ones is precious without wavering in the eyes of the Lord; but to die in war how much more precious and glorious. O life is secure, where conscience is chaste! Life is secure for those who anticipate death without fear, and, on the contrary, desire it greatly with passion and embrace it with devotion! O truly sacred and secure are these knights, and how entirely free of the double jeopardy of those who fight that are not for

Christ. Many times, as worldly knights, you must have feared that the death of an enemy in the flesh should cause the death of your soul, or even perhaps that both your body and soul might be slain by his hands.

Of course, in either peril or victory, the Christian is requited by the affections of his heart, not the fortunes of war. If the combatant fights for the good cause, the purpose of his fight is by no means evil. Just as the final results cannot be judged good if his cause was not good and his intentions not virtuous. If you are killed with the intention of killing another, you die a murderer. If you prevail, are stronger, and with a strong will kill a man, you are a living murderer. It is not acceptable, however, whether dead or alive, victorious or vanquished, to be a murderer. Unfortunate victory is his who has destroyed a man, succumbed to vice, and indulged in vainglory; then wrath and pride are your master.

Nevertheless, what of those who kill neither for jealous revenge nor for monstrous vanity, but only to save themselves. But certainly even this victory, I say is not good, since the death of the body is a lesser evil than death of the soul. The soul need not die when the body does. But the soul that sins will die.

## II. OF WORLDLY KNIGHTS

3. What then is the end result or the fruit of this worldly knighthood, dare I say, but knavery if a lethal murderer sins and experiences the ruin and loss of an eternal death? Well truly, I will borrow the words of the Apostle, and say to him who plows to bind himself to his plow in hope, and whoso threshes, to keep before his eyes the fruits of hope.

For what purpose, O knights, is this stupendous error; what is this uncontrollable madness that causes you to fight to such a degree of labor and zeal to the point of either death or sin? You dress your horses with Chinese silks, and decorate your armor with additional rags of which I am ignorant; paint your shields and saddles; cover your bridles and spurs with gold and silver and expensive gems; and then with all this pomp, shamefully and with thoughtless haste rush to your death. Are these the ornaments of a knight, or the trinkets of a woman? Do you think the swords of your enemies will be repelled by your gold, shrink from your jewels, or be incapable of piercing your Chinese silks?

Finally, as you yourselves have most certainly often experienced, to be a warrior there are three necessary characteristics: namely, a knight should be strong, industrious, and cautious; unencumbered and able to move around; and quick to strike with his sword. Then why, to the contrary, are you blinded by effeminate locks; and trip yourselves up with long and full vestments; and finally bury your delicate and tender hands in ample and cumbersome sleeves? Above all, there is this frightening insecurity of conscience even though you are sufficiently armed, since you have taken a perilous route in such a lighthearted and frivolous manner. There is no doubt that the causes of wars and disputes among you are either irrational, untempered rage, empty appetite for glory, or earthly preoccupation with greed. For such causes, it is certain that it is not safe to kill nor to die at the hands of another.

## III. Of the New Knighthood

4. But in truth the knights of Christ may fight securely in battle for their Lord, and by no means fear either sin if they slay the enemy, or the danger of their own death. Because either to bring about death, or to die for Christ, you have not sin but an abundant right to glory. No matter which the case, Christ wins, for in the first case he willingly accepts the death of the enemy, and in the second freely gives consolation to his knight.

The knight of Christ may strike with honor and perish with honor. For when he strikes he serves Christ, and when he perishes in Christ he serves himself. He does not carry a sword without just cause, for he is a minister of God, and he punishes malicious men for the praise of the truth. If he kills malicious men, he is not a murderer under these circumstances. I say that he is a murderer of wickedness and a champion of Christ. He drives away malicious men and is the defender of the Christian order. On the other hand if he is killed, he has not perished but has come home.

In consequence, when he imposes death, then it is for Christ to profit; when he suffers death, it is his gain. In the death of the pagan is Christian glory because Christ is glorified. The death of a Christian is a marked event in which the King is able to liberally reward his knights. For this reason the just shall be cheerful that he sees justice done. "Tell men: do they delight in justice? Only if it is God who judges in that land." I do not mean that pagans are to be slaughtered, if there is another way to prevent them from their extraordinary aggression and oppression of the faithful. It seems, however, more gracious to slay them than to let them sin strongly, win over the just, and therefore, perhaps the righteous will choose to take sin into their hands.

5. What is certain? If it is not permissible for a Christian to strike with sword, why did the precursor of the Savior teach that the soldiers should be happy with their pay rather than prohibit them from their calling? If, on the other hand, it is truly permissible for those so appointed by God — if they are not called to a more gracious profession — then to whom, I request to know, is it more rightly allowed than to those who hold our hearts and minds in Zion, city of our fortitude?

For they have driven away the transgressors of divine law and secured just people in the truth. Likewise do they overthrow the heathen that love war, and slay those who create our consternation, and drive away the wicked people from the holy city of the Lord. In Jerusalem the evil ones eagerly steal the invaluable riches of the Christian laity; they violate religious relics; they possess the Holy Sanctuary of God. Let the swords of the faithful fall on the necks of the enemy in order to destroy anyone who is himself against the knowledge of God, by which is the faith of Christians, in order that the heathen not say: "Where is their God?"

6. When they have been expelled, he shall return to his home and his property, which kindled his anger in the Gospel. "Behold," he says "your house and your vestments are left behind desolated," and he complains bitterly about it. Accordingly the prophet replies: "Leave behind your house, let go of your inheritance." Moreover with this the other prophecy is fulfilled: "The Lord has ransomed his own people, and set them free, and they will come, and they will rejoice on Mount Zion, and they will rejoice in the good Lord."

Fortunate Jerusalem, learn that now is the time in which you are to be visited. "Rejoice and praise together, desolate Jerusalem, for the Lord consoles his own people, he has redeemed Jerusalem, and the Lord with his holy arm consoles in the sight of all the people of the world." Virgin Israel, desolate, and with no one to lift you up. Now stand up, shake loose of the dust, Virgin, captive daughter Zion. Arise, I say, and stand on high, and you will see the delight that comes to you by the hands of your God. You will no longer be called neglected, nor will you be referred to as desolated, for the Lord delights in you, and your land will become prosperous. Raise your eyes and see all that is around you; all have come together and come to you. This is the help that is sent by the Holiest One. In all respects the ancient prophecy is now fulfilled, "I will rebuild you in the pride of the ages, a great rejoicing from generation to generation; and you will suck up the milk of all the people of the world, and moreover you will suck the milk of the breasts of their royalty." And likewise, "Like a mother comforts her sons, this is how I will console you, and in Jerusalem you will be comforted."

Do you not see how frequently the old prophecies foretold of the new knighthood? Because just as we have heard, we have now seen the city of the Lord of all. Naturally we must not become prejudiced by these explicit fulfillments, for we must remember the celestial nature of these texts. Certainly we should live in hope eternal no matter what portents appear during this time. Otherwise earthly wealth could destroy spiritual hope, and realization fulfilled in advance could interfere with future promises. In other respects the temporary glory of the earthly city does not diminish the glory of the celestial one but prepares the way for it; at least we consider it a form of the one that is in Heaven, which is our mother.

## IV. On the Manner of Life of the Knights of the Temple

7. But now, so that our knights may set forth a standard to shame those knights who fight for the devil, not God, we will tell quickly and briefly the life and death of the Knights of Christ. Just what qualities do they show in public, and what in war? Alternately how different is the knight of God from the knight of the world?

In the first place discipline is not lacking, neither is obedience regarded with contempt. As the Scripture proves, the undisciplined son "will be destroyed: defiance is like the sin of sorcery, and disobedience is like the wicked deed of idolatry." They will depart and return at the will of their leader. He will also give them what they eat and wear, and they do not obtain their provisions from another place. And of the manner of living and of vestments, they are wary of any extravagances like gold, only utilizing the necessities. They live like monks in delightful and sober community, without a wife and without children. And indeed that evangelical perfection is not lacking, for they live apart from the world in one family, anxious to guard the sole unity of spirit in the bonds of peace.

Dedicated all together, they are of one heart and one soul: in this manner no one follows his own individual will, but yields to a leader. Neither do they idly shirk their official obligation, nor wander aimlessly. When they are not on duty, they eat their bread with care, repair either their armor or their torn vestments, or put order to the disordered, and finally they are guided by common necessities and by the commands of their leader.

There are no differences between them, with the exception that deference is shown to deed, not well-known nobility. They rival each other in honor; they carry each others burdens in order that they may complete the work for Christ. No impractical word, useless work, uncontrolled laughter, or any murmur or whisper is left uncorrected when once perceived. They detest gaming and gambling, are averse to the hunt, and do not take delight in that wicked, cruel sport of falconry, which is the custom. They reject the vanity of court jesters, magicians, troubadours, and jousters, and detest their foolish deceits. Their hair is shaved short, according to the words of the Apostle, for it dishonors a man to care for flowing locks. Certainly, they rarely dress up or wash their hair, but rather neglect it all the while until it becomes shaggy and dusty, bearing the marks of armor and the sun.

8. When readying for imminent battle, their inner faith is their protection. On the exterior, steel, not gold, is their security — since they are to strike fear in the enemy, not provoke his avariciousness. They need to have horses that are swift and strong, not pompous and decorated. Their purpose is fighting, not parades. They seek victory, not glory. They would rather strike terror than impress. They are not violent men, and do not thoughtlessly or frivolously rush about, but exercise skilled consideration. With caution and prudence they set themselves in military order, accordingly to the ancient scripture: "Truly Israelites are men of peace, even when they rise up to make war."

But truly when it comes to battle, he sets aside his former state of gentleness, as if to say: "Do I not hate those that hate you, Lord; moreover do I not deplore your enemies." They rush in to attack the adversaries, considering them like sheep. No matter how outnumbered, they do not consider the savage barbarians as formidable multitudes. Not that they are secure in their own abilities, but they trust in the virtue of the Lord Sabaoth to bring them to victory. Certainly they are confident when they remember the words of the Maccabees, "It is easy for a multitude to be driven away by the hands of a few. It makes no difference in the sight of the God of Heaven whether he sets them free by the hands of many or by a select few, because victory in war is not the result of a large army, and fortitude is from Heaven." We have seen one man in hot pursuit put a thousand to flight, and two drive away ten thousand.

Even more amazing is that they can be gentle like a lamb, yet ferocious like a lion. I do not know whether I should address them as monks or as knights; perhaps they should be recognized as both. But as monks they have gentleness, and as knights military fortitude. And of this we can say, "This deed is of the hands of the Lord, and is remarkable in our eyes." These men are appointed by God and searched out by his hand to the limits of the land; honorable men of Israel to guard faithfully and protect vigilantly the tomb, which is the bed of the true Solomon, each man with sword in hand, and skillfully trained to battle.

## V. THE TEMPLE OF JERUSALEM

9. Indeed, their quarters are in the temple of Jerusalem — which is not that ancient and famous structure of King Solomon, unequal to any other building — but the current temple, which is not inferior in glory. Truly, all the magnificence of that first temple lies in corruptible gold and silver, in daises of marble and various woods; while the decorations and beautiful ornamentation of the present temple are the religious piety of its inhabitants and their ordained association. Of the first temple you could imagine the variety of spectacular colors; the current temple is venerable in diverse virtues and saintly actions. By all means holiness is the proper adornment for the House of God, which delights in splendid merits more than polished marble, and is fonder still of chaste hearts than golden walls.

Nevertheless, the facade of the temple is decorated, but with arms not jewels, and in lieu of ancient crowns of gold are hung shields. In place of candelabras, censors, and ewers are bridles, saddles, and lances. With all these signs the knights proclaim their faithfulness and zeal to God, which inspired their leader himself in old times to enter knightly service — when he, immensely inflamed, armed His holy hand, not with a sword, but with a flail that he made from thin cord. He entered the temple, drove out the merchants, overturned the boxes of the money changers, and destroyed the stalls of the dove vendors; judging these activities to be a public defilement and unworthy for the house of prayer.

So greatly moved therefore by the example of their King, devoted knights consider it by far more shameful and more intolerable for the Holy House to be polluted by the hands of infidels than infested by merchants. With horse and armor they remain, and by their own hands repulse filthy infidels and tyrannical madness from the Holy Place. There they occupy themselves day and night in pious efforts as well as utilitarian work. They honor the Temple of God with diligent and un-tainted divine service and continuous devotion — not with the sacri-fice of the flesh of animals according to the custom of the ancients, but with true peaceful sacrifices of fraternal love, faithful obedience, and voluntary poverty.

10. These deeds in Jerusalem have excited the whole world. The islands listen, and the laity of afar consider. They come from the east and the west as a stream carrying God's glory to the Gentiles, and their babbling is as the overflowing river which makes joyous the citizens of God's city. And it is certainly delightful and rewarding to view so great a multitude of mankind flocking to the aid of the few. It is a twofold goodness to see that the wicked, the cruel, the thieves, the sacrilegious, the murderers, and the perjurers, as well as the adulterers, have been converted.

It is yet a double cause of joy since their kinsmen are as happy to be rid of them as their new companions are ready to receive them. Both sides are happy with this, since their former kinsmen are in peace, and their new companions are strengthened. Thus Egypt rejoices in their conversion and their departure, while Mount Zion rejoices and the daughters of Judea are joyful. Indeed the former glory in being delivered from their hands, while the latter expect their freedom will come by means of these same hands. Their former countrymen willingly watch as their cruel devastators leave, while their new companions take joy in welcoming their faithful defenders. Thus the one is comfortably delighted by this, while the other is profitably abandoned.

In this way Christ takes revenge on His enemies, triumphing strongly and gloriously by and through themselves. It is delightful and proper that those who have perpetually fought as His enemy are now His champions who fight for Him in military service, just as Saul, the persecutor, was made Paul, the preacher. Therefore, I am not surprised that it is the testimony of the Savior that the Court of Heaven cries out in joy in the repentance of one sinner rather than the virtues of those who have no need of conversion. Certainly the conversion of so many sinners and evil men will now do as much good as their prior ways did harm.

11. Hail then, Holy Cathedral City sanctified by the Most High, for in His own tabernacle a great many people might be saved in You and through You. Hail, Cathedral City of the Great King from which unusual and delightful miracles emanate for the world. Hail, Lady of the Nations and Queen of the Provinces, Estate of the Patriarchs, Mother of Prophets and Apostles, Initiate of Fidelity, Glory of the Christian Laity. If God has allowed you to be assaulted often, it is to have given brave men a cause to fight for virtue and salvation. Hail, promised land who provided flowing milk and honey to your former inhabitants, now be the nourishment for the prosperous life and the healing salvation for the earth.

Yes, I say yes, you are the good and most beneficial land that received into its fruitful depths the heavenly seed from the heart of the eternal Father. So great a crop of martyrs has been produced from this celestial seed. This fertile land begets all the sacred virtues, some bearing fruit as many as thirtyfold, sixtyfold, and even a hundredfold. Wherefore, they who know you understand your delight and are nourished on a great multitude of riches and powers. To all — even to those who never knew you — and to the ends of the earth, they proclaim and describe your greatness, remarkable glories, and marvels.

Glorious things are told of you, Cathedral City of God. For now, we will set down in this medium some of the affluent delights of the Cathedral City, for the praise and glory of Your Name.

✝ ✝ ✝

*Editor's Note:* This translation by Lisa Coffin is of the first five chapters of *De laude*, which are specifically devoted to the Knights Templar. The remaining eight chapters of the letter are descriptions of the holy sites of Palestine and the biblical events that sanctified them. Bernard's full text is available in English in *The Works of Bernard of Clairvaux*, translated by Conrad Greenia. See the bibliography for the full citation.

*Translator's Note:* The original Latin text from which I translated was published in *St. Bernard's Opera, Vol. III, Tractatus et Opuscula* (Rome: Editiones Cistercienses, 1963). It is my sincerest hope that I have communicated his thoughts both accurately and respectfully. I would like to thank James Wasserman for polishing my stone-in-the-rough and for giving me this opportunity. I would also like to thank my Beloved, Scott Coffin, for his help here and his unending support and love.

# Endnotes

### Chapter 1 — An Introduction to Secret Societies

[1] Iamblichus, *On the Mysteries of the Egyptians, Chaldeans and Assyrians*, trans. Thomas Taylor (1821; reprint, London: Stuart and Watkins, 1968), p. 23.

[2] Hermes Trismegistus, *The Mind to Hermes*, trans. Frances A. Yates in *Giordano Bruno and the Hermetic Tradition* (Chicago: University of Chicago Press, 1964), p. 32.

[3] Crowley, Aleister, *The Book of the Law* (1938; reprint, New York: Samuel Weiser, Inc., 1976), p. 22.

[4] James Bovard, *Freedom in Chains: The Rise of the State and the Demise of the Citizen* (New York: St. Martins Press, 1999), p. 1.


## Part One: Setting the Stage

### Chapter 2 — Historical Background of the Crusades

[1] Norman F. Cantor, *The Civilization of the Middle Ages* (New York: Harper Perennial, 1994), p. 37.

[2] Ibid., p. 42.

[3] David L. Vagi, *Coinage and History of the Roman Empire*, 2 vols. (Sidney, OH: Coin World/Amos Press, 1999), vol. 1, p. 279.

[4] Ibid., p. 352.

[5] Cantor, *The Civilization of the Middle Ages*, pp. 44–45.

[6] Will Durant, *Caesar and Christ*, vol. 3 of *The Story of Civilization* (New York: Simon and Schuster, 1950), p. 659, quoting a letter from the emperor.

[7] Jules Michelet, *Satanism and Witchcraft*, trans. A. R. Allinson (New York: Citadel Press, 1946), pp. 78–80.

[8] Cantor, *The Civilization of the Middle Ages*, p. 155.

[9] Will Durant, *Age of Faith*, vol. 4 of *The Story of Civilization* (New York: Simon and Schuster, 1944), p. 564.

[10] *Cambridge Medieval History*, vol. 7, p. 722, quoted by Durant, *Age of Faith*, p. 556.


## Part Two: The Order of Assassins

### Chapter 4 — Islamic Roots

[1] Durant, *Age of Faith*, p. 197.

[2] Farhad Daftary, *The Ismailis: Their History and Doctrines* (Cambridge: Cambridge University Press, 1994), p. 37.

[3] Martin Lings, *Muhammad: His Life Based on the Earliest Sources* (New York: Inner Traditions, 1983), p. 57.

[4] Ibid., p. 164.

[5] Durant, *Age of Faith*, p. 283.

[6] Farhad Daftary, *The Assassin Legends* (London: I. B. Tauris & Company, 1995), p. 13.

7 Daftary, *The Ismailis*, pp. 160–161.
8 Daftary, *The Assasin Legends*, p. 5.
9 Daftary, *The Ismailis*, p. 198.

CHAPTER 5 — TEACHINGS OF ISMAILISM

1 Daftary, *The Ismailis*, p. 233.
2 Ibid., pp. 141–43.
3 Ibid., p. 137.
4 Aziz Esmail and Azim Nanji, "The Ismailis in History," in *Ismaili Contributions to Islamic Culture*, ed. Seyyed Hossein Nasr (Tehran: Imperial Iranian Academy of Philosophy, 1977), p. 233.
5 Marshall G. S. Hodgson, *The Order of Assassins* (The Hague: Mouton, 1955), pp. 16–18.
6 Daftary, *The Ismailis*, pp. 240–41.
7 Bernard Lewis, *The Assassins: A Radical Sect in Islam* (New York: Basic Books, 1968), p. 30.
8 Edward Burman, *The Assassins: Holy Killers of Islam* (Wellingborough: Aquarian Press, 1987), p. 55.
9 Heinz Halm, discussing Samuel M. Stern's research in Farhad Daftary, *Medieval Ismaili History and Thought* (Cambridge: Cambridge University Press, 1996), p. 91.
10 Samuel M. Stern, *Studies in Early Ismailism* (Jerusalem: The Magness Press, Hebrew University; Leiden: E. J. Brill, 1983), p. 58.
11 Lewis, *The Assassins*, p. 48.
12 Stern, *Studies in Early Ismailism*, p. 61.

CHAPTER 6 — ENTER HASAN

1 Joseph von Hammer-Purgstall, *The History of the Assassins* (1835; reprint, New York: Burt Franklin, 1968), p. 46.
2 Enno Franzius, *The History of the Order of the Assassins* (New York: Funk & Wagnalls, 1969), p. 24.
3 Lewis, *The Assassins*, p. 43, and Daftary, *The Ismailis*, p. 340.
4 Lewis, *The Assassins*, p. 58.
5 Ibid., p. 61. Burman, *The Assassins*, p. 36, has it as June 12.

CHAPER 7 — AN OVERVIEW OF HASAN'S ASSASSINS

1 Hodgson, *The Order of Assassins*, p. 126.
2 Ibid., p. 82.
3 Lings, *Muhammad*, p. 199.
4 Lewis, *The Assassins*, p. 51.
5 Burman, *The Assassins*, p. 37.
6 Hodgson, *The Order of Assassins*, p. 115.
7 Lewis, *The Assassins*, p. 48.
8 Ibid., p. 105.
9 Daftary, *The Assassin Legends*, p. 30.
10 Silvestre de Sacy, "Memoirs on the Dynasty of the Assassins," trans. in Daftary, *The Assassin Legends*. The etymology is discussed on pp. 147–71.

11 Daftary, *The Assassin Legends*, pp. 91–93.
12 Lewis, *The Assassins*, p. 12.
13 Daftary, *The Ismailis*, p. 19.
14 Esmail and Nanji, "The Ismailis in History," p. 250.
15 Hodgson, *The Order of Assassins*, p. 59.

## CHAPTER 8 — AFTER HASAN

1 Daftary, *The Assassin Legends*, p. 41.
2 See Hodgson, *The Order of Assassins*, pp. 153–57, for more on this.
3 Daftary, *The Assassin Legends*, p. 41.
4 Hodgson, *The Order of Assassins*, p. 157.
5 Daftary, *The Ismailis*, p. 392.
6 Muhammad ibn al-Husayn al-Sulami, *The Book of Sufi Chivalry*, trans. Sheikh Tosun Bayrak al-Jerrahi al-Halveti (New York: Inner Traditions, 1983), p. 6.

## CHAPTER 9 — THE SYRIAN ASSASSINS

1 Daftary, *The Assassin Legends*, pp. 68 and 71; *The Ismailis*, p. 398.
2 Lewis, *The Assassins*, pp. 116–17.
3 Ibid., p. 122.
4 Hodgson, *The Order of Assassins*, p. 274.

## CHAPTER 10 — THE NIZARI ISMAILIS TODAY

1 Hodgson, *The Order of Assassins*, p. 276, and Daftary, *The Ismailis*, p. 415.
2 Daftary, *The Ismailis*, p. 454.

# PART THREE: THE KNIGHTS TEMPLAR

## CHAPTER 12 — THE FIRST CRUSADE

1 Steven Runciman, *A History of the Crusades*, 3 vols. (1951; reprint, London: The Folio Society, 1994), vol. 1, p. 140.

## CHAPTER 13 — AN OVERVIEW OF THE ORDER

1 Stephen Howarth, *The Knights Templar* (London: Collins, 1982), p. 48
2 Edward Burman, *The Templars: Knights of God* (Wellingborough: Aquarian Press, 1986), pp. 19–20, and Malcolm Barber, *The New Knighthood* (Cambridge: Cambridge University Press, 1994), pp. 6–7.
3 Burman, *The Templars*, p. 23.
4 Quoted by Cantor, *The Civilization of the Middle Ages*, p. 34.
5 J. M. Upton-Ward, *The Rule of the Templars*, (Suffolk: The Boydell Press, 1992), p. 106.
6 Ibid., pp. 13–16.
7 Ibid., p. 19.
8 Ibid.
9 Burman, *The Templars*, p. 30.

10 Upton-Ward, *The Rule of the Templars*, p. 87.
11 Ibid., p. 79.
12 Ibid., p. 112.
13 Quotations are from "In Praise of the New Knighthood," translated by Lisa Coffin. See appendix 2.
14 Henry Charles Lea, *A History of the Inquisition of the Middle Ages*, 3 vols. (1888; reprint, New York: Russell & Russell, 1955), vol. 3, pp. 250–251. Lea's chapter on the Templars was reprinted in G. Legman, *The Guilt of the Templars* (New York: Basic Books, 1966), pp. 137–244.
15 Burman, *The Templars*, p. 80.
16 Barber, *The New Knighthood*, p. 276.

CHAPTER 14 — THE EARLY YEARS

1 Burman, *The Templars*, p. 36.

CHAPTER 15 — THE SECOND CRUSADE

1 Burman, *The Templars*, p. 56.

CHAPTER 16 — SALADIN AND THE BATTLE OF HATTIN

1 Barber, *The New Knighthood*, p. 89.
2 Howarth, *The Knights Templar*, p. 145.

CHAPTER 17 — THE THIRD CRUSADE

1 For example, Durant, *Age of Faith*, p. 310.

CHAPTER 19 — THE CATHARS AND THE ALBIGENSIAN CRUSADE

1 Malcolm Lambert, *The Cathars*, (Oxford: Blackwell Publishers, 1998), pp. 43–44.
2 Ibid., p. 21.
3 Joseph R. Strayer, *The Albigensian Crusades* (Ann Arbor: University of Michigan Press, 1992), pp. 143–50, provides extracts of Cathar rituals.
4 Matt. 3:11; see also Acts 1:5.
5 Lambert, *The Cathars*, p. 69.
6 Strayer, *The Albigensian Crusades*, p. 75.
7 KJV, 2 Timothy 2:19, and Numbers 16:5. These two biblical verses are offered in support of the historicity of the legate's statement by Malcolm Lambert in *The Cathars*, p. 103.

CHAPTER 22 — THE SEVENTH CRUSADE AND THE RISE OF BAYBARS

1 Christopher Marshall, *Warfare in the Latin East, 1192–1291* (Cambridge: Cambridge University Press, 1992), p. 41, quoting from the contemporary account in the Rothelin manuscript, *Continuation de Guillaume de Tyr de 1229 à 1261*.
2 Burman, *The Templars*, p. 131.
3 John J. Robinson, *Born in Blood* (New York: M. Evans & Co., 1989), p. 60.

CHAPTER 23 — THE EIGHTH CRUSADE AND FINAL DEFEAT

[1] Howarth, *The Knights Templar*, p. 224.
[2] Barber, *The New Knighthood*, p. 171.

CHAPTER 24 — THE LAST YEARS OF THE KNIGHTS TEMPLAR

[1] Lea, *A History of the Inquisition of the Middle Ages*, vol. 3, pp. 243–244.
[2] Barber, *The New Knighthood*, p. 1.
[3] Malcolm Barber, *The Trial of the Templars* (Cambridge: Cambridge University Press, 1978), p. 22.
[4] Barber, *The New Knighthood*, p. 285.
[5] Burman, *The Templars*, p. 156.

CHAPTER 25 — THE END OF THE ORDER

[1] Legman, *The Guilt of the Templars*, p. 16.
[2] Ibid., p. 94.
[3] Barber, *The Trial of the Templars*, p. 68.
[4] *Encyclopedia Britannica*, as quoted by Legman, *The Guilt of the Templars*, p. 46.
[5] Barber, *The Trial of the Templars*, p. 243.
[6] Legman, *The Guilt of the Templars*, p. 3; Barber, *The Trial of the Templars*, p. 126.
[7] Robinson, *Born in Blood*, p. 115.
[8] Barber, *The Trial of the Templars*, pp. 139–43.
[9] Lea, *A History of the Inquisition of the Middle Ages*, vol. 3, p. 316.
[10] Howarth, *The Knights Templar*, p. 305.

CHAPTER 26 — REFLECTIONS ON THE TEMPLAR ORDER

[1] Thomas Wright, "The Worship of the Generative Powers," in *A Discourse on the Worship of Priapus*, Richard Payne Knight (1865; reprinted as *Sexual Symbolism*, *A History of Phallic Worship*, New York: The Julian Press, 1961), p. 106. The portion of Wright's essay dealing with the Templars was also reprinted in Legman, *The Guilt of the Templars*, pp. 247–286.
[2] Matt. 10:34, KJV. Bible.
[3] Lea, *A History of the Inquisition of the Middle Ages*, vol. 3, p. 268.

PART FOUR: AFTERWORD

[1] Ogden Goelet, ed., *The Egyptian Book of the Dead, The Book of Going Forth by Day* (San Francisco: Chronicle Books, 1998), pp. 147–48.
[2] Manly P. Hall, *The Secret Teachings of All Ages* (1925; reprint, Los Angeles: Philosophical Research Society, 1975), p. 17.
[3] Cantor, *The Civilization of the Middle Ages*, p. 558.
[4] "The History of Science," *Encyclopedia Britannica*.
[5] Pauline Matarasso, *The Quest of the Holy Grail* (Middlesex, U.K.: Penguin Books, 1975), pp. 15–16, 20–21.

6  Yates, *Giordano Bruno and the Hermetic Tradition*, pp. 1–2.
7  Christopher McIntosh, *The Rosicrucians* (York Beach, ME: Samuel Weiser, Inc., 1997), pp. 22–23
8  Frances Yates, *The Rosicrucian Enlightenment* (London: Routledge & Kegan Paul, 1974), p. 40.
9  Ibid., p. 39.
10  Ibid., p. 104; McIntosh, *The Rosicrucians*, pp. 49–50.
11  McIntosh, *The Rosicrucians*, p. 43.
12  Peter Partner, *The Murdered Magicians: The Templars and Their Myth* (Oxford: Oxford University Press, 1981), p. 118.
13  Christopher McIntosh, *Eliphas Lévi and the French Occult Revival* (New York: Samuel Weiser, Inc., 1972), p. 24.
14  Eliphas Lévi, *Transcendental Magic*, trans. A. E. Waite (1896; reprint, York Beach: Samuel Weiser, Inc., 1991), p. 394
15  R. Swinburne Clymer, *The Rosicrucian Fraternity in America*, 2 vols. (Quakertown, PA: Rosicrucian Fraternity, 1935), vol. 1, p. 463.
16  Crowley, *The Book of the Law*, p. 5.
17  Aleister Crowley, *The Equinox of the Gods* (1936; reprint, Scottsdale, AZ: New Falcon Publications, 1991) p. 118.
18  Francis King, *Ritual Magic in England* (London: Neville Spearman, 1970), pp. 205–207, and the *Secret Rituals of the O.T.O.* (London: C. W. Daniel Co., 1973),
19  David Annan, "The Ku Klux Klan," in Norman MacKenzie, ed., *Secret Societies* (New York: Crescent Books, 1967), p. 277.
20  Richard Kelly Hoskins, *Vigilantes of Christendom* (Lynchburg, VA: The Virginia Publishing Co., 1990).

# Selected Bibliography

## The Assassins

Al-Sulami, Muhammad ibn al-Husayn. *The Book of Sufi Chivalry.* Trans. Sheikh Tosun Bayrak al-Jerrahi al-Halveti. New York: Inner Traditions, 1983.

Browne, Edward G. *A Literary History of Persia.* 4 vols. 1902. Reprint, London: Cambridge University Press, 1977.

Burman, Edward. *The Assassins: Holy Killers of Islam.* Wellingborough: Aquarian Press, 1987.

Daftary, Farhad. *The Assassin Legends.* London: I. B. Tauris & Company, 1995.

—. *The Ismailis: Their History and Doctrines.* Cambridge: Cambridge University Press, 1994.

—, ed. *Medieval Ismaili History and Thought.* Cambridge: Cambridge University Press, 1996.

De Lacy, O'Leary. *A Short History of the Fatimid Khalifate.* 1923. Reprint, Delhi: Renaissance Publishing House, 1987.

Franzius, Enno. *The History of the Order of the Assassins.* New York: Funk & Wagnalls, 1969.

Hammer-Purgstall, Joseph von. *The History of the Assassins.* 1835. Reprint, New York: Burt Franklin, 1968.

Hodgson, Marshall G. S. *The Order of Assassins.* The Hague: Mouton, 1955.

Khan Sahib Khaja Khan. *The Secret of Ana'l-Haqq.* 1926. Sh. Muhammad Ashraf, Reprint, Lahore Pakistan: 1976.

Khayyam, Omar. *The Rubaiyat.* Trans. and ed. Edward Fitzgerald, New York: Collier Books, 1962.

Lewis, Bernard. *The Assassins: A Radical Sect in Islam.* New York: Basic Books, 1968.

Lings, Martin. *Muhammad: His Life Based on the Earliest Sources.* New York: Inner Traditions, 1983.

Nasr, Seyyed Hossein, ed. *Ismaili Contributions to Islamic Culture*. Tehran: Imperial Iranian Academy of Philosophy, 1977.

Newby, P. H. *Saladin in His Time*. New York: Dorset Press, 1992.

Pickthall, Marmaduke, trans. and ed. *The Meaning of the Glorious Koran*. 1930. Reprint, New York: Alfred A. Knopf, 1992.

Rosebault, Charles J. *Saladin: Prince of Chivalry*. New York: Robert M. McBride & Co., 1930.

Stern, Samuel M. *Studies in Early Ismailism*. Jerusalem: The Magness Press, Hebrew University; Leiden: E. J. Brill, 1983.

Tawfik, Younis. *Islam*. New York: Konecky & Konecky, 1998.

Wilson, Peter Lamborn. *Sacred Drift: Essays on the Margins of Islam*. San Francisco: City Lights Books, 1993.

## The Knights Templar

Barber, Malcolm. *The New Knighthood*. Cambridge: Cambridge University Press, 1994.

—. *The Trial of the Templars*. Cambridge: Cambridge University Press, 1978.

Billings, Malcolm. *The Cross and the Crescent*. New York: Sterling Publishing, 1990.

Bradford, Ernle. *The Knights of the Order*. 1972. Reprint, New York: Dorset Press, 1991.

Burman, Edward. *The Templars: Knights of God*. Wellingborough: Aquarian Press, 1986.

Coss, Peter. *The Knight in Medieval England 1000–1400*. Conshohocken, PA: Combined Books, 1993.

Dudley, Dean. *History of the First Council of Nicaea*. 1925. Reprint, Mokelumne Hill, CA: Health Research, 1966.

Eschenbach, Wolfram von. *Parzival*. Trans. with introduction by Helen M. Mustard and Charles E. Passage, New York: Vintage Books, 1961.

Greenia, Conrad, trans. *The Works of Bernard of Clairvaux*. Vol. 7, *Treatises 3*. The Cistercian Fathers Series, no. 19. Kalamazoo, MI: Cistercian Publications, 1977.

Howarth, Stephen. *The Knights Templar*. London: Collins, 1982.

Knight, Richard Payne and Thomas Wright. *A Discourse on the Worship of Priapus*. 1865. Reprinted as *Sexual Symbolism, A History of Phallic Worship*. New York: The Julian Press, 1961.

Lambert, Malcolm. *The Cathars*. Oxford: Blackwell Publishers, 1998.

Lea, Henry Charles. *A History of the Inquisition of the Middle Ages*. 3 vols. 1888. Reprint, New York: Russell & Russell, 1955.

Legman, G. *The Guilt of the Templars*. New York: Basic Books, 1966.

Marshall, Christopher. *Warfare in the Latin East, 1192–1291*. Cambridge: Cambridge University Press, 1992.

Matarasso, Pauline. *The Quest of the Holy Grail*. Middlesex, U.K.: Penguin Books, 1975.

Michelet, Jules. *Satanism and Witchcraft*. Trans. A. R. Allinson, New York: Citadel Press, 1946.

Partner, Peter. *The Murdered Magicians: The Templars and Their Myth*. Oxford: Oxford University Press, 1981.

Paynes, Robert. *The Dream and the Tomb*. Chelsea: Scarborough House, 1991.

Riley-Smith, Jonathan, ed. *The Atlas of the Crusades*. New York: Facts on File, 1990.

Robinson, John J. *Born in Blood*. New York: M. Evans & Co., 1989.

—. *Dungeon, Fire and Sword*. New York: M. Evans & Co., 1991.

Runciman, Steven. *A History of the Crusades*. 3 vols. 1951. Reprint, London: The Folio Society, 1994.

Simon, Edith. *The Piebald Standard*. London: White Lion Publishers Limited, 1976.

Strayer, Joseph R. *The Albigensian Crusades*. Ann Arbor: University of Michigan Press, 1992.

Upton-Ward, J. M. *The Rule of the Templars*. Suffolk: The Boydell Press, 1992.

Weston, Jessie L. *From Ritual to Romance*. Garden City: Doubleday Anchor Books, 1957.


## General Reference Works

Apuleius, Lucius. *The Transformation of Lucius, Otherwise Known as The Golden Ass*. Trans. Robert Graves. New York: Farrar, Strauss & Giroux, 1951.

Cantor, Norman F. *The Civilization of the Middle Ages*. New York: Harper Perennial, 1994.

Cavendish, Richard, ed. *Man, Myth and Magic: An Illustrated Encyclopedia of the Supernatural*. 24 vols. New York: Marshall Cavendish Corporation, 1970.

Cohn, Norman. *The Pursuit of the Millennium*. 3rd ed. New York: Oxford University Press, 1970.

Crystal, David, ed. *The Cambridge Biographical Encyclopedia*. Cambridge: Cambridge University Press, 1994.

Durant, Will. *The Age of Faith*. Vol. 4 of *The Story of Civilization*. New York: Simon and Schuster, 1944.

—. *Caesar and Christ*. Vol. 3 of *The Story of Civilization*. New York: Simon and Schuster, 1950.

Goelet, Ogden, ed. *The Egyptian Book of the Dead: The Book of Going Forth by Day*. Rev. ed. San Francisco: Chronicle Books, 1998.

Plato. *The Works of Plato*. Trans. B. Jowett. New York: Tudor Publishing Company, n.d.

Potok, Chaim. *Wanderings*. New York: Fawcett Crest, 1980.

Robinson, James M., ed. *The Nag Hammadi Library*. 3rd ed. San Francisco: Harper & Row, 1988.

Vagi, David L. *Coinage and History of the Roman Empire*. 2 vols. Sidney, OH: Coin World/Amos Press, 1999.

## Mystical Secret Societies

Allen, Paul M., ed. *A Christian Rosenkreutz Anthology*. Blauvelt, NY: Rudolf Steiner Publications, 1968.

Beta, Hymenaeus, ed. *The Equinox*, Vol. 3, no. 10. 1986. Reprint, York Beach, ME: Samuel Weiser, Inc., 1990

Clymer, R. Swinburne. *The Rosicrucian Fraternity in America*. 2 vols. Quakertown, PA: Rosicrucian Fraternity, 1935.

Crowley, Aleister. *The Book of the Law*. 1938. Reprint, New York: Samuel Weiser, Inc., 1976.

——. *The Confessions of Aleister Crowley*. Ed. by John Symonds and Kenneth Grant. New York: Hill and Wang, 1969.

——. *The Equinox of the Gods*. 1936. Reprint, Scottsdale, AZ: New Falcon Publications, 1991.

Daraul, Arkon. *A History of Secret Societies*. New York: Citadel Press, 1990.

Godwin, Joscelyn. *The Theosophical Enlightenment*. Albany: State University of New York Press, 1994.

Godwin, Joscelyn, Christian Chanel, and John P. Deveney. *The Hermetic Brotherhood of Luxor*. York Beach, ME: Samuel Weiser, Inc., 1995.

Goodrick-Clarke, Nicholas. *The Occult Roots of Nazism*. New York: New York University Press, 1992.

Grant, Kenneth. *The Magical Revival*. New York: Samuel Weiser, Inc., 1972.

Heckethorn, Charles William. *The Secret Societies of All Ages and Countries*. 2 vols. 1897. Reprint, New Hyde Park: University Books, 1965.

Hall, Manly P. *The Secret Teachings of All Ages*. 1925. Reprint, Los Angeles: Philosophical Research Society, 1975.

Hamill, John. *The Craft*. Wellingborough, U.K.: Aquarian Press, 1986.

Howard, Michael. *The Occult Conspiracy*. Rochester, VT: Destiny Books, 1989.

Howe, Ellic. *Theodor Reuss*. London: Transactions of Quatuor Coronati Lodge, 1978.

Iamblichus. *On the Mysteries of the Egyptians, Chaldeans and Assyrians*. Trans. Thomas Taylor. 1821. Reprint, London: Stuart and Watkins, 1968.

King, Francis. *Ritual Magic in England*. London: Neville Spearman, 1970.

—. *The Secret Rituals of the O.T.O.* London: C. W. Daniel Co., 1973.

—. *Sexuality, Magic and Perversion*. Secaucus, NJ: Citadel Press, 1974.

King, Francis, and Isabel Sutherland. *Rebirth of Magic*. London: Corgi, 1982.

Lévi, Eliphas. *The History of Magic*. Trans. A. E. Waite. 1913. Reprint, London: Rider and Company, 1951.

—. *Transcendental Magic*. Trans. A. E. Waite. 1896. Reprint, York Beach: Samuel Weiser, Inc., 1991.

McIntosh, Christopher. *Eliphas Lévi and the French Occult Revival*. New York: Samuel Weiser, Inc., 1972.

—. *The Rosicrucians*. York Beach, ME: Samuel Weiser, Inc., 1997.

MacKenzie, Norman, ed. *Secret Societies*. New York: Crescent Books, 1967.

Scott, Ernest. *The People of the Secret*. London: The Octagaon Press, 1983.

Shah, Idries. *The Sufis*. Garden City: Doubleday, 1964.

Wasserman, James. *Art and Symbols of the Occult*. Rochester, VT: Destiny Books, 1992.

Webb, James. *The Occult Establishment*. LaSalle, IL: Open Court, 1976.

—. *The Occult Underground*. LaSalle, IL: Open Court, 1974.

Yates, Frances. A. *Giordano Bruno and the Hermetic Tradition*. Chicago: University of Chicago Press, 1964.

—. *The Rosicrucian Enlightenment*. London: Routledge & Kegan Paul, 1974.

## POLITICAL CONSPIRACIES

(*Note*: Some of the books under this heading could as easily appear under the previous heading and vice versa.)

Bailyn, Bernard, ed. *The Debate on the Constitution*. 2 vols. New York: Literary Classics of the United States, Inc., 1977.

Barruel, Augustin. *Memoirs Illustrating the History of Jacobinism*. 1798. Trans. Robert Clifford. Fraser, MI: Real View Books, 1995.

Bastiat, Frederic. *The Law*. 1850. Trans. Dean Russell. Irvington-on-Hudson: The Foundation for Economic Education, 1994.

Bovard, James. *Freedom in Chains: The Rise of the State and the Demise of the Citizen*. New York: St. Martins Press, 1999.

Bushart, Howard L., John R. Craig, and Myra Barnes. *Soldiers of God: White Supremacists and Their Holy War for America*. New York: Kensington Books, 1998.

Courtois, Stéphane, ed. *The Black Book of Communism: Crimes, Terror, Repression*. Trans. Jonathan Murphy and Mark Kramer. Cambridge: Harvard University Press, 1999.

Hoskins, Richard Kelly. *Vigilantes of Christendom*. Lynchburg, VA: The Virginia Publishing Co., 1990.

Huxley, Aldous. *Brave New World*. Garden City: Sun Dial Press, 1932.

Jasper, William F. *Global Tyranny . . . Step by Step*. Appleton, WI: Western Islands Publishers, 1992.

Kelly, Clarence. *Conspiracy Against God and Man*. Boston: Western Islands, 1974.

Kopel, David B., and Paul H. Blackman. *No More Wacos*. Amherst, NY: Prometheus Books, 1997.

LaPierre, Wayne. *Guns, Crime and Freedom*. Washington, D.C.: Regnery Publishing, 1994.

Malcolm, Joyce Lee. *To Keep and Bear Arms*. Cambridge: Harvard University Press, 1994.

McAlpine, Peter. *The Occult Technology of Power*. Port Townsend, MI: Loompanics Unlimited, 1974.

McNulty, Mike, and William Gazicki. *Waco: The Rules of Engagement*. Video documentary. Los Angeles: Somford Entertainment, 1997.

McNulty, Mike, and Rick Van Fleet. *Waco: A New Revelation.* Video documentary. Ft. Collins, CO: MGA Films, Inc., 1999.

Miller, Edith Starr (Lady Queenborough). *Occult Theocracy.* 1933. Reprint, Hawthorne, CA: Christian Book Club of America, 1980.

Orwell, George. *Animal Farm.* 1946. Reprint, New York: New American Library, 1964.

—. *1984.* 1949. Reprint, New York: New American Library, 1984.

Perloff, James. *The Shadows of Power.* Appleton, WI: Western Islands Publishers, 1988.

Quigley, Carroll. *The Anglo-American Establishment.* New York: Books in Focus, Inc., 1981.

—. *Tragedy and Hope.* 1966. Reprint, Hollywood: Angriff Press, 1974.

Rand, Ayn. *Atlas Shrugged.* New York: Random House, 1957.

Robison, John. *Proofs of a Conspiracy.* 1798. Reprint, Boston: Western Islands, 1967.

Ross, John. *Unintended Consequences.* St. Louis: Accurate Press, 1996.

Rummel, R. J. *Death by Government.* New Brunswick, NJ: Transaction Publishers, 1994.

Stoddart, Christina M. *Light-Bearers of Darkness.* 1930. Reprint, Hawthorne, CA: Christian Book Club of America, 1983.

—. *Trail of the Serpent.* Hawthorne, CA: Christian Book Club of America, n.d.

Tabor, James D. and Eugene V. Gallagher. *Why Waco? Cults and the Battle for Religious Freedom in America.* Berkeley: University of California Press, 1995.

Vazsonyi, Balint. *America's 30 Years War: Who Is Winning?* Washington, D.C.: Regnery Publishing, Inc., 1999.

Webster, Nesta H. *Secret Societies and Subversive Movements.* 1924. Reprint, Hawthorne, CA: Christian Book Club, n.d.

Wingus, Neal. *The Illuminoids.* New York: Pocket Books, 1979.

Yallop, David A. *In God's Name.* New York: Bantam Books, 1984.

# INDEX

# ABOUT THE AUTHOR

Photo by Illia Tulloch

James Wasserman was born in 1948. After attending Antioch College, he spent several years studying with various teachers of meditation and other occult disciplines. Settling in New York City in 1973, he began working at Samuel Weiser's, then the world's largest occult bookstore. In 1977, he left to found Studio 31, specializing in book production and graphic design.

In 1976, he joined Ordo Templi Orientis, having explored Aleister Crowley's system of Scientific Illuminism. In 1979, he founded TAHUTI Lodge, one of the oldest continuous O.T.O. Lodges in the world. He has played a key role in numerous seminal publications of the Crowley corpus, and was responsible for the widely acclaimed reclamation of the Papyrus of Ani, *The Egyptian Book of the Dead: The Book of Going Forth by Day*.

*The Templars and the Assassins: The Militia of Heaven* is the result of more than seven years research and writing.

In addition to his interest in religion and creative mythology, he maintains an ardent passion for political liberty. He is a student of the United States Constitution, the writings of the Founding Fathers, and Libertarianism. A lifetime member of the NRA, he lives in New York with his wife and two children.

# BOOKS OF RELATED INTEREST

THE LOST TREASURE OF THE KNIGHTS TEMPLAR
Solving the Oak Island Mystery
*by Steven Sora*

THE KNIGHTS TEMPLAR AND THEIR MYTH
*by Peter Partner*

THE TEMPLARS
Knights of God
*by Edward Burman*

MUHAMMAD
His Life Based on the Earliest Sources
*by Martin Lings*

THE WOMAN WITH THE ALABASTER JAR
Mary Magdalen and the Holy Grail
*by Margaret Starbird*

THE OCCULT CONSPIRACY
Secret Societies—Their Influence and Power in World History
*by Michael Howard*

THE MYSTERY OF THE GRAIL
Initiation and Magic in the Quest for the Spirit
*by Julius Evola*

Inner Traditions • Bear & Company
P.O. Box 388
Rochester, VT 05767
1-800-246-8648
www.InnerTraditions.com

Or contact your local bookseller